CYBER 2023

The Eighth International Conference on Cyber-Technologies and Cyber-Systems

September 25 - 29, 2023

Porto, Portugal

CYBER 2023 Editors

Rainer Falk, Siemens AG, Technology, Germany

Steve Chan, Decision Engineering Analysis Laboratory, USA

Printed from e-media with permission by:

Curran Associates, Inc.
57 Morehouse Lane
Red Hook, NY 12571

Some format issues inherent in the e-media version may also appear in this print version.

Printed with permission by Curran Associates, Inc. (2024)

International Academy, Research, and Industry Association (IARIA)
412 Derby Way
Wilmington, DE 19810

Phone: (408) 893-6407
Fax: (408) 527-6351

petre@iaria.org

Additional copies of this publication are available from:

Curran Associates, Inc.
57 Morehouse Lane
Red Hook, NY 12571 USA
Phone: 845-758-0400
Fax: 845-758-2633
Email: curran@proceedings.com
Web: www.proceedings.com

Table of Contents

CYBER 2023

Forward

The Eighth International Conference on Cyber-Technologies and Cyber-Systems (CYBER 2023), held between September 25th and September 29th, 2023, continued a series of international events covering many aspects related to cyber-systems and cyber-technologies; it is also intended to illustrate appropriate current academic and industry cyber-system projects, prototypes, and deployed products and services.

The increasing size and complexity of the communications and the networking infrastructures are making difficult the investigation of the resiliency, security assessment, safety and crimes. Mobility, anonymity, counterfeiting, are characteristics that add more complexity in Internet of Things and Cloud-based solutions. Cyber-physical systems exhibit a strong link between the computational and physical elements. Techniques for cyber resilience, cyber security, protecting the cyber infrastructure, cyber forensic, and cyber-crimes have been developed and deployed. Some new solutions are nature-inspired and social-inspired, leading to self-secure and self-defending systems. Despite the achievements, security and privacy, disaster management, social forensics, and anomalies/crimes detection are challenges within cyber-systems.

We take here the opportunity to warmly thank all the members of the CYBER 2023 technical program committee, as well as all the reviewers. The creation of such a high-quality conference program would not have been possible without their involvement. We also kindly thank all the authors who dedicated much of their time and effort to contribute to CYBER 2023. We truly believe that, thanks to all these efforts, the final conference program consisted of top-quality contributions. We also thank the members of the CYBER 2023 organizing committee for their help in handling the logistics of this event.

We hope that CYBER 2023 was a successful international forum for the exchange of ideas and results between academia and industry and for the promotion of progress related to cyber-technologies and cyber-systems.

CYBER 2023 Chairs

CYBER 2023 Steering Committee Chair
Steve Chan, Decision Engineering Analysis Laboratory, USA

CYBER 2023 Steering Committee
Carla Merkle Westphall, UFSC, Brazil
Barbara Re, University of Camerino, Italy
Rainer Falk, Siemens AG, Corporate Technology, Germany
Daniel Kästner, AbsInt GmbH, Germany
Anne Coull, University of New South Wales, Australia
Steffen Fries, Siemens, Germany

CYBER 2023 Publicity Chairs
Laura Garcia, Universitat Politecnica de Valencia, Spain

Lorena Parra Boronat, Universitat Politecnica de Valencia, Spain

CYBER 2023
Committee

CYBER 2023 Steering Committee Chair

Steve Chan, Decision Engineering Analysis Laboratory, USA

CYBER 2023 Steering Committee

Carla Merkle Westphall, UFSC, Brazil
Barbara Re, University of Camerino, Italy
Rainer Falk, Siemens AG, Corporate Technology, Germany
Daniel Kästner, AbsInt GmbH, Germany
Anne Coull, University of New South Wales, Australia
Steffen Fries, Siemens, Germany

CYBER 2023 Publicity Chairs

Laura Garcia, Universitat Politecnica de Valencia, Spain
Lorena Parra Boronat, Universitat Politecnica de Valencia, Spain

CYBER 2023 Technical Program Committee

Aysajan Abidin, imec-COSIC KU Leuven, Belgium
Shakil Ahmed, Iowa State University, USA
Cuneyt Gurcan Akcora, University of Manitoba, Canada
Oum-El-Kheir Aktouf, Grenoble Institute of Technology, France
Abdullah Al-Alaj, Virginia Wesleyan University, USA
Khalid Alemerien, Tafila Technical University, Jordan
Usman Ali, University of Connecticut, USA
Aisha Ali-Gombe, Towson University, USA
Mohammed S Alshehri, University of Arkansas, Fayetteville, USA
Alina Andronache, University of West of Scotland, UK
Abdullahi Arabo, University of the West of England, UK
A. Taufiq Asyhari, Coventry University, UK
Syed Badruddoja, University of North Texas, USA
Morgan Barbier, ENSICAEN, France
Samuel Bate, EY, UK
Vincent Beroulle, Univ. Grenoble Alpes, France
Clara Bertolissi, Aix-Marseille University | LIS | CNRS, France
Khurram Bhatti, Information Technology University (ITU), Lahore, Pakistan
Michael Black, University of South Alabama, USA
Davidson R. Boccardo, Clavis Information Security, Brazil
Felix Boes, University of Bonn, Germany
Ravi Borgaonkar, SINTEF Digital / University of Stavanger, Norway
Florent Bruguier, LIRMM | CNRS | University of Montpellier, France
Enrico Cambiaso, Consiglio Nazionale delle Ricerche (CNR), Italy

Nicola Capodieci, University of Modena and Reggio Emilia (UNIMORE), Italy
Pedro Castillejo Parrilla, Technical University of Madrid (UPM), Spain
Steve Chan, Decision Engineering Analysis Laboratory, USA
Christophe Charrier, Normandie Universite, France
Bo Chen, Michigan Technological University, USA
Mingwu Chen, Langara College, Canada
Lu Cheng, ArizonaState University, USA
Ioannis Chrysakis, FORTH-ICS, Greece / Ghent University, Belgium
Anastasija Collen, University of Geneva, Switzerland
Giovanni Costa, ICAR-CNR, Italy
Domenico Cotroneo, University of Naples, Italy
Anne Coull, University of New South Wales, Australia
Heming Cui, University of Hong Kong, Hong Kong
Monireh Dabaghchian, Morgan State University, USA
Dipanjan Das, University of California, Santa Barbara, USA
João Paulo de Brito Gonçalves, Instituto Federal do Espírito Santo, Brazil
Vincenzo De Angelis, University of Reggio Calabria, Italy
Lorenzo De Carli, Worcester Polytechnic Institute, USA
Noel De Palma, University Grenoble Alpes, France
Luigi De Simone, Università degli Studi di Napoli Federico II, Italy
Jerker Delsing, Lulea University of Technology, Sweden
Patrício Domingues, Polytechnic Institute of Leiria, Portugal
Paul Duplys, Robert Bosch GmbH, Germany
Soultana Ellinidou, Cybersecurity Research Center | University Libre de Bruxelles (ULB), Belgium
Rainer Falk, Siemens AG, Corporate Technology, Germany
Omair Faraj, Internet Interdisciplinary Institute (IN3) | UOC, Barcelona, Spain
Yebo Feng, University of Oregon, USA
Eduardo B. Fernandez, Florida Atlantic University, USA
Steffen Fries, Siemens Corporate Technologies, Germany
Somchart Fugkeaw, Thammasat University, Thailand
Damjan Fujs, University of Ljubljana, Slovenia
Steven Furnell, University of Nottingham, UK
Gina Gallegos Garcia, Instituto Politécnico Nacional, Mexico
Huangyi Ge, Purdue University, USA
Kambiz Ghazinour, SUNY Canton, USA
Konstantinos Giannoutakis, University of Macedonia, Greece
Uwe Glässer, Simon Fraser University - SFU, Canada
Ruy Jose Guerra Barretto de Queiroz, Federal University of Pernambuco, Brazil
Ekta Gujral, Walmart Global Tech, USA
Chunhui Guo, San Diego State University, USA
Amir M. Hajisadeghi, AmirkabirUniversity of Technology, Iran
Arne Hamann, Robert Bosch GmbH, Germany
Zecheng He, Princeton University, USA
Ehsan Hesamifard, University of North Texas, USA
Gahangir Hossain, West Texas A&M University, Canyon, USA
Mehdi Hosseinzadeh, Washington University in St. Louis, USA
Yaodan Hu, Idaho State University, USA
Zhen Huang, DePaul University, USA

Maria Francesca Idone, University of Reggio Calabria, Italy
Christos Iliou, Information Technologies Institute | CERTH, Greece / Bournemouth University, UK
Shalabh Jain, Research and Technology Center - Robert Bosch LLC, USA
Kevin Jones, University of Plymouth, UK
Georgios Kambourakis, University of the Aegean - Karlovassi, Samos, Greece
Sayar Karmakar, University of Florida, USA
Saffija Kasem-Madani, University of Bonn, Germany
Daniel Kästner, AbsInt GmbH, Germany
Basel Katt, Norwegian University of Science and Technology (NTNU), Norway
Mazaher Kianpour, Norwegian University of Science and Technology, Norway
Lucianna Kiffer, Northeastern University, USA
Sotitios Kontogiannis, University of Ioannina, Greece
Tanya Koohpayeh Araghi, University Oberta de Catalunya, Spain
Dragana S. Krstic, University of Nis, Serbia
Fatih Kurugollu, University of Derby, UK
Cecilia Labrini, University of Reggio Calabria, Italy
Ruggero Lanotte, University of Insubria, Italy
Petra Leimich, Edinburgh Napier University, Scotland, UK
Rafał Leszczyna, Gdansk University of Technology, Poland
Eirini Liotou, National and Kapodistrian University of Athens, Greece
Jing-Chiou Liou, Kean University - School of Computer Science and Technology, USA
Hao Liu, University of Cincinnati, USA
Xing Liu, Kwantlen Polytechnic University, Canada
Qinghua Lu, CSIRO, Australia
Yi Lu, Queensland University of Technology, Australia
Mahesh Nath Maddumala, Mercyhurst University, Erie, USA
Jorge Maestre Vidal, Universidad Complutense de Madrid, Spain
Louai Maghrabi, Dar Al-Hekma University, Jeddah, Saudi Arabia
Yasamin Mahmoodi, Tübingen University | FZI (Forschungszentrum Informatik), Germany
David Maimon, Georgia State University, USA
Ivan Malakhov, Università Ca' Foscari Venezia, Italy
Timo Malderle, University of Bonn, Germany
Mahdi Manavi, Mirdamad Institute of Higher Education, Iran
Sathiamoorthy Manoharan, University of Auckland, New Zealand
Michael Massoth, Hochschule Darmstadt - University of Applied Sciences / CRISP – Center for Research in Security and Privacy, Darmstadt, Germany
Vasileios Mavroeidis, University of Oslo, Norway
Mohammadreza Mehrabian, University of the Pacific, USA
Golizheh Mehrooz, University of Southern Denmark, Denmark
Weizhi Meng, Technical University of Denmark, Denmark
Carla Merkle Westphall, UFSC, Brazil
Massimo Merro, University of Verona, Italy
Caroline Moeckel, Open University, UK
Yasir F. Mohammed, University of Arkansas, USA
Lorenzo Musarella, University Mediterranea of Reggio Calabria, Italy
Vasudevan Nagendra, Stony Brook University, USA
Roberto Nardone, University Mediterranea of Reggio Calabria, Italy
Niels Nijdam, University of Geneva, Switzerland

Klimis Ntalianis, University of West Attica, Greece
Jason Nurse, University of Kent, UK
Riccardo Ortale, Institute for High Performance Computing and Networking (ICAR) of the National Research Council of Italy (CNR), Italy
Jordi Ortiz, University of Murcia, Spain
Richard E. Overill, King's College London, UK
Antonio Pecchia, University of Sannio, Italy
Eckhard Pfluegel, Kingston University, London, UK
Mila Dalla Preda, University of Verona, Italy
Muhammad Haris Rais, Virginia Commonwealth University, USA
Paweł Rajba, Hitachi Energy / University of Wroclaw, Poland
Massimiliano Rak, Università della Campania, Italy
Alexander Rasin, DePaul University, USA
Danda B. Rawat, Howard University, USA
Barbara Re, University of Camerino, Italy
Leon Reznik, Rochester Institute of Technology, USA
Jan Richling, South Westphalia University of Applied Sciences, Germany
Giulio Rigoni, University of Florence / University of Perugia, Italy
Antonia Russo,University Mediterranea of Reggio Calabria, Italy
Peter Y. A. Ryan, UniversityofLuxembourg, Luxembourg
Asanka P. Sayakkara, University of Colombo School of Computing (UCSC), Sri Lanka
Florence Sedes, Université Toulouse 3 Paul Sabatier, France
Abhijit Sen, Kwantlen Polytechnic University, Canada
Shirin Haji Amin Shirazi, University of California, Riverside, USA
Srivathsan Srinivasagopalan, AT&T CyberSecurity (Alien Labs), USA
Zhibo Sun, Drexel University, USA
Ciza Thomas, Government of Kerala, India
Zisis Tsiatsikas, Atos Greece / University of the Aegean, Greece
Tobias Urban, Institute for Internet Security - Westphalian University of Applied Sciences, Gelsenkirchen, Germany
Eric MSP Veith, OFFIS e.V. - Institut für Informatik, Germany
Mudit Verma, Arizona State University, Tempe, USA
Simon Vrhovec, University of Maribor, Slovenia
Stefanos Vrochidis, ITI-CERTH, Greece
James Wagner, University of New Orleans, USA
Khan Ferdous Wahid, Airbus Digital Trust Solutions, Germany
Gang Wang, Emerson Automation Solutions, USA
Qi Wang, Stellar Cyber Inc., USA
Ruoyu "Fish" Wang, Arizona State University, USA
Zhiyong Wang, Utrecht University, Netherlands
Zhen Xie, JD.com American Technologies Corporation, USA
Cong-Cong Xing, Nicholls State University, USA
Ping Yang, State University of New York at Binghamton, USA
Wuu Yang, National Chiao-Tung University, HsinChu, Taiwan
George O. M. Yee, Aptusinnova Inc. & Carleton University, Ottawa, Canada
Serhii Yevseiev, National Technical University - Kharkiv Polytechnic Institute, Ukraine
Kailiang Ying, Google, USA
Wei You, Renmin University of China, China

Yicheng Zhang, University of California, Irvine, USA
Piotr Zwierzykowski, Poznan University of Technology, Poland

Copyright Information

Cyber and Space: Information Warfare and Joint All Domain Effects in the Youngest Domains

Joshua A. Sipper
Air Command and Staff College
Air University
Maxwell AFB, AL, United States
Email: joshua.sipper.1@us.af.mil

Abstract— **Cyberspace and space operations are examined here as interdependent, cross-functional, and co-dependent on the electromagnetic spectrum. The research methodologies used here are survey research and comparative analysis leveraging the myriad entanglements between space, cyberspace, and electromagnetic spectrum technologies. To get a closer look at how space and interdisciplinary cyber operations can achieve these effects, cyber and space technological relationships, doctrine, operations, and cross-domain integration are analyzed and discussed. Through this analysis, it is found that these technologies have the intrinsic potential to affect deep enclaves of the electromagnetic spectrum, critical infrastructure, information infrastructure, information-related capabilities, and joint all-domain operations. These various technological and operational connections suggest various vulnerabilities and consequences if they are not properly secured and managed. However, if space and cyber can combine and interact across the full range of operations, there is a greater possibility of achieving sustained victory and peace.**

Keywords- cyber; space; infrastructure; electromagnetic; spectrum; security.

I. INTRODUCTION

The domains of space and cyber share many similarities, especially the fact that both are operationally akin to flying an aircraft that never lands, especially when referring to satellite operations. This, among other things, means that you never bring the airframe to depot for maintenance and refueling always takes place while the plane is flying. These and other similar properties were the impetus for the original assignment of Air Force Network Operations (AFNetOps), now cyber, under Air Force Space Command. Not only did the operational needs and mechanisms flow well together, the space doctrine and instructions made the most sense initially for establishing cyber guidance and procedures. Essentially, both domains follow the motto of the 26th Network Operations Squadron; Always On, Always Ready [1]. These two domains flow well together philosophically and operationally as both domains are mutually supportive, complementary, and critical enablers of Joint All-Domain Operations (JADO).

The most inherently positive correlations between space and cyber operations are their technological prowess and global empowerment of JADO. Joint All-Domain Operations require that cyber and space, from a domain perspective, focus on enabling capabilities to ensure strategic overmatch against foreign adversaries [2]. Through conjoined technological enhancements, cyber and space both push boundaries within their respective battlespaces and the kinetic, traditional domains. This fact coupled with the interlaced operational constructs of space and cyber technological capabilities brings additional power to bear in situations where networks, Global Positioning Systems (GPS), timing servers, and communications are of paramount importance to JADO. Further analysis of these technological capabilities will be examined later and special attention will be given to the specific enabling actions and effects produced using space and cyber together.

Doctrine is always at the forefront of any discussion concerning warfighting domains as it contains the best practices found in service and joint policy that guide and give weight to how wars are prosecuted. As with any highly technical subject matter, service and joint doctrine have historically found it difficult to capture the operational and tactical aura of the space and cyber domains. However, as further understanding concerning these domains and their capabilities has developed, an inclusion of their placement in JADO has begun to develop. This is vitally important as it relates to the aforementioned fact that space and cyber share a parallel function as critical enablers for all domains. Doctrine currently exists that points to joint capabilities that cross domains as this foundation is necessary for continued expansion and development of the domains and their intertwined nature [3]. Doctrine is and will continue to be an extremely important method for stating in service and joint terms how space and cyber will operate together and support JADO now and into the future.

Every domain includes specific operational capacities and limitations. However, within the space and cyber domains, these proclivities tend to reach much farther into other domains than others might into their more technical and abstract auspices. It is in these specific operational spaces that a deep exploration must take place in order to grasp how space and cyber press and change what have been considered impenetrable boundaries in the past. It is in these "technological zones" [4] that cyber and space have significant impact, spanning operational Command, Control, Communication, and Computers (C4) while saturating Intelligence, Surveillance, and Reconnaissance (ISR) and Electromagnetic Warfare (EW) as well. Operationally, space and cyber act not only as conduits for furthering operations in other domains, but also as equal partners, benefiting from one another and the air, sea, and land feedback loops, furthering the cyber and space situational awareness and ISR counterbalance. It is in this fundamentally cyclical and interdisciplinary construct that true combined JADO effects can take place.

Finally, interdisciplinary cross-domain effects are of peak concern when considering the combinatory power and effects of cyber and space within the JADO construct. As Laird put it, "A future war might first begin with attack-defense confrontation in space and network space, and seizing command of space and network dominance will become the crux to obtaining comprehensive dominance rights on the battlefield to further conquer the enemy and gain victory [5]." It is easy to sense the rhizomatic nature of space and cyber in this image of future conflicts. With the immediate battlefield advantage offered through feeding power into other domains with technological overmatch, all other domain spaces would naturally follow. Of course, this is dependent on numerous, complex factors within the space and cyber domains proper, not to mention the other domains. Some of these complexities will be underlined in later analysis.

The remainder of the paper structure is organized as follows. In section 2, space and cyberspace technical relationships are discussed to add context concerning the various linkages and dependencies across these domains. Section 3 presents an analysis of cyberspace and space doctrinal connections and overlaps for appropriate interactions within joint and service doctrinal enclaves. Section 4 delves into the complex interrelationships between cyberspace and space operations to include linkages through the Electromagnetic Spectrum (EMS) and satellite communications and telemetry. Section 5 analyzes the cross-domain synthesis and operability between space and cyberspace domains. Finally, section 6 summarizes and closes the paper and gives a forward perspective as cyberspace and space operations continue to coalesce and fuse. Technology, doctrine, operations, and cross-domain integration and effects are by no means the only considerations when exploring the cyber and space domains and their growing influence within military operational and strategic constructs. Nevertheless, these are areas of great importance that set the stage for many other issues of significance and consideration. Through analyzing and understanding these areas, a firmer comprehension of the overarching methodologies and constructs can be grasped.

II. SPACE AND CYBER TECHNOLOGICAL RELATIONSHIPS

Space and cyber are two domains, intimately linked in a constant technological surge for superiority and supremacy, both in military and civilian capacities. This linkage serves to produce ever more interesting and far reaching progress technologically while simultaneously presenting entangled complexity and problems. This is characterized by the amazing, and what Mills [6] characterizes as miraculous, technological leaps innate in cyber and space technologies, but also in security concerns and concurrent adversary advancement technologically and interdisciplinarily. These areas of import will serve as the crux of the following discussion concerning space and cyber technology, but also as a running theme represented not only here, but in the real world as cyber and space professionals have noted numerous times [7].

Technology in space and cyber are, although different, irrevocably intertwined and interdependent. As Madelyn R. Creedon, former Assistant Secretary of Defense Global Strategic Affairs, states, "the different physics and technical realities of space and cyberspace result in somewhat different threats. But despite the differences in our use of space and cyberspace, there are many similarities in the challenges [2]." These technological similarities are what drive space and cyber to continue the development of new and better technical methodologies for operations to meet the strategic concerns often seen on the horizon both domestically and abroad. These concerns are generally presented through vulnerabilities in cyber and space technologies, however, the technical realities of how space and cyber systems work together and are advancing offer ways to meet these challenges and work through and around them. For instance, the increasing capability to introduce more granular and advanced cyber and onboard space network information protection measures has increased and continues to increase rapidly. "More and more information can be stored and transported at ever-smaller scales, using profoundly fewer atoms and less energy per unit [6]." The accompanying miniaturization of components that can store increasingly more information more securely and stably offers cyber and space technological applications a way to protect against and drive past many of the current strategic concerns being forewarned. Additionally, as compared with legacy computer systems, current technology consumes over 100 million times less energy per logic operation, while working in a physical space more than one million times smaller with this same trend continuing exponentially on a daily basis [6]. And this doesn't even account for nascent technologies such as artificial intelligence, machine learning, deep learning, nanotech, and quantum computing; areas showing great promise toward increasing storage, speed, and computing at a distance through entanglement of subatomic particles. The technological interleaving of the space and cyber domains strategically and operationally offer seemingly limitless opportunities going forward, however, with any great step comes potentially great opportunity to stumble as further discussion regarding security and adversary competition shall bear out.

Security is a constant concern when dealing with any technology. The overwhelming desire of nation-state, terrorist, criminal, and corporate actors to gain access to information about and within bleeding edge cyber and space technologies presents a constant barrage of attacks and probes attempting to gain access and insight. But, even more sinister is the parallel desire to deny, degrade, deceive and destroy cyber and space assets. Adversaries across the spectrum from individuals and small groups to state and state sponsored cyber attackers, if not already, will soon have tools at their disposal to enact anti-satellite cyberattacks [8]. The consistent prodding and pushing to develop ways into cyber and space technological systems presents a growing risk to all domains of warfare, not just space and cyber. The continuing dependence of air, land, and sea operations for cyber and space situational awareness, navigation, and C4ISR carries with it myriad opportunities for mission failure. GPS is one of several examples of cyber enable satellite technology that could bring a rapid breakdown in operational capability if degraded. "These troubling trends are driving defense spending increases in resiliency and redundancy, including considerations of how best to achieve GPS-dependent Position, Navigation, and Timing (PNT) assurance [8]." It is only in protecting cyber and space technologies through mission assurance that operations can be continued, even in the most contested and congested of operational and information environments.

Peer and near-peer adversaries present several risks strategically and operationally to both cyber and space in the technological sphere. As has been reported and confirmed on numerous occasions, peer adversaries China and Russia engage constantly in industrial espionage, working vociferously to catch and surpass the United States technological aptitude and advances. "Washington views Russia's and China's pursuit of Anti-Satellite weapons (ASAT), including laser-armed, satellite-hunting aircraft, as an attempt 'to reduce U.S. and allied military effectiveness' and 'to offset any perceived US military advantage derived from military, civil, or commercial space systems [8]." With increasing regularity and persistence, China especially has sought to maintain a foothold in United States cyber and space systems, adding to the threat of espionage and sabotage on a massive scale. This can be seen in China's strategic move to establish its Strategic Support Force (SSF) which, among other things, consolidates space and cyber power to advance China's strategic interests in economic growth and technological development [9]. These advancements strategically undergird China's dream to further their space program and pass that of the United States, reaching farther into space than has been previously imagined. With this enhanced reach and power, China could set itself up for economic and technological power projection launching the country far ahead of all other competition. "China aims to establish a manned space station by 2020–22 and a space-based solar power station by 2050 to meet its burgeoning economic and energy needs, develop space science and technology, explore outer space, and land on Mars [7]." With strategic aims such as these, China stands a great chance of surpassing US technological capabilities and reaching the potentially vast resources contained in the inner solar system and belt.

Technological reach, while only one area of interest and concern within the cyber and space operational domains, is nevertheless extremely important, probabilistically affecting every other domain and area of strategic interest including doctrine, operations, and cross-domain integration. With the technological piece firmly planted in the consciousness of military and government psyches, further considerations must be made to advance cyber and space technological growth and integration, security protections and mission assurance, and peer competition. Only through continued technological advancement in these arenas will the US be able to continue to lead the way in every area of global and space power insertion.

III. CYBER AND SPACE DOCTRINE

The interlacing of doctrine concerning disparate domains has always been an area of difficulty and potential breakdown, especially when it comes to highly technical and complex domain infrastructures such as space and cyber. The level of competency and understanding the technical and architectural requirements related to operations and strategic concerns, not to mention the deep tactical intricacies, in the cyber and space domains often makes tying these areas into other operations difficult. This is true not only for the traditional domains, but even more so between space and cyber since the technologies are always growing and advancing in capability and complexity. Doctrinally, the areas cogent to this discussion are space and cyber operational entanglement, operational thresholds regarding war and potential escalation, and the operational systems associated with these domains across the spectrum of conflict.

As technologically diverse and discrete fields often are, space and cyber tie closely together due to their technological dependence for operations while simultaneously holding their own entrenched technical specificities. Regardless of any disparities, however, the space and cyber domains experience what can best be described as entanglement; the quality of a technological cause and effect relationship. This can be seen across the operational spectrum within space and cyber as certain areas of networking for cyber operations are space dependent and many areas of space operations from a networking and C4ISR perspective are supported, enabled, and driven by cyber operations. Cybersecurity supports and defends space assets, provides authentication and encryption to space assets, and uses filtering shielding, and spread-spectrum techniques to guard against electromagnetic interference, jamming, and other attack [10]. The transverse is true as space assets provide over-the-horizon communications, data linkages and network capability, network command and control, and ISR data for cyber operations, creating a continuous, complementary feedback loop. As doctrine concerning these cross-domain interactions is developed and specified, these relationships will become clearer and more defined.

Both cyber and space domains share a similar kinetic/non-kinetic threshold as well. When it comes to the level of conflict that may lead to escalation and potential acts of war, both space and cyber present advantages and complexities. For instance, both space and cyber may be used consistently to degrade, deny, and deceive adversaries, leading to conflict below the threshold of kinetic operations that may extend into potential kinetic conflict leading to war. It is important from a doctrinal perspective to draw these lines and intimate the contrasts involved in these conflict situations. Questions such as what level of operations define the level of Anti-Satellite (ASAT) weapons, whether lasing or jamming are considered ASAT, for example, persist [11]. Differentiation must also be expressed regarding the various actions potential during wartime and peacetime. "Possibly only probing and reversible cyber-type attacks would be allowed in peacetime, but more permanent, damaging attacks could be executed in general wartime situations [12]." These issues must be discussed within space and cyber doctrine in order to help operators and strategists in both disciplines create opportunities and battlefield effects across the spectrum of conflict.

The operational systems used to drive those operations are integral to the success of space and cyber operational integration. While it is usually not wise from a doctrinal standpoint to specify systems, it is nevertheless important to note that systems do exist and interleave. This is true for many domains and will only become more important as JADO continues to grow and ramify. However, space and cyber operational systems are often interdependent, leading to even more need to understand these entanglements and ensure they are spelled out in doctrine. For instance, "The term space systems refers to the equipment required for space operations, which is comprised of nodes and links. This includes all the devices and organizations forming the space network, which consists of spacecraft; ground and airborne stations; and data links among spacecraft, mission, and user terminals [13]." All of the data links, nodes, and other network linkages mentioned here are cyber driven and controlled. Unfortunately, this is not always specifically, explicitly stated in doctrinal sources. While some might cite the implicit understanding, it may not always come through to operators trying to ensure space and cyber assets and operational systems are integrated and working together.

As doctrine inevitably shifts and changes with the stand-up of the new United States Space Force (USSF), it will be increasingly important to ensure that space and cyber are linked and operationally related in every way possible. With the JADO concept of operations continuing to gain strength and significance, this will become even more important to ensure all-domain operation and superiority. As cyber and space entanglement grow continuously, the operational dependencies naturally present will need to be noted and explained in doctrine. The operational thresholds also must be framed and dictated to ensure the appropriate measures are prescribed across the spectrum of conflict. Also, operational systems related to both space and cyber domains must be interlocked and explicitly discussed in doctrine to ensure clear and concise operational understanding and future integration.

IV. CYBER AND SPACE OPERATIONS

As relatively new warfare domains, space and cyber both operate in distinct ways compared to the traditional air, land, and sea battlespaces. This can be seen primarily in the technological emphasis inherent in space and cyber, but also in several other operationally vital areas. Many of the operational support, training, and auxiliary elements associated with space and cyber are uniquely attuned to the specialized technical and navigability requirements for these domains. Without the proper equipment and operational understanding of that equipment, for instance, the space and cyber missions are intractable. Both space and cyber also contain imbedded operational vulnerabilities special to their battlespace environs. While space suffers the tyranny of distance, cyber suffers a tyranny of locality, both of which present different and convoluted vulnerabilities. Space and cyber, while young domains, also have grown and matured rapidly over the last decade, bringing with them amazing and powerful capabilities that have revolutionized warfare, making JADO and Information Warfare (IW) realities. The following areas of space and cyber operational elements, operational vulnerabilities, and operational maturity serve as major topics of understanding going forward.

The operational elements associated with cyber and space are integral to the domains' ability to interleave and prosecute missions. While some areas such as intelligence, education, and training are definitively carried over into these domains operationally [14] others such as land- and sea-based nuclear operations, cyberspace operations, and the overall missile defense mission have been suggested to be set aside as tangential [15]. While it could be understood how some of these areas might be considered tangential and need to be somewhat decentralized within their own domain structures, it is imperative that some (cyber especially) be closely held and integrate into space operations from launch to landing. This is not to say that USSF needs to hold operational control of US Cyber Command, but that the elements should work closely to ensure space and cyber operations carry forward for JADO, IW, and cross-domain support. Without this solid operations linkage, mission assurance could disintegrate rapidly.

The potential disintegration relates directly to the various, specialized vulnerabilities present within the space and cyber operational constructs. As these domains continue operating together, they tend to rub off on one another to some extent as they both are highly dependent on their respective and combined technological scaffolds. "Technology can be lost in microseconds through cyber espionage, giving rogue nations the ability to catch up without the time or investment devoted by first movers [11]." The technical, strategic, and economic vulnerabilities to space and cyber are often related to what has become an increasingly lower level of entry into these spheres; one that will continue to present risks. Integration of C2 and other systems also introduces potential problems into operations as bugs and zero day vulnerabilities may lie unpatched [16]. These issues are various and plentiful and must be considered as space and cyber integration proceeds.

Conversely, as the youthful domains of space and cyber have grown preternaturally over the last decade, they have taken on many, extremely complex operational responsibilities, leading to the development of JADO and IW strategic and operational concepts. As enabling and singularly capable operation domains, space and cyber have both found purchase in every area of warfare, leading to combinations and effects heretofore unheard of. For instance, both domains offer power and stability to information related capabilities such as Information Operations (IO), Electromagnetic Warfare (EW), and ISR that have allowed the integration and cross-disciplinary operation of all of these elements to produce IW effects. Consequently, "space and cyberspace have… grown from their original manifestations as supporting capabilities into warfighting arenas in their own right [17]." As space and cyber continue to develop and mature, the capabilities and technologies associated with and shared by both domains will doubtless continue to take new and conjoined shapes.

Operationally, space and cyber are distinct, yet linked in numerous ways. Both share elements that can be integrated and moved fluidly through both domains while still being irrevocably linked to their own operational area. Training, education, and ISR are a good example as these can easily overlap operationally, feeding necessary information between all domains, further enhancing the JADO and IW concepts. Space and cyber also share similar vulnerabilities. While space vulnerabilities are ones associated with distance such as communications and networks, they also relate with the cyber domain vulnerabilities of the same ilk which are most often made difficult in the local, global ability of adversaries to affect devices at light speed instantaneously from a distance. Ultimately, the maturity of both domains have lent them the ability to operate together, exponentially increasing each other's potential and effectiveness while also enhancing JADO and IW battlespace efficacy.

V. CYBER AND SPACE CROSS-DOMAIN CONSIDERATIONS

As IW and JADO strategic scaffolds proliferate throughout joint and service philosophy, space and cyber cross-domain effects and concepts will continue to pervade every domain. This fact makes understanding and performing space and cyber cross-domain effects all the more important and integral to operations at every level. While there are potentially copious ways to ensure cross-domain considerations are attended to, the most vital components for discussion are cross-domain platforms, hardening across technologies, and IW and JADO superiority. Platforms within any domain are the bedrock, tangible resources upon which most operations rest. If platforms are not well designed and integrated, mission success is constantly in question. Hardening of these platforms and systems directly affects whether or not they can function since the protective measures from hardening often spell the difference between operational success and failure. If space and cyber missions are active, assured, and ready, IW and JADO can be mission assured, leading to victory across all domains, disciplines, and battle spaces.

Cross-domain operations are, more often than not, supported and assured through platform integration and interoperability. This can be seen in the more traditional domains through close air support, ground support to naval activities, and other integral platform-dependent undertakings. The same types of integration can be seen in network support to space operations and space platform network support to cyber operations and numerous other examples of platform interlocking. Position, Navigation, and Timing (PNT) is one critical area associated with cross-platform integration. "PNT information is a critical enabler for the delivery of numerous types of Precision-Guided Munitions (PGMs) including aircraft missiles, naval gunnery and land-based artillery shells. Synchronous timing provided by space-based PNT services is also a vital element of many military communication and information systems [18]." Another cross-platform solution deeply related to PNT is GPS through which coordination of cross-domain, JADO, and IW activities can be coordinated globally. These and other cross-platform necessities must be considered heavily in order to ensure operational stability.

To ensure cross-platform permanency, vulnerabilities must be identified, addressed, and continuously reevaluated as new threats arise. While threats to space and cyber sometimes differ, they tend to overlap often as the technological vulnerabilities associated with electronic traffic through the EMS pervade every corner of space and cyber operations. Various attacks across the EMS and networks are possible including jamming, spoofing and hacking attacks on communication networks via space infrastructure, attacks on satellites, targeting their control systems or mission packages, perhaps taking control of a satellite to exploit its capabilities, shut it down, alter its orbit, or "cook" or "grill" its solar cells through deliberate exposure to damaging levels of radiation attacks on ground infrastructure, such as satellite control centers, associated networks and data centers, leading to potential global cascading effects on critical information infrastructure and networks [18]. With this level of destruction at adversaries' fingertips, it is vitally important to consider ways in which to harden and protect the cross-platform infrastructures and information transmission dependencies necessary for mission completion. "Debilitating loss of space capabilities from a surprise attack; direct assaults with ballistic and cruise missiles; cyber strikes; or, in the near future, space-based weaponry could be anticipated within minutes [15]." Thus, hardening must reach outside of the kinetic norms while continuing to consider the wide array of possible adversary attack options. Several options exist for hardening including air gapping, strong encryption, and layer authentication protocols, many of which are already in use. However, space and cyber operators must always be vigilant as new attacks, vulnerabilities, and weak spots in human diligence are always present.

Although cross-domain dependencies specifically between space and cyber are extremely important, the strategic and operational landscapes of IW and JADO must also be given full attention as these nascent concepts are growing in power and profusion. IW is currently defined as the interdisciplinary combination of information related capabilities (Cyber, ISR, EW, and IO) to produce effects. This is an extremely powerful panoply and lends its strength potentially to JADO as IW operational effects have the potential to create major weaknesses in adversary defensive and operational constructs. A prime example of this is the Israeli Air Force operation carried out in September of 2007 against the joint Syrian/North Korean nuclear operations in Syria where Israel used a combination of cyber, ISR, EW, and IO along with its kinetic air capabilities to destroy the Syrian reactor. [20] This lethal combination is just one instance where the use of IW and JADO/MDO was an unparalleled success. Space factors well into these types of operations as well as the space-eye view enables ISR, cyber, and numerous other domain and information areas close access to battlespaces. "A state may, over time, create a resilient constellation of hundreds of networked satellites (national, commercial, and allied) that may be able to convince an adversary that its forces will not be able to accomplish their objective of denying space-derived information [19]." The same can be seen in the IW sphere as combinations of information related capabilities produce a united front during conflict by leveraging space, cyberspace, and electronic warfare assets [3] as well as ISR through imagery and other intelligence disciplines [17]. The decisive victory to be gained through JADO and IW interactions and integration with space and cyber cannot be overstated. Through a full-spectrum junction of this cornucopia of capabilities, space and cyber power can create and sustain effects profoundly into every space of engagement.

VI. CONCLUSION

Cyber and space, while the youngest of the warfighting domains, have risen rapidly in prominence, capability, and maturity to become the key JADO and IW critical enablers. This can be seen in the constant operation constructs of space and cyber as ongoing missions; planes that never land. Additionally, the technical prowess and capabilities of space and cyber make them integral parts of every mission area within every domain. Through the C4ISR and cross-domain enablement found in these young domains, information flows and operations succeed. Doctrine is an area constantly striving to maintain pace with technologically agile areas and must continue to shape and expand to fill gaps and tie together warfighting concepts as they evolve. From and operational standpoint, space and cyber represent the Gemini in warfighting constructs, complementing and completing each other while offering their superior operational technological scaffold for use in IW and JADO. The possibilities are seemingly limitless as are the challenges, but if space and cyber can combine and interact across the full range of operations, there is a much greater possibility of achieving sustained victory and peace.

REFERENCES

[1] 26th NOS motto, retrieved 9 July 2020: https://www.afhra.af.mil/About-Us/Fact-Sheets/Display/Article/432510/26-network-operations-squadron-afspc/

[2] M. Creedon, "Space and Cyber: Shared Challenges, Shared Opportunities", Strategic Studies Quarterly, Vol. 6, No. 1, SPRING 2012, pp. 3-8.

[3] J. Caton, "The Land, Space, and Cyberspace Nexus: Evolution of the Oldest Military Operations in The Newest Military Domains", Strategic Studies Institute, US Army War College, 2018.

[4] J. Hay, "The Invention of Air Space, Outer Space, and Cyberspace," Rutgers University Press, 2019.

[5] B. Laird, "Space and Cyberspace Operations," Center for a New American Security, 2017.

[6] M. Mills, "Making Technological Miracles", The New Atlantis, Spring 2017, No. 52, pp. 37-55.

[7] N. Gowswami, "China in Space: Ambitions and Possible Conflict", Strategic Studies Quarterly, Vol. 12, No. 1, SPRING 2018, pp. 74-97.

[8] C. Kavanagh, "New Tech, New Threats, and New Governance Challenges: An Opportunity to Craft Smarter Responses?" Carnegie Endowment for International Peace, 2019.

[9] A. Ni, "Dreams in Space" ANU Press, 2020.

[10] Annex 3-14 - Counterspace Operations, retrieved 7/16/2020 from https://www.doctrine.af.mil/Doctrine-Annexes/Annex-3-14-Counterspace-Ops/

[11] T. Harrison, "Defining Space Warfare and Space Weapons," Center for Strategic and International Studies (CSIS), 2020.

[12] P. Szymanski, "Techniques for Great Power Space War" Strategic Studies Quarterly, Vol. 13, No. 4, WINTER 2019, pp. 78-104.

[13] C. King, D. Young, E. Byrne, and P. Konyha, "AU-18 Space Primer," Air Command and Staff College and Space Research Electives Seminars Air University Press, 2009.

[14] RAND Corporation, "Creating a Separate Space Force: Challenges and Opportunities for an Effective, Efficient, Independent Space Service," RAND Corporation, 2020.

[15] E. Dolman, "Space Force Déjà Vu," Strategic Studies Quarterly, Vol. 13, No. 2, SUMMER 2019, pp. 16-22.

[16] G. McCleod, G. Nacouzi, P. Dreyer, M. Eisman, M. Hura, K. Langeland, D. Manheim, and G. Torrington, "Resilience and Air Force Space Operations," RAND Corporation, 2016.

[17] D. Grant, and M. Neil, "The Case for Space: A Legislative Framework for an Independent United States Space Force," Air University Press, 2020.

[18] M. Davis, "Why maintaining space access matters," Australian Strategic Policy Institute, 2019.

[19] J. Moltz, "The Changing Dynamics of Twenty-First-Century Space Power," Strategic Studies Quarterly, Vol. 13, No. 1, SPRING 2019, pp. 66-94.

[20] V. Holath and H. Stark, "How Israel Destroyed Syria's Al Kibar Nuclear Reactor," Der Spiegel, retrived 13 August 2023: https://www.spiegel.de/international/world/the-story-of-operation-orchard-how-israel-destroyed-syria-s-al-kibar-nuclear-reactor-a-658663.html

DISCLAIMERS:

The views expressed are those of the author and do not necessarily reflect the official policy or position of the Air Force, the Department of Defense, or the U.S. Government.

DoD School Policy. DoD gives its personnel in its school environments the widest latitude to express their views. To ensure a climate of academic freedom and to encourage intellectual expression, students and faculty members of an academy, college, university, or DoD school are not required to submit papers or material that are prepared in response to academic requirements and not intended for release outside the academic institution. Information proposed for public release or made available in libraries or databases or on web sites to which the public has access shall be submitted for review.

Physical-World Access Attestation

Rainer Falk and Steffen Fries
Siemens AG
Technology
Munich, Germany
e-mail: {rainer.falk|steffen.fries}@siemens.com

Abstract—**Virtualized automation functions can be used in a cyber-physical system to influence the real, physical world using sensors and actuators connected via input-output modules. Other virtualized automation functions may be used for planning, testing, or optimization. It has to be distinguished reliably which instances in fact interact with the real, physical world, and which ones are used for other, less critical purposes. A reliable method for determining whether a certain virtualized automation function has access to the real, physical world is proposed, based on a cryptographically protected physical-world access attestation issued by an input/output module. It confirms whether a certain virtualized automation function has in fact access to the real-physical world.**

Keywords–cyber physical system; attestation, industrial security; cybersecurity.

I. INTRODUCTION

A Cyber Physical System (CPS) contains control devices that interact with the real, physical world using sensors and actuators. Which automation and control devices are connected via sensors and actuators to the real, physical world has implicitly been clear from the structure of physical control devices, sensors, actuators and their cabling.

Digital twins supporting the simulation of the CPS and its control devices provide the possibility to perform plausibility checks of the measured real-world behavior and the expected, simulated behavior in parallel. This eases the detection of unexpected system behavior, which may indicate a failure situation or even an attack. In addition, virtualization of control devices is increasing, allowing to deploy multiple instances of virtualized control devices that look and behave identically [1]. A virtualized control device can be realized as virtual machine or container hosted on an app-enabled edge device or on a cloud infrastructure by a virtualized Automation Function (vAF). In such a deployment, it has to be distinguished which vAF instances in fact interact with the real, physical world, and which ones are used for other purposes as, e.g., training, optimization, planning, virtual commissioning, simulation, or for testing. The vAF instance that in fact has access to the real physical world is the one that is the most critical, as its operation affects the real world.

In this paper, we propose a reliable method for determining whether a certain vAF instance has access to the real, physical world. A cryptographically protected Physical-World Access Attestation (PWAA) issued by an Input/Output (IO) module confirms whether a certain vAF instance has access to that IO module. The IO module itself provides the connectivity to the real, physical world via the connected sensors and actuators.

The remainder of the paper is structured as follows: Section II gives an overview on related work. Section III describes the concept of physical world access attestations, and Section IV presents a usage scenario in an industrial Operation Technology (OT) environment. Section V provides a preliminary evaluation of the presented approach. Section VI concludes the paper and gives an outlook towards future work.

II. RELATED WORK

Cybersecurity for Industrial Automation and Control Systems (IACS) is specified in the standard series IEC62443 [2]. This series provides a security framework as a set of security standards defining security requirements for the development process and the operation of IACS as well as technical cybersecurity requirements on automation systems and the used components.

The Trusted Computing Group (TCG) defined attestation as the process of vouching for the accuracy of information [3]. An attestation is a cryptographically protected data structure that asserts the accuracy of the attested information.

The Remote Attestation procedureS (RATS) working group of the Internet Engineering Task Force (IETF) described various attestation use cases [4]. Examples are the attestation of platform integrity and the attestation of the implementation approach for a cryptographic key store. An attestation allows a communication peer to reliably determine information about the (remote) platform besides the authenticated identity.

III. PHYSICAL WORLD ACCESS ATTESTATION

A cryptographically protected PWAA is issued by an input/output (IO) module confirming in a reliable way that a certain vAF instance has in fact access to that IO module, i.e., that it has access to the physical world. This information can be used for monitoring the CPS operations as well as for adapting access permissions of the vAF. It can be reliably determined whether the intended vAFs have in fact access to the physical world. Furthermore, only those vAFs having the privilege of accessing the physical world can be granted access to perform security-critical operations during production, e.g., providing production data to a product database.

A. *CPS System Model*

Figure 1 shows an example of a CPS where multiple vAFs monitor and control the physical world via sensors and actuators connected to IO Modules (IOM). The vAFs are executed on an industrial edge compute system by an industrial edge RunTime Environment (RTE). It would also be possible that vAFs are executed on different edge compute systems or on a backend compute system (cloud-based control).

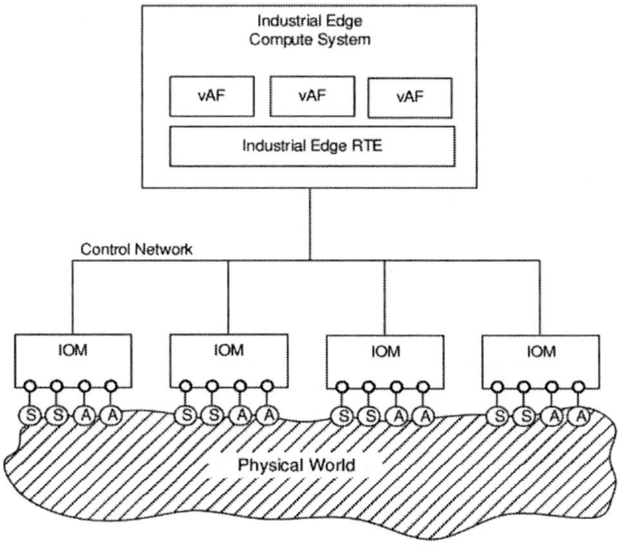

Figure 1. CPS system model

As depicted in Figure 1, an IOM is directly connected to sensors and actuators that in turn provide the interaction with the real, physical world. Thus, these IO modules are crucial as they control on one hand the actions to be performed in the physical world, but also provide monitoring data received from the physical world via the sensors.

B. *Physical-World Access Attestation*

An IOM authenticates the vAF that is accessing the IOM, e.g., by using a mutual certificate-based Transport Layer Security (TLS) authentication. The IOM creates a cryptographically protected attestation (the aforementioned PWAA) that confirms reliably which vAF is accessing this IOM, thereby confirming that the identified vAF has access to the sensors/actuators connected to the IOM, and thereby consequently having access to the physical world. The PWAA confirms, based on the authenticated communication session between a vAF and the IOM, that the authenticated vAF has currently access to the physical world via this IOM. In addition, the PWAA may also provide additional information like information about the sensors and actuators connected to the IOM, or about its location.

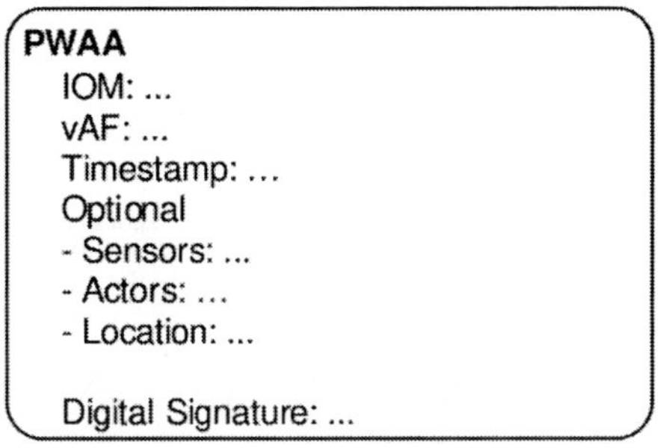

Figure 2. Physical world access attestation

Figure 2 visualizes the main elements of a PWAA. It indicates the IOM, the vAF, and it includes furthermore a timestamp to ensure freshness, and a digital signature of the IOM issuing the PWAA. The identification of the IOM and also the vAF may be done based on the credentials used for the mutual authentication between both. Optionally, the PWAA can comprise also an information on the sensors and actuators to which the indicated vAF has access, or on its location. The digital signature ensures that any manipulation of the PWAA can be detected.

C. *IO-Module with Real-world Access Attestation*

An IOM includes an attestation unit that creates and provides the cryptographically protected PWAA.

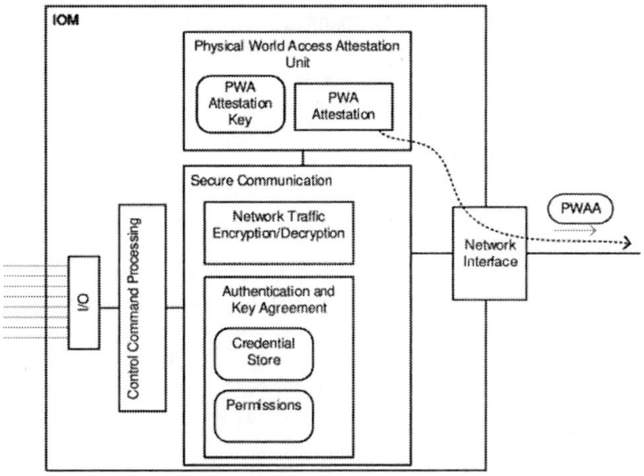

Figure 3. IO module with physical world access attestation

Figure 3 shows an IOM that includes an attestation unit that determines and provides the PWAA to a relying party, e.g., a CPS management system . The IOM comprises an input-output interface (I/O) to which sensors and actuators can be connected. The IOM can be accessed via its network interface using a mutually authenticated secure communication session. The physical world access attestation unit determines which vAF has been authenticated by the IOM to establish a secure communication session, and builds a cryptographically protected PWAA. The digital signature of the PWAA may be build using the same credentials as used for mutual authentication or by distinct ones.

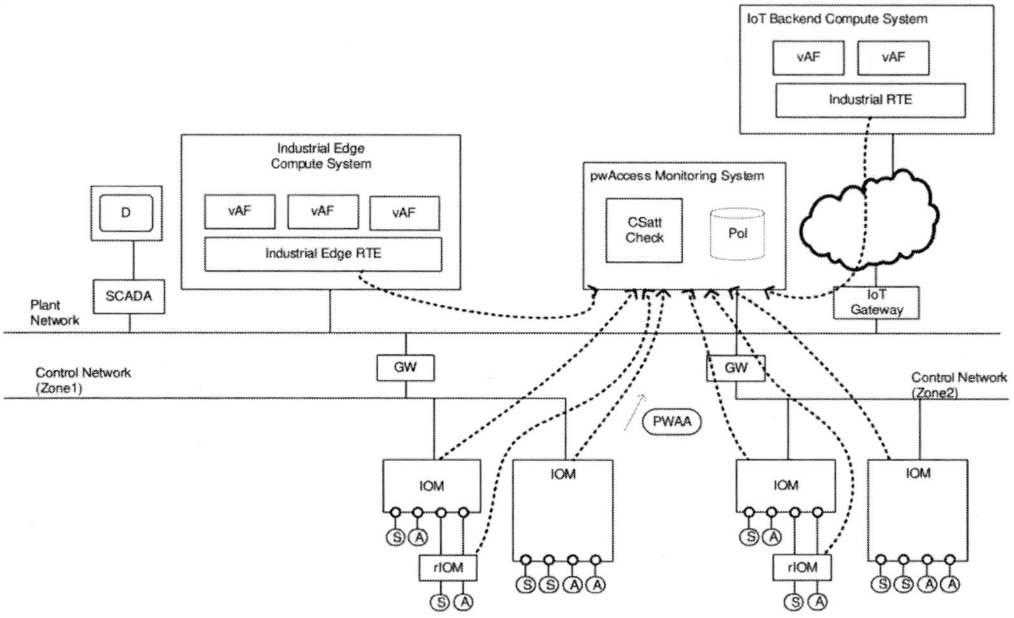

Figure 4. Example PWAA usage scenario

D. Adapting Access Permissions

The PWAA provided by an IOM is verified by a relying party, e.g., a production management system to adapt access information related to the vAF indicated by the PWAA. The PWAA can be seen as a context information used in access control decision. This is related to a zero-trust security approach, where context information of the requester and also the responder is taken into account for access control decisions.

E. Integrating with System Integrity Monitoring

The PWAAs provided by IOMs can also be used by a CPS integrity monitoring systems as described in [6]. It allows to reliably determine which vAF instances are the "real" ones that in fact have access to the physical world. Those vAFs are the ones that are subject to the operative CPS integrity monitoring. Other vAF instances may be used for simulations, tests, or as redundant backup functions.

IV. USAGE EXAMPLE

This section describes the usage of PWAA for CPS in an exemplary way. Figure 4 shows a CPS usage scenario. It shows two control networks for two production networks (zone1, zone2) and a plant network. The automation system is virtualized, i.e., it is realized by virtual automation functions (vAF) that are execute on an on-premise compute infrastructure (Industrial Edge Compute System) or in a backend computing infrastructure, e.g., a hyperscaler cloud or a multiaccess edge computing infrastructure of a mobile communication network.

In addition to the IOMs connected to the control network, also remote IO modules (rIOM) connected to the IOMs can be used. The IO modules (IOM, rIOM) provide PWAA to a physical world access monitoring system. Optionally, also the RTEs executing the vAFs can provide attestations confirming to which IOMs a vAF is connected.

The physical world access monitoring system determines which vAFs have access to the physical world. Depending on the monitoring results, an authorization token, e.g., an OAuth token [7], a verifiable credential [8], or an attribute certificate, can be provided to the vAF, or it can be granted the permission to perform a startup procedure of a technical system, e.g., a production machine.

It is also possible to adapt access permissions of a vAF, e.g., to access a production management system or a Supervisory Control And Data Acquisition (SCADA) system.

Moreover, based on the context information contained in the PWAA, a pwAccess monitoring system as shown in Figure 4 can use this information to derive a system state based on specific sensor and actuator information. This system state can characterize if the system is operating in normal mode, in alert mode, or even in emergency mode, based on the evaluation of the actual measured values with potentially simulated and thus expected values. This derived system state in turn may influence further access decisions. This may be specifically important for systems in a critical infrastructure, like a power generation or distribution facility. Here, it may be important to bind access decisions on the overall system state to ensure reliable operation of the system.

Furthermore, external provided system state information may also influence the access decision. An example may be the information about a maintenance period, to ensure that certain operation of a system is not possible during this time.

The physical world access monitoring system is shown as dedicated component. However, it is also possible to realize it as virtualized function, e.g., as virtual machine or as container executed on an edge computing platform.

V. Evaluation

This section gives a preliminary evaluation of the presented PWAA concept from the perspective of the operator of a CPS, and from the perspective of IO module implementation, performance impact, and provisioning.

Operator perspective: Availability and the flexibility to adapt to changing production requirements are important requirements for OT operators [5]. The proposed approach allows to apply strict cybersecurity controls automatically only when really needed, i.e., for operational real-world systems. The information may be utilized to report a system overall health state, which in turn can be considered in further access decisions. Other installations can be handled more openly, providing more flexibility.

Implementation perspective: The IOMs have to provide cryptographic attestations. This required support for basic cryptographic operations (cryptographic algorithms, key store, key management) is already available on IO modules that allow authenticated network access. So, only the additional functionality to create and provide attestations has to be implemented.

Performance perspective: The creation of an attestation is expected to have a negligible impact on the real-time performance of the IOM. For example, the signature can be generated during the authentication and key agreement phase of the secure communication protocol between IOM and vAF. Certain parts of the PWAA may also be prepared based on the locally available sensor information to require only minor lookup and completing of the information structure during the actual authentication and authorization phase.

Provisioning perspective: Additional key material has to be provisioned for protecting attestations, as the attestation key should be different to the device authentication key of IO module to have separate key material for different cybersecurity usages. Here, it may be assumed that for certificate management an automated interaction based on typical certificate management protocols like the Certificate Management Protocol CMP [10], Enrollment over Secure Transport EST [11], or the Simple Certificate Enrolment Protocol SCEP [12] is applied to overcome the burden of manual administration. In this context, a separate attestation key pair may be managed in addition to device authentication keys.

VI. Conclusion and Future Work

The physical-world access attestation proposed in this paper allows to determine reliably which vAFs have in fact access to the real, physical world, i.e., to operational real-world technical systems. This information allows to apply stricter cybersecurity controls automatically specifically to those vAFs and their hosting platforms that are determined to be critical for the real-world CPS operation.

The exact implementation size and performance overhead of a technical realization has still to be evaluated, considering that cryptographic building blocks that are needed, e.g., for secure communications, can be reused. From a practical perspective, it is considered to be more important to determine the usefulness in practical use, i.e., to what degree it allows to enhance flexibility in CPS planning and operation, and to increase operational efficiency by reducing the time needed for reconfiguring real-world technical systems while still being compliant with the required cybersecurity level.

References

[1] M. Gundall, D. Reti, and H. D. Schotten, "Application of Virtualization Technologies in Novel Industrial Automation: Catalyst or Show-Stopper?", arXiv:2011.07804v1, Nov. 2020, [Online]. Available from: https://arxiv.org/abs/2011.07804 [retrieved: Aug., 2023]

[2] IEC 62443, "Industrial Automation and Control System Security" (formerly ISA99), [Online]. Available from: http://isa99.isa.org/Documents/Forms/AllItems.aspx [retrieved: Aug., 2023]

[3] Trusted Computing Group, "Glossary", 2012, [Online]. Available from https://trustedcomputinggroup.org/wp-content/uploads/TCG_Glossary_Board-Approved_12.13.2012.pdf [retrieved: Aug., 2023]

[4] H. Birkholz, D. Thaler, M. Richardson, N. Smith, and W. Pan, "Remote ATtestation procedureS (RATS) Architecture", Internet Request for Comments RFC9334, 2023, [Online]. Available from: https://datatracker.ietf.org/doc/rfc9334/ [retrieved: Aug., 2023]

[5] R. Falk and S. Fries, "System Integrity Monitoring for Industrial Cyber Physical Systems", Journal on Advances in Security, vol 11, no 1&2, July 2018, pp. 170-179, [Online]. Available from: www.iariajournals.org/security/sec_v11_n12_2018_paged.pdf [retrieved: Aug., 2023]

[6] R. Falk and S. Fries, "Dynamic Trust Evaluation of Evolving Cyber Physical Systems", CYBER 2022, The Seventh International Conference on Cyber-Technologies and Cyber-Systems, pp.19-24, 2022, [Online]. Available from: http://thinkmind.org/index.php?view=article&articleid=cyber_2022_1_30_80022 [retrieved: Aug., 2023]

[7] D. Hardt (Editor), " The OAuth 2.0 Authorization Framework", Internet Request for Comments RFC6749, 2012, [Online]. Available from: https://datatracker.ietf.org/doc/rfc6749/ [retrieved: Aug., 2023]

[8] D. Longley and M. Sporny, "Verifiable Credential Data Integrity 1.0 – Securing the Integrity of Verifiable Credential Data", W3C Working Draft 15 May 2023, [Online]. Available from: https://www.w3.org/TR/vc-data-integrity/ [retrieved: Aug., 2023]

[9] "Information technology - Open Systems Interconnection - The Directory: Public-key and attribute certificate frameworks", ITU-T X.509, October 2019, [Online]. Available from: https://www.itu.int/rec/T-REC-X.509-201910-I/en [retrieved: Aug., 2023]

[10] C. Adams, S. Farrell, T. Kause, and T. Mononen, "Internet X.509 Public Key Infrastructure Certificate Management Protocol (CMP)", Internet Request for Comments RFC4210, 2005, [Online]. Available from: https://datatracker.ietf.org/doc/rfc4210 [retrieved: Aug., 2023]

[11] M. Pritikin, P. Yee, and D. Harkins, "Enrollment over Secure Transport", Internet Request for Comments RFC7030, 2013, [Online]. Available from: https://datatracker.ietf.org/doc/rfc7030 [retrieved: Aug., 2023]

[12] P. Gutmann, "Simple Certificate Enrolment Protocol", Internet Request for Comments RFC8894, 2020, [Online]. Available from: https://datatracker.ietf.org/doc/rfc8894 [retrieved: Aug., 2023]

You Are Doing it Wrong - On Vulnerabilities in Low Code Development Platforms

Miguel Lourenço
Instituto Universitário de Lisboa
(ISCTE-IUL), ISTAR
Lisbon, Portugal
email: miguel_ponte@iscte-iul.pt

Tiago Espinha Gasiba
T CST SEL-DE
Siemens AG
Munich, Germany
email: tiago.gasiba@siemens.com

Maria Pinto-Albuquerque
Instituto Universitário de Lisboa
(ISCTE-IUL), ISTAR
Lisbon, Portugal
email: maria.albuquerque@iscte-iul.pt

***Abstract*—Low-Code Development Platforms (LCDPs) are gaining more and more traction, even in the industrial context, as a means for anyone with less coding experience to develop and deploy applications. However, little is known about the vulnerabilities resulting from this new software development model. This paper aims to understand vulnerabilities in applications developed and deployed on these platforms. We show that these vulnerabilities can be considered from three perspectives: platform, developer, and plugins. We determine the top three vulnerabilities for each perspective based on a review of the literature and expert interviews. Our results contribute to understanding LCDP applications' security and raise awareness of industry practitioners by providing typical LCDP security pitfalls.**

***Keywords–low code*; *software development*; *web applications*; *cybersecurity*; *industry*; *low code development platforms*; *vulnerabilities*.**

I. INTRODUCTION

Low-Code Development Platforms [1], a relatively new technology to develop software, trace their roots to software development tools from the 1990s and early 2000s. These platforms allow applications to be developed without writing code or only requiring small amounts of coding. The main idea is to enable application development for everyone - any user can quickly develop applications without needing to be a software developer or having too much knowledge about software development. Low-code development platforms bring several additional advantages compared to traditional software development. As such, developing software using LCDP is not only easier but can be more prevalent. In a 2021 study by Gartner [2], it was predicted that there would be an increase of 23% in the low-code development market due to the surge of remote development during the pandemic. Hyperautomation [3] was seen as one of the causes of the adoption of the low-code through 2022, which came to be true in the most recent study in 2023 by Gartner [4]. This latter study predicts that the low-code development technologies market will grow by 20% in 2023. The same study predicts a significant increase in the low-code application platforms, with an estimated growth of 25% during the year 2023, achieving almost $10 billion in revenue. Furthermore, the study predicts that the revenue will increase to $12 billion by 2024.

In addition to the lesser need to develop software, low-code development platforms can bring additional advantages. According to North [5], some advantages that key players in the market advertise include a shorter time to market, cost savings, an increase in productivity, easier maintenance, and support of digital transformation. The usage of LCDP is also impacting and gaining traction in industrial software development.

Bargury [6] and Liu [7] investigated cybersecurity incidents resulting from the usage of LCDP. Their work shows that cybersecurity incidents have steadily increased over the last few years. Security incidents can cause serious problems, from financial loss to loss of life, and are particularly important in the industrial context, especially in cases that affect critical infrastructure. Industrial cybersecurity standards, such as IEC 62.443 [8], provide several guidelines for the secure development of software and applications for the industry.

A study by the Department of Homeland Security (DHS) [9] calls attention to the fact that the root cause of more than 90% of cybersecurity incidents can be traced back to poor software quality. Developers can introduce these vulnerabilities through written code or by including external third-party components in products and services. While one of the main goals of LCDPs is to reduce the amount of software being developed, thus ideally reducing the number of security incidents, more understanding is needed to know about the security implications of developing applications using LCDP. In particular, there needs to be more understanding of the underlying vulnerabilities resulting from deploying and developing LCDP applications. This lack of knowledge is likely related to the fact that LCDP is a new technology.

In this work, we want to address these issues and increase our knowledge of LCDP vulnerabilities. Therefore, our work aims to generate an artifact - a list of relevant vulnerabilities that can affect applications developed and deployed using LCDPs. Our study approaches the issues by 1) conducting a lightweight systematic literature review relevant to the topic, 2) performing relevant database searches for known vulnerabilities, and 3) conducting interviews with cybersecurity experts from the industry.

Our work contributes to industry and academia, enabling the development of more secure applications and stimulating research in the field. To the best of our knowledge, the present work is the first to address and understand the vulnerabilities and pitfalls of application development through low-code development platforms. Therefore, through the present work, industry practitioners can better understand the security pitfalls of developing and deploying applications using LCDP and thus actively address these pitfalls during the development of the applications. Furthermore, the present work can serve as an additional motivation for academic research and contributes to the cybersecurity body of knowledge through empirical evidence.

Our work is structured in the following way. Section II briefly overviews previous work related to the present study. In Section III, we provide details on the research method, describe our approach to the problem, and also provide a description of our experiment setup. Our results are presented in Section IV and are discussed in detail in Section V. Finally, we conclude our work with Section VI, which provides a quick overview of our main results and details for further work.

II. RELATED WORK

This section characterizes the standards that influenced this work and discusses relevant blogs and articles found during the Lightweight Systematic Literature Review (LWLR) carried out during the research.

The IEC 62443 cybersecurity standard provides guidelines under which this research [8] is conducted. This standard aims to increase system security by reducing the number of system vulnerabilities. The increased security is achieved by specifying technical security requirements that industrial system elements must comply with. The IEC 62443 standard is especially relevant for industries that deliver products and services for critical infrastructures. One of the premises in the standard aims to identify and secure valuable system assets.

The MITRE Corporation, a US-based organization, maintains the Common Weakness and Enumeration (CWE) standard. While the MITRE Corporation drives this standard, the cybersecurity community influences it through open contributions. As of 2023, the CWE standard identifies over 1000 software vulnerability types. Although this standard aims to enumerate software vulnerabilities, it is general enough to be used in other areas of cybersecurity. Due to the lack of LCDP cybersecurity standards, in the present work, we use this standard to specify security vulnerabilities.

We conducted surveys and LWLR in the present work. Our survey design methodology finds its roots in work from Grooves et al. [10]. As input to the design of our survey, we conducted LWLR, a simplified version of the systematic literature review method by Kitchenham et al. [11].

In this method, we used a handful of keywords to search for literature about this topic, as follows: "low-code", "low-code development", "low-code platform", "low-code development platform", and "security in low-code development". With these keywords, we put them on five different databases: Google Scholar [12], IEEE Xplore [13], Springer Link [14], ACM Digital Library [15] and ResearchGate [16]. To conduct a selection of works, we defined a set of inclusion and exclusion parameters. The inclusion parameters are as follows: documents are single works (articles, papers, and book chapters), papers discuss LCDPs, and papers are available electronically in full-text form. The exclusion parameters are as follows: papers prior to 2020, papers not written in English, and studies conducted that do not cover LCDP. This process resulted in a small list of 10 articles listed in Table III in the appendix section.

However, these articles show a need for more knowledge regarding the security and vulnerabilities of LCDPs and applications developed using LCDPs. This issue is relevant since there has been an increase in cybersecurity incidents. As such, we expect this work to consolidate already-known information and introduce new knowledge.

III. METHODOLOGY

The present section describes the methodology followed in this work, which was used to create our artifact – a list of top LCDP vulnerabilities. This work separates the process into two focuses: the research method followed and the approach used based on the research method.

A. Research Method

For the present work, we took inspiration from the Design Science Research method by Peffers et al. [17], and Hevner et al. [18]. Based on the guidelines provided by Peffers et al. and our experience, we adopted four relevant guidelines for this research: 1) design as an artifact, 2) problem relevance, 3) rigor, and 4) contributions.

Regarding the first point, our designed artifact consists of a table of the top 3 vulnerabilities. Furthermore, this work's problem is relevant for the industry since cybersecurity is essential in developing products and services. We aim to achieve rigor in our research by using diversified sources of information. In particular, we use existing information in databases and blog posts and validate our work through cybersecurity experts' opinions and experience. Regarding the last guideline related to DSR methodology, our work aims to contribute to a better understanding of vulnerabilities in low-code development platforms. Additionally, the present work contributes to academia by deepening the existing knowledge on this subject.

According to our experience in cybersecurity in the industry, we decided to focus on three different perspectives to derive the top LCDP vulnerabilities: *platform*, *developer*, and *plugins*. We considered the platform perspective to be related to the vulnerabilities of the environment where the application is developed or runs, thus covering the LCDP application deployment aspect. We specify the developer perspective as the problems the LCDP developer causes or introduces to the LCDP-developed application throughout the software development lifecycle. This perspective focuses on problems generated by the developer of the application him or herself and does not consider problems incurred through the usage of external components. Lastly, we defined the plugin's perspective as the problems that may occur in the developed solution due to the inclusion of third-party components, e.g., from the LCDP plugin marketplace.

To better understand the vulnerabilities of each of the perspectives, we designed an approach that would fit our research. This approach not only covers theoretical research but also a more practical one.

B. Approach

To address our research goal and create our artifact, we collected data from different sources and validated the results through expert review. Figure 1 visually represents our approach. Data collection was carried out in three ways: 1) lightweight literature review, 2) database search, and 3) expert interviews. The last step (4) consisted of the consolidation of the results through expert review.

The lightweight literature review method which was followed is inspired by Kitchenham and Charters' Systematic Literature Review [11], but on a smaller scale. In particular, we did not conduct a review using the snowball method, and our selection process and reporting on the review are simplified. The following search engines and repositories were taken into consideration: IEEE [13], ACM [15], Springer [14], Research Gate [16], and Google Scholar [12]. We searched for papers with publishing dates between 2019 and 2023. The keywords used for the search were: "Low-Code", "Low-Code Development Platforms", "Security in Low-Code Platforms", and derived terms from these.

Regarding the database search, it was conducted on the Common Vulnerability and Exposures(CVE Details) [19] database, a free-of-use database on common vulnerabilities and exposures on most software available worldwide. To get a list of relevant LCDPs, we consulted the "Magic Quadrant for Enterprise Low-Code Application Platforms" provided by Gartner [20], along with the following additional sources: [21], [22]. With the list of LCDPs, we searched for any vulnerabilities for these platforms in CVE Details. From this, we obtained the vulnerabilities for each platform, their corresponding CWE ID [23] and a brief description of the vulnerability. It is essential to mention that, despite searching for all platforms, not all were in the database. Therefore, we consider the following low-code development platforms: Mendix [24], OutSystems [25], Salesforce [26], ServiceNow [27], Appian [28], Pega [29], Oracle Apex [30], Zoho [31], Claris Filemaker [32], Airtable [33], Blueprism [34], Processmaker [35], Wavemaker [36], HCL Domino [37], 1C [38], Intrexx [39], Agilepoint NX [40], Joget Dx [41], Openedge [42], Decisions [43], and Nintex [44]. Also, some vulnerabilities did not have a CWE ID, meaning they were either unmapped or unspecified. Thus, those vulnerabilities were not taken into consideration for the research. The list of vulnerabilities and affected platforms and their impact were collected in an Excel table. After obtaining this data, we grouped all vulnerabilities by their CWE ID and calculated the number of occurrences of each vulnerability across all frameworks. Finally, we ordered them by the number of occurrences and impact, and when two or more vulnerabilities had the same frequency value, we asked for security experts' opinions as a means for a tie-breaker.

Based on the gathered list of vulnerabilities, we designed a simple survey. The following process resulted from the design: 1) present our findings from database search and literature review, 2) ask if the experts agree with the findings, and 3) ask what the experts would change. We used the survey to interview six security experts in the industry. The industry professionals had diversified years of field experience, which ranged from beginners (two experts with less than five years of experience) to senior developers (four experts with more than twenty years of experience). These interviews were performed during May 2023, were recorded with the respondents' consent, and lasted between 30 and 60 minutes. The format was an open discussion using a questionnaire based on our findings. With all the gathered data, the information was coded and grouped into each perspective from the artifact, as shown in Table I. Following this, each perspective's vulnerabilities were prioritized to get a top 3 for the developer and plugins' perspective.

In the last step, all gathered data and information were reviewed by experts from the industry to validate and approve all the research and interviews done. To do this, we consulted three industry experts to validate all the information gathered. Also, we appealed to the experts to help narrow down and prioritize the list in case of double results. For example, when a double vulnerability result appeared, we consulted them to have a better prioritization, according to their experience.

Table I summarizes the mapping between the data input and the LCDP vulnerability perspective.

TABLE I
MAPPING OF INFORMATION

	LWLR	CVE Details	Interview
Platform		•	
Developer			•
Plugins	•		•

This table shows that the CVE details database mainly influences our understanding of platform vulnerabilities. Security expert interviews mainly influence our understanding of developer vulnerabilities. Finally, the lightweight literature review and the conducted security expert interviews mainly influence the understanding of plugin vulnerabilities.

IV. RESULTS

In this section, we present the main results from our research in the following sub-sections: mainly identified vulnerabilities from the CVE details database, results of experts' interviews, and final consolidated results in the form of an artifact containing the top LCDP vulnerabilities.

A. Platforms' Vulnerabilities

The bar chart in Figure 2 summarizes the ten most recurrent vulnerabilities identified in the analyzed platforms and the number of findings. We observe that the vulnerability which contains the highest number of recorded data is the CWE-79, i.e., the *cross-site scripting* vulnerability. In the second place, we found CWE-89 and CWE-352, with six findings each. These vulnerabilities correspond to *SQL injection* and *cross-site request forgery*. In the third place, we found CWE-20, with five findings, a vulnerability related to *improper input validation*. In the fourth place, with four findings each,

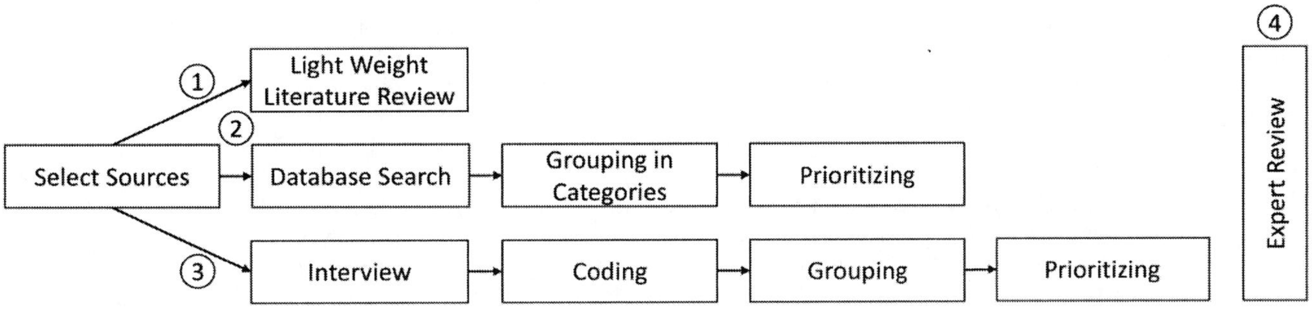

Figure 1. Process of approach for this work.

we found CWE-668, CWE-918, CWE-269, CWE-400, and CWE-287, which correspond to *resource exposure*, *server-side request forgery*, *improper privilege management*, *uncontrolled resource consumption*, and *improper authentication*, respectively. Finally, in the fifth place, we found CWE-611 with three findings corresponding to the *XML external entity* vulnerability.

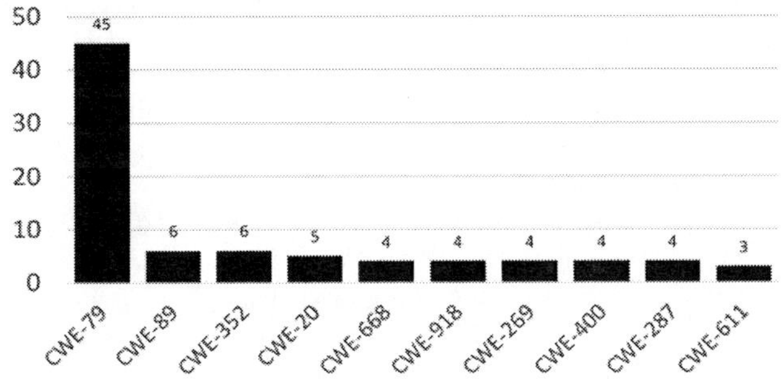

Figure 2. Identified CWE IDs together with the number of identified platform vulnerabilities from CVE details database.

B. Experts' Interview

After presenting the initial artifact, the six experts agreed with the obtained results, with few exceptions. In particular, we obtained feedback on the topic of "access control", "administrative features", and "injection vulnerabilities". The experts claimed that the two first topics could be grouped as they could be seen to overlap. Furthermore, the experts raised the point that injection vulnerabilities have not been considered, and, according to their experience, these are significant enough to belong to the list. Based on the results of the interview with the experts, not only did we validate our findings, but we could also improve and extend them.

C. Final Results

Table II shows each perspective's final results on the top vulnerabilities. The table briefly describes the vulnerability and the associated CWE ID.

Our results show that from the platform perspective, the collected top three LCDP vulnerabilities are: T.1-1 – *cross-site scripting*, T.1-2 – *SQL injection*, T.1-3 – *cross-site request forgery*. Regarding the developer perspective, our collected top three LCDP vulnerabilities are: T.2-1 – *access control and administrative features*, T.2-2 – *business logic*, and T.2-3 – *injections*. Regarding the plugins perspective, our collected top three LCDP vulnerabilities are: T.3-1 – *custom-made plugins and interfaces*, T.3-2 – *data breaches*, and T.3-3 – *unauthorized access to systems*. We note that, in Table II, for each individual perspective, the three found vulnerabilities are listed according to their impact, e.g. T.1-1 has higher impact than T.1-3.

TABLE II
FINAL RESULTS ON TOP THREE VULNERABILITIES, FOR EACH PERSPECTIVE

Perspective	Ref.	CWE-ID	Vulnerability Description
Platform	T.1-1	*79*	Cross-Site Scripting
	T.1-2	*89*	SQL Injection
	T.1-3	*352*	Cross-Site Request Forgery
Developer	T.2-1	284	Access Control and Administrative Features
	T.2-2	840	Business Logic
	T.2-3	250	Injections
Plugins	T.3-1	–	Custom-made plugins and interfaces
	T.3-2	200	Data Breaches
	T.3-3	285	Unauthorized access to systems

V. DISCUSSION

This section focuses on discussing all the results obtained from the research and some possible threats to validity.

The present work considers three vulnerabilities for each perspective ordered by importance. However, we note that the order of vulnerabilities between different perspectives has yet to be considered. For example, while T.1-1 - *cross-site scripting* is the top vulnerability from the platform perspective, we do not compare its importance to T.2-1 - *access control and administrative features* of the developer perspective.

Concerning the platform's perspective, the results achieved were expected by the authors. The outcome of developing software with LCDP is a web application. As such, the results obtained according to the platforms' perspective were unsurprising, i.e., not only do they constitute typical web vulnerabilities, according to the OWASP Top 10 project [45], but they also match previous known platform incidents. Our results provide an indicator that the deployment of the LCDP platform itself should be carefully monitored, hardened, and patched. Our experience has shown that the problems present in the platform perspective only occur sometimes in the applications developed within LCDP.

Regarding the developer's perspective, our results indicate that wrong configurations and implementation of business logic are the main concerns when developing LCDP applications. These results are not surprising, as the typical LCDP developer is inexperienced. However, a surprising result is the inclusion of the CWE-250 in the developer perspective. An application developed using an LCDP is typically well protected against injection attacks. However, injection problems can occur when custom components need to be developed. Thus, our results indicate that the vulnerabilities that occur using pre-defined or pre-packaged components by the LCDP vendor consist of configuration and business logic issues (T.2-1, and T.2-2). However, when custom-written components are integrated into the application, typical web development problems can occur (T.2-3).

Concerning the perspective of plugins, except for the T.3-1, the resulting findings also align with the authors' experience in the industry. The major problem we have identified is the usage of custom-made plugins and interfaces (T.3-1). This problem relates to the fact that plugins included in the LCDP application are typically custom developed, might only implement some security features, and might even lack security documentation. Therefore, custom-made plugins possess a security risk when integrated into LCDP applications without careful checking. Additionally, including externally developed plugins can lead to data leakages and data breaches, e.g., when the integrated plugin connects to an external unknown or authorized party (e.g., the plugin's vendor). This problem can lead to unauthorized access to systems (T.3-3) due to the vendor's potentially malicious usage of the components.

Finally, most analyzed platforms have a dedicated marketplace where LCDP developers can get plugins. The main idea is that the developers need not worry about security since the plugins are developed and tested by the respective vendors, and the vendors build a security stance and reputation within the marketplace. Although plugins are being vetted in the marketplace, it is still necessary to be cautious not to integrate any form of malware into the environment and projects. Acquiring third-party components through external marketplaces or specialized companies is also possible. In this case, according to our experience in the industry, it is advisable to be extra careful regarding discontinued products, obsolete versions, and malware.

A. Threats to Validity

Our lightweight literature review methodology might not have considered all existing articles on low-code-development platforms, thus potentially skewing our results. Furthermore, using the CVE Details database as the single source for the platform's vulnerabilities can bias our conclusions. Further work should therefore consider additional sources to provide a more solid validation of our results.

The present study considers a limited number of interviews with industry experts. While this small number of interviews is typical for work performed in an industrial context, this can lead to skewed and situated results. LCDPs are a new technology that, according to the author's experience, is assumed to improve and become more mature. Therefore, our results might only partially apply to current or future versions of LCDPs. As the present study is carried out in an industrial setting, it is subject to its inherent limitations in terms of the available number of experts. Nevertheless, the results obtained in the study are in agreement with the authors' experience. These results are not only corroborated by additional experts through their insightful reviews but also through practical real-world examples as obtained from feedback from the interviewed pentesters. We also note that more precise results might be obtained when the LCDP field is more mature.

Furthermore, our work summarizes vulnerabilities across different LCDPs. Due to its nature, different results might be obtained for each platform. Nevertheless, our work aims to capture an overall picture; therefore, the authors do not focus on individual platforms.

VI. CONCLUSION AND FUTURE WORK

Low-code development platforms constitute a new technology that is revolutionizing software development. Thanks to these platforms being end-user friendly, even people with little or no coding experience can develop software applications according to their ideas and requirements. With more convenient access to software development and the increase of citizen developers, it is necessary to raise awareness of the security aspects of these platforms. With this work, we study common vulnerabilities when developing and deploying applications created with LCDPs. Towards this goal, we conducted a lightweight literature review, analyzed openly known platform vulnerabilities, and interviewed six industry security experts. Our results shed light on the top three vulnerabilities of applications developed using LCDPs into three perspectives: platform, developer, and plugins. We show that not only typical software development vulnerabilities can occur but also additional vulnerabilities due to the development and deployment platform itself and the inclusion of third-party plugins. In future work, we intend to further understand and validate our results by taking a broader approach to the topic, considering additional information from a more significant number of sources, and conducting a large-scale survey. Furthermore, the authors would like to conduct a longitudinal study approach to understand the evolution of CWE vulnerabilities in LCDPs over time. This detailed study can contribute to acknowledge on the dynamic nature of vulnerabilities, their relevancy and their potential changes.

ACKNOWLEDGEMENTS

Portuguese national funds partially finance this work through FCT–Fundação para a Ciência e Tecnologia, I.P., under the projects FCT UIDB/04466/2020 and FCT UIDP/04466/2020. Furthermore, Miguel Lourenço and Maria Pinto-Albuquerque thank the Instituto Universitário de Lisboa and ISTAR for their support.

Siemens acknowledges funding for project CONTAIN by the Federal Ministry of Education and Research under project number 13N16585.

REFERENCES

[1] M. K. Pratt, "What are Low-Code and No-Code Development Platforms?" https://www.techtarget.com/searchsoftwarequality/definition/low-code-no-code-development-platform, [Online, 2023.09.18].
[2] Gartner, "Gartner Forecasts Worldwide Low-Code Development Technologies Market to Grow 23% in 2021," https://www.gartner.com/en/newsroom/press-releases/2021-02-15-gartner-forecasts-worldwide-low-code-development-technologies-market-to-grow-23-percent-in-2021, [Online, 2023.05.10].
[3] Gartner, "Definition of Hyperautomation - Gartner Information Technology Glossary," https://www.gartner.com/en/information-technology/glossary/hyperautomation, [Online, 2023.05.10].
[4] Gartner, "Gartner Forecasts Worldwide Low-Code Development Technologies Market to Grow 20% in 2023," https://www.gartner.com/en/newsroom/press-releases/2022-12-13-gartner-forecasts-worldwide-low-code-development-technologies-market-to-grow-20-percent-in-2023, [Online, 2023.05.10].
[5] J. North, "Will Low-Code Replace Developers?" https://www.101ways.com/is-low-code-development-a-threat-to-software-engineering/, [Online, 2023.05.10].
[6] M. Bargury, "Major Security Breach From Business Users' Low-Code Apps Could Come in 2023, Analysts Warn," https://www.darkreading.com/edge-articles/major-security-breach-from-business-users-low-code-apps-could-come-in-2023-analysts-warn, [Online, 2023.05.10].
[7] N. Liu, "Forrester: Low-Code, Citizen Development Will Lead to Major Data Breach in 2023," https://www.sdxcentral.com/articles/analysis/forrester-low-code-citizen-development-will-lead-to-major-data-breach-in-2023/2022/11/, [Online, 2023.05.10].
[8] International Electrotechnical Commission, "Understanding IEC 62443," https://www.iec.ch/blog/understanding-iec-62443, [Online, 2023.05.10].
[9] Department of Homeland Security, US-CERT, "Software Assurance," https://tinyurl.com/y6pr9v42, [Online, 2020.09.07].
[10] R. M. Groves, F. J. Fowler Jr, M. P. Couper, J. M. Lepkowski, E. Singer, and R. Tourangeau, *Survey methodology*. John Wiley & Sons, 06 2009.
[11] B. Kitchenham and S. Charters, "Guidelines for Performing Systematic Literature Reviews in Software Engineering," *Information and Software Technology*, vol. 2, pp. 1–65, 01 2007.
[12] Google, "Google Scholar Website," https://scholar.google.com, [Online, 2023.05.10].
[13] IEEE, "IEEE Xplore," https://ieeexplore.ieee.org/Xplore/home.jsp, [Online, 2023.05.10].
[14] Springer Nature, "Springer - International Publisher," https://www.springer.com/gp, [Online, 2023.05.10].
[15] Association for Computing Machinery, "ACM Digital Library," https://dl.acm.org, [Online, 2023.05.10].
[16] ResearchGate GmbH, "ResearchGate Website," https://www.researchgate.net, [Online, 2023.05.10].
[17] K. Peffers, T. Tuunanen, M. Rothenberger, and S. Chatterjee, "A Design Science Research Methodology for Information Systems Research," *Journal of Management Information Systems*, vol. 24, pp. 45–77, 01 2007.
[18] A. Hevner, S. Chatterjee, A. Hevner, and S. Chatterjee, "Design Science Research in Information Systems," *Design research in information systems: theory and practice*, pp. 9–22, 2010.
[19] MITRE Corporation, "CVE Details Website," https://www.cvedetails.com/, [Online, 2023.05.10].
[20] Gartner, "Magic Quadrant for Enterprise Low-Code Application Platforms," https://www.gartner.com/en/documents/4022825, 12 2022, [Online, 2023.05.10].
[21] Gartner, "Enterprise Low-Code Application Platforms Reviews and Ratings," https://www.gartner.com/reviews/market/enterprise-low-code-application-platform, [Online, 2023.05.10].
[22] G2.com, "Top Free Low-Code Development Platforms," https://www.g2.com/categories/low-code-development-platforms/free, [Online, 2023.05.10].
[23] MITRE, "CWE List Version 4.11," https://cwe.mitre.org/data/, [Online, 2023.05.10].
[24] Mendix, "Mendix Website," https://www.mendix.com, [Online, 2023.05.10].
[25] OutSystems, "OutSystems Website," https://www.outsystems.com, [Online, 2023.05.10].
[26] Salesforce, "Salesforce Website," https://www.salesforce.com/eu/, [Online, 2023.05.10].
[27] ServiceNow, "ServiceNow Website," https://www.servicenow.com, [Online, 2023.05.10].
[28] Appian, "Appian Website," https://appian.com, [Online, 2023.05.10].
[29] Pega, "Pega Website," https://www.pega.com/, [Online, 2023.05.10].
[30] Oracle, "Oracle APEX Website," https://apex.oracle.com/en/, [Online, 2023.05.10].
[31] Zoho, "Zoho Website," https://www.zoho.com, [Online, 2023.05.10].
[32] Claris Filemaker, "Claris Filemaker Website," https://www.claris.com/filemaker/, [Online, 2023.05.10].
[33] Airtable, "Airtable Website," https://www.airtable.com, [Online, 2023.05.10].
[34] Blueprism, "Blueprism Website," https://www.blueprism.com, [Online, 2023.05.10].
[35] Processmaker, "Processmaker Website," https://www.processmaker.com, [Online, 2023.05.10].
[36] Wavemaker, "Wavemaker Website," https://www.wavemaker.com, [Online, 2023.05.10].
[37] HCLDomino, "HCLDomino Website," https://www.hcltechsw.com/domino, [Online, 2023.05.10].
[38] 1C, "1C Website," https://1c-dn.com, [Online, 2023.06.18].
[39] Intrexx, "Intrexx Website," https://www.intrexx.com, [Online, 2023.06.18].
[40] AgilepointNX, "AgilepointNX Website," https://www.agilepoint.com, [Online, 2023.06.18].
[41] JogetDx, "JogetDx Website," https://www.joget.org/product/joget-dx/, [Online, 2023.06.18].
[42] Openedge, "Openedge Website," https://www.progress.com/openedge, [Online, 2023.06.18].
[43] Decisions, "Decisions Website," https://decisions.com, [Online, 2023.06.18].
[44] Nintex, "Nintex Website," https://www.nintex.com, [Online, 2023.06.18].
[45] Open Web Application Security Project, "OWASP Top Ten," https://owasp.org/www-project-top-ten, [Online, 2023.06.18].
[46] F. Sufi, "Algorithms in Low-Code-No-Code for Research Applications: A Practical Review," *Algorithms*, vol. 16, no. 2, 2023.
[47] J. Cabot and R. Clarisó, "Low Code for Smart Software Development," *IEEE Software*, vol. 40, no. 1, pp. 89–93, 2023.
[48] D. Di Ruscio, D. Kolovos, J. de Lara, A. Pierantonio, M. Tisi, and M. Wimmer, "Low-Code Development and Model-Driven Engineering: Two Sides of the Same Coin?" *Softw. Syst. Model.*, vol. 21, no. 2, pp. 437–446, 2022.
[49] A. Trigo, J. Varajão, and M. Almeida, "Low-Code Versus Code-Based Software Development: Which Wins the Productivity Game?" *IT Professional*, vol. 24, no. 5, pp. 61–68, 2022.
[50] A. Bucaioni, A. Cicchetti, and F. Ciccozzi, "Modelling in Low-Code Development: A Multi-Vocal Systematic Review," *Softw. Syst. Model.*, vol. 21, no. 5, pp. 1959–1981, 2022.
[51] S. Käss, S. Strahringer, and M. Westner, "Practitioners' Perceptions on the Adoption of Low Code Development Platforms," *IEEE Access*, vol. 11, pp. 29 009–29 034, 2023.
[52] J. Kirchhoff, N. Weidmann, S. Sauer, and G. Engels, "Situational Development of Low-Code Applications in Manufacturing Companies," in *Proceedings of the 25th International Conference on Model Driven Engineering Languages and Systems: Companion Proceedings*, ser. MODELS '22, 2022, p. 816–825. [Online]. Available: https://doi.org/10.1145/3550356.3561560
[53] D. Pinho, A. Aguiar, and V. Amaral, "What About the Usability in Low-Code Platforms? A Systematic Literature Review," *Journal of Computer Languages*, vol. 74, p. 101185, 2023. [Online]. Available: https://www.sciencedirect.com/science/article/pii/S259011842200082X
[54] F. Khorram, J.-M. Mottu, and G. Sunyé, "Challenges & Opportunities in Low-Code Testing," in *Proceedings of the 23rd ACM/IEEE International Conference on Model Driven Engineering Languages and Systems: Companion Proceedings*, ser. MODELS '20, New York, NY, USA, 2020. [Online]. Available: https://doi.org/10.1145/3417990.3420204
[55] A. Sahay, A. Indamutsa, D. Di Ruscio, and A. Pierantonio, "Supporting the Understanding and Comparison of Low-Code Development Platforms," in *2020 46th Euromicro Conference on Software Engineering and Advanced Applications (SEAA)*, 2020, pp. 171–178.

APPENDIX

TABLE III
FINAL LIST OF REVIEWED ARTICLES FROM LIGHTWEIGHT LITERATURE REVIEW

Title	Year	Reference	Short Summary
Algorithms in Low-Code-No-Code for Research Applications: A Practical Review	2023	[46]	This work gives us information about the advantages and downsides of the LCDPs, supported by some examples. It also shows how to create artificial intelligence (AI) without coding, followed by an example of an algorithm that monitors cyber-attacks through a LCDP.
Low Code for Smart Software Development	2022	[47]	In this article, the authors explore the potential and challenges of low-code environments, which enable quick delivery of AI-enhanced software solutions, and provide a "wish list" for developers to consider in these tools.
Low-code development and model-driven engineering: Two sides of the same coin?	2022	[48]	This expert-voice paper compares low-code and model-driven approaches, identifying differences, commonalities, strengths, and weaknesses, and suggests cross-pollination directions.
Low-Code Versus Code-Based Software Development: Which Wins the Productivity Game?	2022	[49]	This article presents an experiment comparing low-code and code-based software development technologies, aiming to answer which technology enhances productivity. Results show clear productivity gains can be achieved using low-code technology in management information system development. The article reviews concepts, methodology, results, discussion, and limitations and suggests future research.
Modeling in low-code development: a multi-vocal systematic review	2022	[50]	This article presents a systematic review of low-code development, focusing on its relationship with model-driven engineering. The article, based on 58 primary studies, provides a comprehensive snapshot of low-code development during its peak of inflated expectations technology adoption phase.
Practitioners' Perceptions on the Adoption of Low Code Development Platforms	2022	[51]	In this work, a study was conducted in which 17 experts identified 12 drivers and 19 inhibitors for LCDP adoption. The consensus was that these factors are crucial, but the ranking is context-dependent. The study validates these factors, adds six new drivers and six new inhibitors to the knowledge, and analyzes their importance.
Situational development of low-code applications in manufacturing companies	2022	[52]	This paper presents an initial version of a situational software development method for manufacturing companies, enabling low-code application development. The method can be customized based on application requirements, low-code platform features, and team characteristics. Feedback from expert interviews supports the method's usefulness.
What about the usability in low-code platforms? A systematic literature review	2022	[53]	In this article, the authors performed a Systematic Literature Review procedure on the usability of LCDPs to understand the advantages and disadvantages of these platforms. Also, in their work, they point out that the drag-and-drop feature and end-user ability to develop software are among the characteristics more commonly mentioned in literature.
Challenges & Opportunities in Low-Code Testing	2020	[54]	This paper analyzes five commercial Low-Code Development Platforms (LCDP) testing components to present business advancements in low-code testing. It proposes a feature list for low-code testing, a baseline for comparison, and a guideline for building new ones. Challenges include the role of citizen developers, high-level automation, and cloud testing.
Supporting the understanding and comparison of low-code development platforms	2020	[55]	The authors worked on a technical review comparing eight representative LCDPs' characteristics and a short report on the experience of using each one. They conclude a set of features covering functionalities and each platform's services. This work aims to raise the understanding of how LCDPs can cover user requirements.

I Think This is the Beginning of a Beautiful Friendship - On the Rust Programming Language and Secure Software Development in the Industry

Tiago Espinha Gasiba
T CST SEL-DE
Siemens AG
Munich, Germany
email: tiago.gasiba@siemens.com

Sathwik Amburi
T CST SEL-DE
Siemens AG
Technical University of Munich
Munich, Germany
email: sathwik.amburi@{siemens.com, tum.de}

***Abstract*—Since the Rust programming language was accepted into the Linux Kernel, it has gained significant attention from the software developer community and the industry. Rust has been developed to address many traditional software problems, such as memory safety and concurrency. Consequently, software written in Rust is expected to have fewer vulnerabilities and be more secure. However, a systematic analysis of the security of software developed in Rust is still missing. The present work aims to close this gap by analyzing how Rust deals with typical software vulnerabilities. We also compare Rust to C, C++, and Java, three widely used programming languages in the industry, regarding potential software vulnerabilities. Our results are based on a literature review, interviews with industrial cybersecurity experts, and an analysis of existing static code analysis tools. We conclude that, while Rust improves the status quo compared to the other programming languages, writing vulnerable software in Rust is still possible. Our research contributes to academia by enhancing the existing knowledge of software vulnerabilities. Furthermore, industrial practitioners can benefit from this study when evaluating the use of different programming languages in their projects.**

***Keywords–Cybersecurity*; *Software development*; *Industry*; *Software*; *Vulnerabilities*.**

I. INTRODUCTION

Rust, a systems programming language that originated in 2010, has significantly increased in popularity over the past decade. According to a market overview survey by Yalantis [1], which conducted more than 9,300 interviews, 89% of developers prefer Rust over other widespread programming languages like C and C++ due to its robust security properties. Despite its steep learning curve, industry professionals argue that the time invested in learning Rust yields added benefits and fosters better programming skills, according to Garcia [2]. Stack Overflow [3] notes that developers appreciate Rust's focus on system-level details since it helps prevent null and dangling pointers and its memory safety without needing a garbage collector. These factors contribute to its growing adoption in the industry. This sentiment is echoed by the industry's push toward adopting the Rust programming language. Furthermore, according to Stack Overflow Developer Surveys, Rust has been the most loved and admired language since 2016. In the most recent Stack Overflow 2023 Developer Survey [4], Rust secured the position of the most admired language, with over 80% of the 87,510 responses favoring it.

Due to its focus on memory safety and concurrency, Rust has become the language of choice for many tools developed for Linux, FreeBSD, and other operating systems. Rust's adoption in Linux Kernel development [5], [6] underlines its growing significance in an industrial context. Major platforms like Google have started including Rust in systems, such as Android [7], and forums like RustSec [8] provide real-time updates and insights into the current state of Rust security.

Rust promotes itself as being safer than traditional languages like C and C++, which are widely used in an industrial context, by borrowing many aspects from functional languages like Haskell. However, in the realm of industry, particularly in critical infrastructures, safety is not synonymous with security. As the industry is obliged to follow secure development standards, such as IEC 62443 [9], [10], the notion of safety in Rust must be understood not just from a memory management perspective but also from a security standpoint.

Developing industrial products and services follows strict guidelines, especially for those products and services aimed at critical infrastructures. In these cases, cybersecurity incidents can severely negatively impact companies and society in general. Therefore, the security of industrial products must be tightly controlled. Consequently, Rust is considered a good candidate for industrial software development.

While Rust has been celebrated for its safety features, less research has been conducted on its security aspects. This lack of research is primarily because this programming language is still relatively young compared to longstanding players in the industry, such as C, C++, and Java. Furthermore, developers and users often conflate safety with security, potentially leading to software vulnerabilities. Therefore, this paper aims to understand to what extent vulnerable software can be written in Rust. We approach this topic in two ways:

1) Evaluating the difficulty of writing vulnerable software based on industry-recognized security standards like SysAdmin, Audit, Network, Security (SANS) Institute TOP 25 [11], Open Web Application Security Project (OWASP) 10 [12], and 19 Deadly Sins [13], and
2) Analyzing past known vulnerabilities in the Rust language and its ecosystem.

This study's contributions are as follows: firstly, through the present work, the authors aim to raise awareness, as defined by Gasiba et al. [14], about Rust security and its pitfalls within the industry (for both industrial practitioners and academia); secondly, our work provides expert opinions from industry security experts on how to mitigate such issues when developing software with Rust; furthermore, our work contributes to academic research and the body of knowledge on Rust security by adding new insights and fostering a deeper understanding of Rust security; finally, our work serves as motivation for further studies in this area.

The rest of this paper is organized as follows: Section II discusses previous work that is either related to or served as inspiration for our study. Section III briefly discusses the methodology followed in this work to address the research questions. In Section IV, we provide a summary of our results, and in Section V, we conduct a critical discussion of these results. Finally, in Section VI, we conclude our work and outline future research.

II. RELATED WORK

A significant contribution to understanding Rust's security model comes from Sible et al. [15]. Their work offers a thorough analysis of Rust's security model, focusing on its memory and concurrency safety features. However, they also highlight Rust's limitations, such as handling memory leaks. While Rust offers robust protections, the authors emphasize that these protections represent only a subset of the broader software security requirements. Their insights are invaluable for understanding both the strengths and limitations of Rust's security model.

In 2023, Wassermann et al. [16] presented a detailed exploration of Rust's security features and potential vulnerabilities. They highlighted issues when design assumptions do not align with real-world data. The authors stress the importance of understanding vulnerabilities from the perspective of Rust program users. They advocate for tools that can analyze these vulnerabilities, even without access to the source code. Discussions also touched upon the maturity of the Rust software ecosystem and its potential impact on future security responses. They suggest that the Rust community could benefit from the Rust Foundation either acting as or establishing a related CVE Numbering Authority (CNA). Their study further enriches the understanding of Rust's security model.

Qin et al. [17] conducted a comprehensive study revealing that unsafe code is widely used in the Rust software they examined. This usage is often motivated by performance optimization and code reuse. They observed that while developers aim to minimize the use of unsafe code, all memory-safety bugs involve it. Most of these bugs also involve safe code, suggesting that errors can arise when safe code does not account for the implications of associated unsafe code. The researchers identified Rust's 'lifetime' concept, especially when combined with unsafe code, as a frequent source of confusion. This misunderstanding often leads to memory-safety issues. Their findings underscore the importance of fully grasping and correctly implementing Rust's safety mechanisms.

A. Security Standards and Guidelines

Various security standards and guidelines can be applied to Rust programming. The International Electrotechnical Commission Technical Report (IEC TR) 24772 [18] standard, "Secure Coding Guidelines Language Independent," provides guidelines suitable for multiple programming languages, including Rust. ISO/IEC 62.443 [9], especially sections 4-1 and 4-2, sets the industry standard for secure software development [10]. The Common Weakness Enumeration (CWE) by MITRE [19] offers a unified set of software weaknesses.

The French Government's National Agency for the Security of Information Systems (ANSSI) has published a guide titled "Programming Rules to Develop Secure Applications with Rust" [20], which is a valuable resource for developers.

B. Security Documentation and Tools

Rust's safety guarantees and performance have led to its growing adoption across various domains. Notably, Google has integrated Rust into the Android Open Source Project (AOSP) to mitigate memory safety bugs, a significant source of Android's security vulnerabilities [7]. Updates and discussions about Rust security are frequently shared on blogs, forums, and other platforms.

Several Static Application Security Testing (SAST) tools are available for Rust, such as those listed on the Analysis Tools platform [21]. These tools play a crucial role in the secure software development lifecycle.

Community-driven initiatives like RustSec [8] offer advisories on vulnerabilities in Rust crates. Real-time updates from RustSec and other platforms are invaluable for developers to stay updated on potential security issues in Rust packages.

C. Secure Coding Guidelines

The paper "Secure Coding Guidelines - (un)decidability" by Bagnara et al. [22] delves into the challenges of secure coding. It mainly focuses on the undecidability of specific rules, such as "Improper Input Validation". The authors argue that determining adherence to specific secure coding guidelines can be complex due to factors like context.

D. Secure Code Awareness

Secure code awareness is crucial, especially in critical infrastructures. A study by Gasiba et al. [23] explored the factors influencing developers' adherence to secure coding guidelines. While developers showed intent to follow these guidelines, there was a noticeable gap in their practical knowledge. This highlights the need for targeted, secure coding awareness campaigns. The authors introduced a game, the CyberSecurity Challenges, inspired by the Capture The Flag (CTF) genre, as an effective method to raise awareness.

The Sifu platform [24] was developed in line with these challenges. Sifu promotes secure coding awareness among developers by combining serious gaming techniques with cybersecurity and secure coding guidelines. It also uses artificial intelligence to offer solution-guiding hints. Sifu's successful deployment in industrial settings showcases its efficacy in enhancing secure coding awareness.

III. METHODOLOGY

Our research methodology, aimed at examining the security in the Rust programming language compared to Java and C, and its interaction with security assessment tools, was composed of four main stages:

- Literature Exploration
- Interviews with Security Experts
- Mapping to CWE/SANS, OWASP, and 19 Deadly Sins
- Analysis with Rust/SAST Tools

A. Literature Exploration

Due to the scarcity of academic resources, we commenced with an integrated literature review, primarily focusing on gray literature, such as reports and blog posts. We also conducted an academic literature review using the ACM, IEEE Xplore, and Google Scholar databases, with search terms including "Rust Security", "Java Security", "C Security", and "Static Application Security Testing". The time frame was set from 2010 to 2023.

B. Interviews with Security Experts

We held discussions with five industry security experts with experience with Rust, Java, C, and security assessment tools. The experts from the industry are consultants with more than ten years of experience and work on the topic of secure software development. Their insights contributed significantly to our understanding and interpretation of the literature. Additionally, we conducted informal interviews with two students who regularly use Rust and contribute to open-source projects developed in the same programming language. The student's background is a master's in computer science with five years of programming experience with Rust. The informal interviews with industry experts and computer science students were conducted in August 2023 and lasted about thirty minutes.

C. Mapping to CWE/SANS, OWASP, and 19 Deadly Sins

In this phase, we categorized Rust security issues according to the Common Weakness Enumeration (CWE), SANS Top 25, and OWASP 10 and 19 deadly sins. This step helped in classifying and understanding the security threats relevant to Rust.

D. Analysis with Rust/SAST Tools

A comparative study was undertaken with Rust and Static Application Security Testing (SAST) tools to assess the effectiveness of these tools in identifying Rust's security vulnerabilities.

E. Definitions

In our research, we employed three categories to assess the level of security protection against specific issues in Rust: Rare and Difficult (RD), Safeguarded (SG), and Unprotected (UP).

- **Rare and Difficult (RD)**: This category refers to security issues Rust's inbuilt features or mechanisms can fully mitigate or prevent. The language itself provides robust protection against such issues. Security vulnerabilities falling into this category are rare and difficult to spot. They occur infrequently, making it challenging to encounter them. Rust's inherent protections are usually effective in addressing these issues, **unless unsafe blocks are used**. These issues are often not commonly observed and may require specific circumstances or careful analysis, often associated with a Common Vulnerabilities and Exposures (CVE) identifier.
- **Safeguarded (SG)**: Issues falling under this category benefit from protective measures provided by Rust. The programming language offers safeguards to mitigate these issues, reducing their likelihood or impact. However, additional precautions or interventions may be necessary in specific scenarios.
- **Unprotected (UP)**: This category encompasses security issues that the language does not inherently guard against or if the CWE does not apply to the language. The language lacks built-in mechanisms to protect against these issues. Addressing them requires utilizing external libraries or tools or a comprehensive understanding of the language and underlying systems. In cases where a particular CWE is irrelevant to the language, it is also categorized as UP.

We utilized this methodology to evaluate the SANS Top 25, OWASP Top 10, and 19 Deadly Sins of Software Security within the context of Rust. Additionally, we created Proof-of-Concept (PoC) Rust code [25] to validate its feasibility, containing vulnerabilities for the following weaknesses: Command Injection, Integer Overflow, Resource Leakage, SQL Injection, and Time-of-Check-Time-of-Use (TOCTOU).

IV. RESULTS

A. SANS 25 (2023)

This section presents the findings of our analysis concerning vulnerabilities in Rust, with a particular focus on evaluating vulnerable software based on the SANS Top 25 list. Table I summarizes the protection levels for different CWE vulnerabilities in Rust. These are categorized into three groups: Rare and Difficult (RD), Safeguarded (SG), and Unprotected (UP). It is crucial to note that complete protection is extended to all code that does not use 'unsafe' blocks.

Among the analyzed CWE vulnerabilities, the following are identified as having Full Protection in Rust: CWE-787, CWE-125, CWE-416, CWE-476, CWE-362, and CWE-119. This finding suggests that Rust offers robust protection against these vulnerabilities, thereby minimizing the likelihood of their occurrence in Rust-based software, provided the code does not employ 'unsafe' blocks.

Conversely, several vulnerabilities, including CWE-79, CWE-22, CWE-352, CWE-434, CWE-502, CWE-287, CWE-798, CWE-862, CWE-306, CWE-276, CWE-918, and CWE-611, exhibit No Protection in Rust. This finding implies that Rust lacks built-in mechanisms to prevent or mitigate these vulnerabilities, even when 'unsafe' blocks are not in use. It is vital for developers working with Rust to be cognizant of these vulnerabilities and implement additional security measures to counteract them.

For certain vulnerabilities, such as CWE-79, CWE-20, CWE-78, CWE-190, CWE-77, CWE-400, and CWE-94, Rust provides some protection and safeguards. This result indicates that Rust incorporates certain features or constructs that can help diminish the likelihood of these vulnerabilities. However, additional precautions may still be necessary to mitigate the associated risks fully.

These findings underscore the importance of understanding the vulnerabilities inherent in Rust and implementing suitable security measures. While Rust provides strong protection against specific CWE vulnerabilities, there are areas where additional precautions are necessary. Developers should exercise caution when dealing with vulnerabilities categorized as UnProtected, as these require meticulous attention and specialized security practices.

In addition to analyzing the vulnerabilities in Rust, it is insightful to contrast the protection levels Rust offers with those provided by other prominent programming languages, such as C, C++, and Java. Table II facilitates a side-by-side comparison across these languages. In this table, the protection levels are denoted as follows: Rare and Difficult (RD), Safeguarded (SG), and Unprotected (UP) for C, C++, and Java.

Upon examining Table II, it is evident that C, being an older language, demonstrates fewer protections compared to C++ and Java, especially regarding memory-related vulnerabilities like CWE-787. For instance, C does not provide safeguards for CWE-787, while C++ and Java offer robust protections.

Java, owing to its managed memory model and sandboxed execution environment, shows strong defenses against some vulnerabilities that are particularly problematic in C and C++, such as CWE-416.

Interestingly, for some vulnerabilities like CWE-79 and CWE-22, all three languages - C, C++, and Java - display limited or no protection. This observation accentuates the importance of following secure coding practices irrespective of the language used.

Furthermore, C++ seems to find a middle ground between C and Java regarding protection levels, which could be attributed to its evolution from C and its incorporation of modern language features.

Developers must be cognizant of these variations in protection levels across languages and carefully weigh the security aspects alongside other factors, such as performance and ecosystem, when choosing a language for their projects.

B. OWASP 10

The OWASP Top 10 is a standard awareness document for developers and web application security. It represents a broad consensus about web applications' most critical security risks. The following is an assessment of how the Rust language can offer protection against these vulnerabilities, according to the OWASP standard from 2021:

TABLE I
SANS TOP 25 CWE VS. PROTECTION LEVELS IN RUST

CWE ID	Short Description	RD	SG	UP
CWE-787	Out-of-bounds Write	•		
CWE-79	Cross-site Scripting			•
CWE-89	SQL Injection		•	
CWE-20	Improper Input Validation		•	
CWE-125	Out-of-bounds Read	•		
CWE-78	OS Command Injection		•	
CWE-416	Use After Free	•		
CWE-22	Path Traversal			•
CWE-352	Cross-Site Request Forgery			•
CWE-434	Unrestricted Dangerous File Upload			•
CWE-476	NULL Pointer Dereference	•		
CWE-502	Deserialization of Untrusted Data			•
CWE-190	Integer Overflow or Wraparound		•	
CWE-287	Improper Authentication			•
CWE-798	Use of Hard-coded Credentials			•
CWE-862	Missing Authorization			•
CWE-77	Command Injection		•	
CWE-306	Missing Critical Function Authentication			•
CWE-119	Buffer Overflow	•		
CWE-276	Incorrect Default Permissions			•
CWE-918	Server-Side Request Forgery			•
CWE-362	Race Condition	•		
CWE-400	Uncontrolled Resource Consumption		•	
CWE-611	Improper Restriction of XXE			•
CWE-94	Code Injection		•	
		24%	28%	48%

TABLE II
SANS TOP 25 CWE VS. PROTECTION LEVELS IN C, C++, AND JAVA

CWE	C			C++			Java		
	RD	SG	UP	RD	SG	UP	RD	SG	UP
CWE-787			•		•		•		
CWE-79			•			•			•
CWE-89			•		•			•	
CWE-20			•			•		•	
CWE-125			•			•	•		
CWE-78			•			•		•	
CWE-416			•		•		•		
CWE-22			•			•			•
CWE-352			•			•			•
CWE-434			•			•			•
CWE-476			•		•		•		
CWE-502			•			•			•
CWE-190			•			•			•
CWE-287			•			•			•
CWE-798			•			•			•
CWE-862			•			•			•
CWE-77			•			•		•	
CWE-306			•			•			•
CWE-119			•		•		•		
CWE-276			•			•			•
CWE-918			•			•			•
CWE-362			•			•		•	
CWE-400			•		•			•	
CWE-611			•			•			•
CWE-94			•			•		•	
	0%	0%	100%	0%	24%	76%	20%	28%	52%

- **A01-Broken Access Control (SG):** While Rust does not inherently provide web application access control, its strong type system and ownership model can help prevent logical errors that might lead to such vulnerabilities.
- **A02-Cryptographic Failures (SG):** Although Rust does not provide built-in cryptographic features, it has high-quality cryptographic libraries that can help mitigate these failures to some extent.
- **A03-Injection (SG):** Rust's strong type system and ap-

proach to handling strings can help prevent injection attacks. However, poor programming practices may still result in these attacks; see PoC code in [25].

- **A04-Insecure Design (UP):** This vulnerability is more about the design of the application rather than the language itself. While Rust offers memory safety, it does not inherently protect against insecure design, which encompasses many issues.
- **A05-Security Misconfiguration (UP):** This vulnerability is more about the application and environment configuration than the language itself.
- **A06-Vulnerable and Outdated Components (SG):** Rust's package manager, Cargo, and its ecosystem can help manage dependencies and their updates.
- **A07-Identification and Authentication Failures (UP):** Rust does not inherently provide user authentication and session management features.
- **A08-Software and Data Integrity Failures (UP):** Rust's ownership model and type system can help ensure data integrity, but it is up to the programmer to leverage these features effectively.
- **A09-Security Logging and Monitoring Failures (UP):** This vulnerability is more about the application's logging and monitoring capabilities than the language itself.
- **A10-Server-Side Request Forgery (SSRF) (UP):** Rust does not inherently protect against SSRF attacks.

We note that in literature, the numbering of the OWASP vulnerabilities can also appear together with the date of the OWASP standard, e.g., A01:2021.

TABLE III
MAPPING OF OWASP TOP 10 FROM 2021 TO RUST PROTECTION LEVELS

OWASP Vulnerability	RD	SG	UP
A01-Broken Access Control		•	
A02-Cryptographic Failures		•	
A03-Injection		•	
A04-Insecure Design			•
A05-Security Misconfiguration			•
A06-Vulnerable and Outdated Components		•	
A07-Identification and Authentication Failures			•
A08-Software and Data Integrity Failures		•	
A09-Security Logging and Monitoring Failures			•
A10-Server-Side Request Forgery			•
	0%	50%	50%

C. 19 Deadly Sins of Software Security

The book "19 Deadly Sins of Software Security: Programming Flaws and How to Fix Them" identifies and guides how to fix 19 common security flaws in software programming. Rust, a programming language, is designed to prevent some of the most common security vulnerabilities. Below is a brief analysis of how Rust addresses the 19 sins:

- **Buffer Overflows (RD)**: Rust has built-in protection against buffer overflow errors. It enforces strict bounds checking, preventing programs from accessing memory they should not.
- **Format String Problems (SG)**: Rust does not support format strings in the same way as languages like C, thereby reducing the risk of this issue. It provides strong protection against format string problems through its type-safe formatting mechanism. The std::fmt module in Rust offers a rich set of formatting capabilities while enforcing compile-time safety.
- **Integer Overflows (SG)**: In Rust, integer overflow is considered a "fail-fast" error. By default, when an integer overflow occurs during an operation, Rust will panic and terminate the program. This behavior helps catch bugs early in development and prevents potential security vulnerabilities. It also offers ways to handle integer overflows gracefully.
- **SQL Injection (SG)**: Rust itself doesn't inherently protect against SQL injection. This protection is usually provided by libraries that parameterize SQL queries, such as rusqlite; see PoC code in [25].
- **Command Injection (SG)**: Rust offers strong protections against command injection vulnerabilities through its string handling and execution mechanisms. The language's emphasis on memory safety and control over system resources helps mitigate the risk of command injection; see PoC code in [25].
- **Cross-Site Scripting (XSS) (UP)**: Rust does not provide inherent protection against XSS. However, web frameworks in Rust, such as Rocket and Actix, have features to mitigate XSS.
- **Race Conditions (RD)**: Rust's ownership model and type system are designed to prevent data races at compile time.
- **Error Handling (RD)**: Rust encourages using the Result type for error handling, which requires explicit handling of errors.
- **Poor Logging (SG)**: Poor logging is more of a design problem than a language issue. Rust offers powerful logging libraries, such as log and env_logger.
- **Insecure Configuration (UP)**: Although Rust's strong typing can catch some configuration errors at compile time, it does not offer direct protections against insecure configurations.
- **Weak Cryptography (SG)**: Rust has libraries that support strong, modern cryptography. However, the correct implementation depends on the developer.
- **Weak Random Numbers (RD)**: Rust's standard library includes a secure random number generator.
- **Using Components with Known Vulnerabilities (SG)**: This is more related to the ecosystem than the language itself. Rust's package manager, Cargo, simplifies updating dependencies.
- **Unvalidated Redirects and Forwards (UP)**: Protection against this is usually provided by web frameworks.
- **Injection (SG)**: Rust's strong typing and absence of eval-like functions lower the risk of code injection.
- **Insecure Storage (UP)**: Not directly related to the language itself.
- **Denial of Service (SG)**: Rust's memory safety and

control over low-level details can help build resilient systems, but it does not inherently protect against all types of DoS attacks.
- **Insecure Third-Party Interfaces (UP)**: This issue is usually independent of the programming language.
- **Cross-Site Request Forgery (CSRF) (UP)**: Typically, handled by web frameworks rather than the language itself.

TABLE IV
MAPPING OF NINETEEN DEADLY SINS OF SOFTWARE SECURITY TO RUST PROTECTION LEVELS

Security Flaw	RD	SG	UP
Buffer Overflows	•		
Format String Problems		•	
Integer Overflows		•	
SQL Injection		•	
Command Injection		•	
Cross-Site Scripting (XSS)			•
Race Conditions	•		
Error Handling	•		
Poor Logging		•	
Insecure Configuration			•
Weak Cryptography		•	
Weak Random Numbers	•		
Using Known Vulnerable Components		•	
Unvalidated Redirects and Forwards			•
Injection		•	
Insecure Storage			•
Denial of Service		•	
Insecure Third-Party Interfaces			•
Cross-Site Request Forgery (CSRF)			•
	21%	47%	32%

In summary, Rust provides strong protections against several of the "19 deadly sins", particularly those related to memory safety and data races. However, some issues, particularly those related to web development or design decisions, are not directly addressed.

In the following sections, we will delve deeper into the analysis of past vulnerabilities in the Rust language and its ecosystem and shed light on the time taken to address these vulnerabilities and the current open issues in the Rust security landscape. This comprehensive analysis aims to provide a better understanding of the vulnerabilities in Rust and guide developers and researchers in effectively addressing security concerns in Rust-based software.

D. CVEs Addressed by Rust Security Advisory

A quick search on CVE Mitre with the keyword "Rust" returns over 400 vulnerabilities at the time of writing. Various researchers have analyzed the CVEs, and the Rust community actively fixes them once discovered [8], [26]. However, Rust's security advisory only addresses six of these vulnerabilities: CVE-2021-42574 [27], CVE-2022-21658 [28], CVE-2022-24713 [29], CVE-2022-36113 [30], CVE-2022-36114 [30], and CVE-2022-46176 [31].

The most recent CVE acknowledged by the Rust security advisory on their blog is CVE-2022-46176 [31]. This vulnerability, found in Cargo's Rust package manager, could allow for man-in-the-middle (MITM) attacks due to a lack of SSH host key verification when cloning indexes and dependencies via SSH. All Rust versions containing Cargo before 1.66.1 are vulnerable. Rust version 1.66.1 was released to mitigate this, which checks the SSH host key and aborts the connection if the server's public key is not already trusted.

E. Comparison of Rust Static Analysis Tools with Python, Java, and C++

Rust has been gaining traction due to its focus on safety and performance. As a young language, Rust's ecosystem of static analysis tools is still in rapid development. The primary tool for static analysis in Rust is the Rust compiler, which includes a robust type system and borrow checker that prevents many bugs at compile time. Moreover, tools like Clippy provide lints to catch common mistakes and improve Rust code.

In contrast, languages like Python, Java, and C++ have been around for a considerable time and have a mature set of static analysis tools. Python, a dynamically typed language, relies on tools like PyLint, PyFlakes, and Bandit for static analysis. With its static type system, Java uses tools like FindBugs, PMD, and Checkstyle. C++, known for its complexity and flexibility, employs tools like cppcheck and Clang Static Analyzer.

While each language has its unique set of static analysis tools, the effectiveness of these tools can vary based on the language's features and characteristics. The rapidly evolving Rust ecosystem is a testament to the language's growing popularity and commitment to safety and performance. On the other hand, the mature toolsets of Python, Java, and C++ provide robust support for detecting potential bugs and improving code quality, backed by years of development and refinement.

V. DISCUSSION

In this study, we have explored the security implications of using the Rust programming language, which is gaining traction in the software industry due to its claims of safety and security. Our findings indicate that while Rust offers certain security advantages, it is not immune to vulnerabilities, and there are areas where it falls short compared to other, more mature languages.

Our research has shown that writing vulnerable software in Rust is possible. This finding is essential, as it challenges the perception that Rust is inherently secure. While Rust's design does make some types of vulnerabilities harder to introduce, it is not a panacea. Other security aspects are as problematic in Rust as in any other language. This point underscores the fact that while language choice can influence the security of a software system, it is not the only factor. Good security practices are essential, regardless of the language used.

Some vulnerabilities are hard or impossible to solve through an improved programming language as these belong to a "non-decidable" category. Therefore, writing a compiler or defining a programming language that identifies and eliminates such problems is impossible. However, we have observed that Rust does offer improvements over other languages in handling these issues, which is a positive sign.

One of the challenges we encountered in our research is the relative immaturity of Rust compared to other languages. There are fewer studies on Rust security, and the tools and support for secure development are not as robust. For example, SonarQube [32], a popular tool for static analysis of code to detect bugs, code smells, and security vulnerabilities, does not currently support Rust. This lack of tooling can significantly impede Rust's adoption in an industrial context, where such tools are critical for finding vulnerabilities and passing cybersecurity certifications.

Our discussions with industry experts found that Rust's high learning curve is another potential barrier to its adoption. More investigation is needed to understand the security consequences of this compared to other languages that might be easier to learn. The lack of a "competent" workforce skilled in Rust is another challenge that needs to be addressed.

In our analysis of the SANS Top 25, Rust provides inherent protections against 24% of the vulnerabilities, some safeguards against 28% of vulnerabilities, and does not offer protection or does not apply to 48% of the vulnerabilities. We made notable observations when comparing Rust with other programming languages like C, C++, and Java. C does not offer any inherent protections against the vulnerabilities listed in the SANS Top 25, as it was designed to be minimal and efficient. C++, on the other hand, provides safeguards against particular vulnerabilities, such as CWE-787 and CWE-15. Examples of language features that can protect against these vulnerabilities include the C++ Standard Template Library (STL) and other features. Nevertheless, the C++ programming language does not inherently protect against them. In our study, we observe that C++ safeguards against only 24% of the vulnerabilities in the SANS Top 25. However, Java utilizes a garbage collector that inherently protects against memory-related issues. This feature puts Java closer to Rust in terms of protection.

Our analysis of the OWASP findings revealed that not a single finding is of the type RD, which is to be expected, as Rust is more a system-level programming language rather than a programming language for web technologies. Compared to C, C++, and Java, which are widely used in the industry, Rust shows promise but has limitations.

Our analysis of the 19 Deadly Sins showed that Rust provides inherent protections against 21% of these sins, offers safeguards for 47% of them, and leaves 32% of the sins unprotected.

We do not expect any current or future programming language to be able to cover 100% of the vulnerabilities, as many coding guidelines in CWE are non-decidable. However, our work shows that Rust does a commendable job addressing many CWE guidelines.

Our inspiration to use a three-point scale (RD, SG, and UP) in our analysis is based on the work by Jacoby (1971) [33], who argued that "Three-point Likert scales are good enough."

The authors consider the present work essential as Rust's usage for software development continues to grow. Without awareness of potential vulnerabilities, we risk replacing one problem with another. It is crucial to emphasize the security limitations of Rust early on rather than treating security as an add-on feature. Security should be prioritized from the inception of every project. Furthermore, due to Rust being a relatively new language, standardized testing tools for assessing compliance with ISO/IEC security standards are not yet available, or very few. This lack of tools makes it challenging to introduce Rust into the industry.

The present work does not focus on finding novel software weaknesses specific to the Rust programming language but rather on comparing well-known vulnerabilities, e.g., as present in secure programming standards, and their relation to the Rust programming language. Additional investigation is needed to understand potential vulnerabilities when developing software in Rust which are caused by the language itself.

In conclusion, our work contributes to scientific knowledge and industry practice by shedding light on the security implications of using Rust. While Rust is rising in significance and the industry is starting to adopt it, there is a lack of studies on its security aspects. Our work closes this gap and shows that while it is still possible to write vulnerabilities in Rust, some problems are well-considered. As Rust continues to grow in popularity, we hope our findings will help guide its development in a direction that prioritizes security and that our work will serve as a foundation for further research in this area.

While the interviews carried out in the present work include a limited number of participants, the results of the present work are validated. The authors did not only confirm some vulnerabilities with proof-of-concept code but also conducted interviews with highly experienced security experts. Nevertheless, the mapping to protection levels, while dependent on the authors' and interviewees' experience, can also change in future releases of the Rust programming language.

VI. CONCLUSION AND FUTURE WORK

Our research provided valuable insights into the security implications of the Rust programming language. While Rust has significantly enhanced software security, we have demonstrated that it is not immune to vulnerabilities. Our findings challenge the notion that Rust is inherently secure and highlight the need for robust security practices, regardless of the language used.

Our study has also shed light on the challenges associated with Rust's relative immaturity compared to other, more established languages. The lack of comprehensive studies on Rust security, the absence of robust tooling for secure development, and the high learning curve associated with Rust are all areas that require attention. Furthermore, the shortage of a skilled workforce in Rust is a significant barrier that needs to be addressed to facilitate its broader adoption in the industry.

Despite these challenges, Rust shows promise. Its design makes specific vulnerabilities harder to introduce and offers improvements over other languages in handling "non-decidable" problems. As Rust continues gaining traction in the software industry, it is crucial to investigate its security implications and develop tools and practices to mitigate potential vulnerabilities.

As the following steps, there are several avenues for future work. One of the critical areas is the development of tools to support secure development in Rust. These tools include static application security testing tools like SonarQube, which are critical for finding vulnerabilities and passing cybersecurity certifications. Another area of focus is the development of comprehensive training programs to lower Rust's learning curve and build a competent workforce skilled in Rust. In further research, the authors would like to understand the security consequences of Rust's high learning curve through comparative studies of software projects developed in different programming languages.

As more software is developed in Rust, it is crucial to maintain a sense of urgency in highlighting its security shortcomings. Security should not be an afterthought but should be integrated from the beginning of every project. We hope our work will contribute to developing safer and more secure software systems.

REFERENCES

[1] Yalantis, "Rust Market Overview," 2023, accessed: July 16, 2023. [Online]. Available: https://yalantis.com/blog/rust-market-overview/

[2] E. D. C. Garcia, "Rust Makes Us Better Programmers," 2023, accessed: July 16, 2023. [Online]. Available: https://thenewstack.io/rust-makes-us-better-programmers/

[3] S. O. Ryan Donovan, "Why the developers who use Rust love it so much," Jun 2020, accessed: July 16, 2023. [Online]. Available: https://stackoverflow.blog/2020/06/05/why-the-developers-who-use-rust-love-it-so-much/

[4] S. Overflow, "Stack Overflow Developer Survey 2023," 2023, accessed: July 16, 2023. [Online]. Available: https://survey.stackoverflow.co/2023/#section-admired-and-desired-programming-scripting-and-markup-languages

[5] J. Barron, "Rust's Addition to the Linux Kernel Seen as 'Enormous Vote of Confidence' in the Language," *SD Times*, Nov. 2022, accessed: July 16, 2023. [Online]. Available: https://sdtimes.com/software-development/rusts-addition-to-the-linux-kernel-seen-as-enormous-vote-of-confidence-in-the-language/

[6] Writing Linux Kernel Modules in Rust. [Online]. Available: https://www.linuxfoundation.org/webinars/writing-linux-kernel-modules-in-rust

[7] G. S. Team, "Memory-safe languages in Android 13," 2022, accessed: July 16, 2023. [Online]. Available: https://security.googleblog.com/2022/12/memory-safe-languages-in-android-13.html

[8] "RustSec Advisory Database," 2023, accessed: July 16, 2023. [Online]. Available: https://rustsec.org/advisories/

[9] "IEC 62443," international Electrotechnical Commission (IEC) Standards.

[10] International Electrotechnical Commission, "Understanding IEC 62443," https://www.iec.ch/blog/understanding-iec-62443, accessed: July 16, 2023.

[11] SANS Institute, "Top 25 Software Errors," https://www.sans.org/top25-software-errors/, accessed: July 16, 2023.

[12] OWASP Foundation, "OWASP Top Ten," https://owasp.org/www-project-top-ten/, accessed: July 16, 2023.

[13] M. Howard, D. LeBlanc, and J. Viega, *19 Deadly Sins of Software Security: Programming Flaws and How to Fix Them*. New York: McGraw-Hill, 2005, accessed: July 16, 2023.
Conference on Software Engineering: Software Engineering Education and Training (ICSE-SEET), 2021, pp. 241–252, accessed: July 16, 2023.

[14] T. Espinha Gasiba, U. Lechner, M. Pinto-Albuquerque, and D. Méndez, "Is Secure Coding Education in the Industry Needed? An Investigation Through a Large Scale Survey," in *2021 IEEE/ACM 43rd International*

[15] J. Sible and D. Svoboda, "Rust Software Security: A Current State Assessment," Carnegie Mellon University, Software Engineering Institute's Insights (blog), Dec 2022, accessed: July 16, 2023. [Online]. Available: https://doi.org/10.58012/0px4-9n81

[16] G. Wassermann and D. Svoboda, "Rust Vulnerability Analysis and Maturity Challenges," Carnegie Mellon University, Software Engineering Institute's Insights (blog), Jan 2023, accessed: July 16, 2023. [Online]. Available: https://doi.org/10.58012/t0m3-vb66

[17] B. Qin, Y. Chen, Z. Yu, L. Song, and Y. Zhang, "Understanding Memory and Thread Safety Practices and Issues in Real-World Rust Programs," in *Proceedings of the 41st ACM SIGPLAN Conference on Programming Language Design and Implementation*, ser. PLDI 2020. New York, NY, USA: Association for Computing Machinery, 2020, p. 763–779, accessed: July 16, 2023. [Online]. Available: https://doi.org/10.1145/3385412.3386036

[18] I. J. S. 22, "ISO/IEC TR 24772-1:2019 - Programming languages — Guidance to avoiding vulnerabilities in programming languages — Part 1: Language-independent guidance," Online, 12 2019, accessed: July 16, 2023. [Online]. Available: https://www.iso.org/standard/71091.html

[19] T. M. Corporation, "Common Weakness Enumeration (CWE)," Online, 2023, accessed: July 16, 2023. [Online]. Available: https://cwe.mitre.org/

[20] ANSSI, "Publication: Programming Rules to Develop Secure Applications With Rust," https://www.ssi.gouv.fr/guide/programming-rules-to-develop-secure-applications-with-rust/, 2023, (accessed July 16, 2023).

[21] "Rust - Analysis Tools," 2023, accessed: July 16, 2023. [Online]. Available: https://analysis-tools.dev/tag/rust

[22] R. Bagnara, A. Bagnara, and P. M. Hill, "Coding Guidelines and Undecidability," *arXiv*, Dec 2022, accessed: July 16, 2023. [Online]. Available: http://arxiv.org/abs/2212.13933

[23] T. Espinha Gasiba, U. Lechner, M. Pinto-Albuquerque, and D. Mendez Fernandez, "Awareness of Secure Coding Guidelines in the Industry - A First Data Analysis," in *2020 IEEE 19th International Conference on Trust, Security and Privacy in Computing and Communications (TrustCom)*, 2020, pp. 345–352, accessed: July 16, 2023.

[24] T. Espinha Gasiba, U. Lechner, and M. Pinto-Albuquerque, "Sifu - a Cybersecurity Awareness Platform with Challenge Assessment and Intelligent Coach," *Cybersecurity*, vol. 3, no. 1, p. 24, 12 2020, accessed: July 16, 2023.

[25] S. Amburi, "Sathwik-Amburi/secure-software-development-with-rust: Secure Software Development with Rust," https://github.com/Sathwik-Amburi/secure-software-development-with-rust, Aug. 2023, last accessed: 2023-08-14. [Online]. Available: https://doi.org/10.5281/zenodo.8247155

[26] H. Xu, Z. Chen, M. Sun, Y. Zhou, and M. R. Lyu, "Memory-Safety Challenge Considered Solved? An In-Depth Study with All Rust CVEs," *ACM Transactions on Software Engineering and Methodology (TOSEM)*, vol. 31, no. 1, sep 2021, accessed: July 16, 2023. [Online]. Available: https://doi.org/10.1145/3466642

[27] The Rust Security Response WG, "Security advisory for rustc (CVE-2021-42574)," November 2021, accessed: July 16, 2023. [Online]. Available: https://blog.rust-lang.org/2022/01/20/cve-2022-21658.html

[28] ——, "Security advisory for the standard library (CVE-2022-21658)," January 2022, accessed: July 16, 2023. [Online]. Available: https://blog.rust-lang.org/2022/01/20/cve-2022-21658.html

[29] ——, "Security advisory for the regex crate (CVE-2022-24713)," March 2022, accessed: July 16, 2023. [Online]. Available: https://blog.rust-lang.org/2022/03/08/cve-2022-24713.html

[30] ——, "Security advisories for Cargo (CVE-2022-36113, CVE-2022-36114)," September 2022, accessed: July 16, 2023. [Online]. Available: https://blog.rust-lang.org/2022/09/14/cargo-cves.html

[31] ——, "Security advisory for Cargo (CVE-2022-46176)," January 2023, accessed: July 16, 2023. [Online]. Available: https://blog.rust-lang.org/2023/01/10/cve-2022-46176.html

[32] SonarSource, "SonarQube," https://www.sonarqube.org, [retrieved July 16, 2023]. [Online]. Available: https://www.sonarqube.org

[33] J. Jacoby and M. S. Matell, "Three-Point Likert Scales Are Good Enough," *Journal of Marketing Research*, vol. 8, no. 4, pp. 495–500, 1971, accessed: July 16, 2023. [Online]. Available: https://doi.org/10.1177/002224377100800414

Towards Explainable Attacker-Defender Autocurricula in Critical Infrastructures

Eric MSP Veith and Torben Logemann
Carl von Ossietzky University Oldenburg
Research Group Adversarial Resilience Learning
Oldenburg, Germany
Email: {eric.veith,torben.logemann}@uol.de

***Abstract*—Agent systems have become almost ubiquitous in smart grid research. Research can be roughly divided into carefully designed (multi-) agent systems that can perform known tasks with guarantees, and learning agents based on technologies such as Deep Reinforcement Learning (DRL) that promise real resilience by learning to counter the unknown unknowns. However, the latter cannot give guarantees regarding their behavior, while the former are limited to the set of problems known at design time. In this paper, we present work in progress towards explaining strategies learned in autocurriculum settings in Critical National Infrastructures (CNIs), such as the power grid. We show how our equivalent representation of DRL policies allows to study agent behavior and ascertain learned strategies for resilient CNI operation.**

Keywords*—*adversarial resilience learning; agent systems; reinforcement learning; explainable reinforcement learning; resilience; power grid

I. Introduction

Over the last years, agent systems and especially Multi-Agent Systems (MASs) [1]–[4] have emerged as one of the most important tools to facilitate management of complex energy systems. As swarm logic, they can handle numerous tasks, such as maintaining real power equilibria, voltage control, or automated energy trading [5]. The fact that MASs implement proactive and reactive distributed heuristics allows to analyze their behavior and give certain guarantees, a property that has helped in their deployment.

However, modern energy systems have also become valuable targets. Cyber-attacks have become more common [6], [7], and establishing local energy markets, although being an attractive concept of self-organization, can also be exploited, e. g., through artificially created congestion [8]. Attacks on power grids are no longer carefully planned and executed, but also learned by agents, such as market manipulation or voltage band violations [9]. Thus, carefully designing software systems that provide protection against a widening field of adversarial scenarios has become a challenge, especially considering that (interconnected) Cyber-Physical Systems (CPSs) are inherently exploitable due to their complexity [10].

Learning agents, particularly those based on DRL, have gained traction as a potential solution: If a system faces *unknown unknowns*, a learning agent can devise strategies against it. In the past, researchers have employed DRL-based agents for numerous tasks related to power grid operations, such as voltage control [11]. Especially the approach to use DRL for vulnerability assessment, cyber security attack mitigation, and general resilient operation have gained traction among researchers in the recent years [12]–[16]. In general, DRL constitutes an attractive family of algorithms as it is at the core of many noteworthy successes, such as MuZero [17], with modern algorithms such as Twin-Delayed DDPG (TD3) [18], Proximal Policy Gradient (PPO) [19], and Soft Actor Critic (SAC) [20] having proved to be able to tackle complex tasks.

While the scientific corpus agrees that DRL-based agents are a valuable topic of research in terms of cyber-security in CNIs, their effectiveness can only be stated in a manner that is (1) indirect and (2) case-based. Indirect, because there is no direct method available that would ascertain a DRL agent's policy. Publications offer analysis of rewards and simulation states; however, it is well known that optimizing a metric (i. e., maximizing the reward) is not necessarily the same as solving the problem behind it. Second, many publications lack long-term simulations, but consider certain well-described scenarios. Thus, a DRL-based agent's ability to generalize is inferred, but not entirely proven.

eXplainable Reinforcement Learning (XRL) [21] promises to fill this gap at least partially. However, the most common techniques, such as saliency maps, give only indirect interpretation and are useful for experts in the DRL domain, but not for practitioners in CNIs. Recent approaches to convert a DRL agent's policy network into a rule-based representation, e. g., as decision tree [22], will satisfy the outlined requirements. In a recent publication, we have presented an equivalent transformation of a DRL agent's policy network into a compressed decision tree, called *NN2EQCDT* [23]. We have also argued that such an equivalent representation should be a default module in any modern architecture for learning agents in CNIs and presented the Adversarial Resilience Learning (ARL) agent architecture in this regard [24].

In this paper, we present an approach to explaining and validating DRL autocurricula in CNIs, such as the power grid. Previous publications have indicated that employing competing agents can lead to faster learning and robust strategies, and we have presented our ARL methodology to take advantage of this [12]. In ARL, two agents (often dubbed "attacker" and "defender") work with an inversible reward function: The defender aims to operate the CNI in a resilient manner, the attacker aims to destabilize the CNI. The competition improves the sample efficiency of the agents, which also learn more robust strategies. As the goal of the ARL research is to develop an actually deployable defender, an extended architecture (the

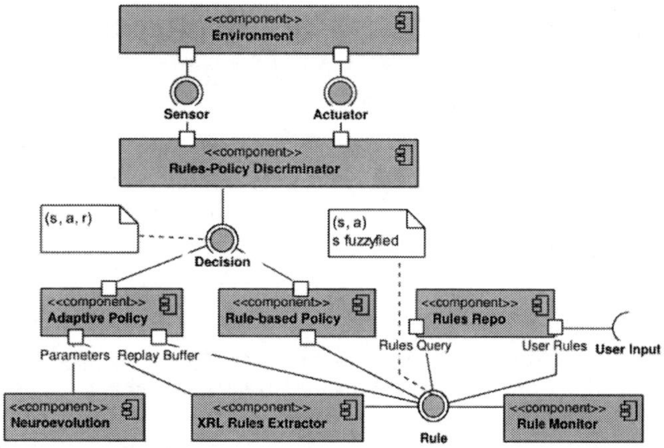

Figure 1. Simplified components view of the ARL agent architecture.

ARL architecture) has been created. In this paper, we will outline how the generation of an equivalent representation of a policy network can be integrated in an agent architecture and provide the first steps towards explaining DRL autocurriculae for resilient operation of smart grids.

The remainder of this work-in-progress paper is structured as follows: Section II gives a concise summary of our NN2EQCDT algorithm and its integration into the ARL agent architecture. In Section III, we then present a scenario that we explain using NN2EQCDT. Section IV offers a discussion of our approach and the experiment's results. Finally, we outline the next steps in Section V.

II. A Self-Explaining Deep Reinforcement Learning Agent

The concept of the ARL agent assumes two parallel policies: An *Adaptive Policy* that is based on DRL, and a *Rules-based Policy* that works on a decision tree. When an agent observes the environment, the *Discriminator* chooses between the two policies based on a trust value. Both policies are queried, and in their *Decision*, they give the action and the reward value they expect from executing the action. The Discriminator checks both proposals against its internal world model and chooses the one whose reward deviates the least from the reward the world model returns. Then, each policy's trust value is modified according to a Linear Time-Invariant (LTI) system:

$$pt1(y, u, t) = \begin{cases} u & \text{if } t = 0 \\ y + \dfrac{u - y}{t} & \text{otherwise,} \end{cases} \quad (1)$$

where y signifies the current trust value of the respective policy module and u is the reward the world model yielded for the policy's decision proposal. The Discriminator's world model is based on data provided by the CNI operator.

The truest approach also means that the adaptive policy will naturally be trusted for situations not covered by rules, but is able to gain more trust to yield innovative strategies over the course of the agent's existence, while the LTI ensures that mistakes do not immediately void the trust.

Whenever the DRL policy retrains, the new policy network is transformed into a new decision tree using the *XRL Rules Extractor*, which implements our NN2EQCDT algorithm [23]. Figure 1 depicts the component architecture of the ARL agent, while Figure 2 shows the procedure described.

The NN2EQCDT algorithm works according to Figure 3. The weight and bias matrices $\boldsymbol{W}_i$ and $\boldsymbol{B}_i$ from the Feed-Forward Deep Neural Network (FF-DNN) model are processed layer by layer. These are used to compute rules that are used to add subtrees to the overall Decision Tree (DT). From the second layer, when multiplying the weight and bias matrices, it is necessary to take into account the position of the node to which the generated subtree will be attached. This is done by applying the slope vector $\boldsymbol{a}$ to the current weight matrices. It represents the node position of the connection, since it is the vector of choices according to the Rectified Linear Unit (ReLU) activation function along the path from the root to the connection node.

When adding a node of a newly created subtree to the overall tree, each path from the root to the node in question is checked for satisfiability. If there can be no input so that its evaluation of the DT that takes this path, the node in question and thus further subtrees are not added to keep the size of the DT dynamically small.

Finally, the last checks are converted into expressions, and the DT can be further compressed by removing unnecessary checks, since they are evaluated the same for all possible inputs.

III. Example of Application

The ability to compress policies is important for an effective operation of the hybrid DRL/rules-based agent. Not only inference, but also analysis of extracted rules (e. g., changes with regards to previous iterations) takes advantage of a small tree. Considering that the ARL agent will run on edge devices that are memory- and CPU-constrained, the ability to compress the tree becomes an important feature of the algorithm. As a first step in our work in progress, we experimentally tested how an extrated decision tree is dependent on the size of the policy network, even if the strategy the agent has learned is seemingly simple.

To test this, we constructed a power grid with a simple linear branch feeder. From the 110 kV/20 kV transformer extends a branch with four nodes:

1) an inverter (Photovoltaics, PV), controlled by a "attacker" agent
2) an inverter (PV), controlled by a "defender" agent
3) an independent hospital
4) an independent wind park.

True to the ARL autocurriculum setting, we provided two largely invertable objectives to the agent, both of which targeted the voltage band. The attacker's task was to violate the voltage band, whereas the defender should keep it within acceptable boundaries. We used a bell-shaped curve centered at $1.0\,\text{pu}$. The defender maximum reward was at $1.0\,\text{pu}$, while the attacker used the inverted curve, with maximum reward at $V < 0.8\,\text{pu}$ and $V > 1.1\,\text{pu}$, respectively. Consider the reward function:

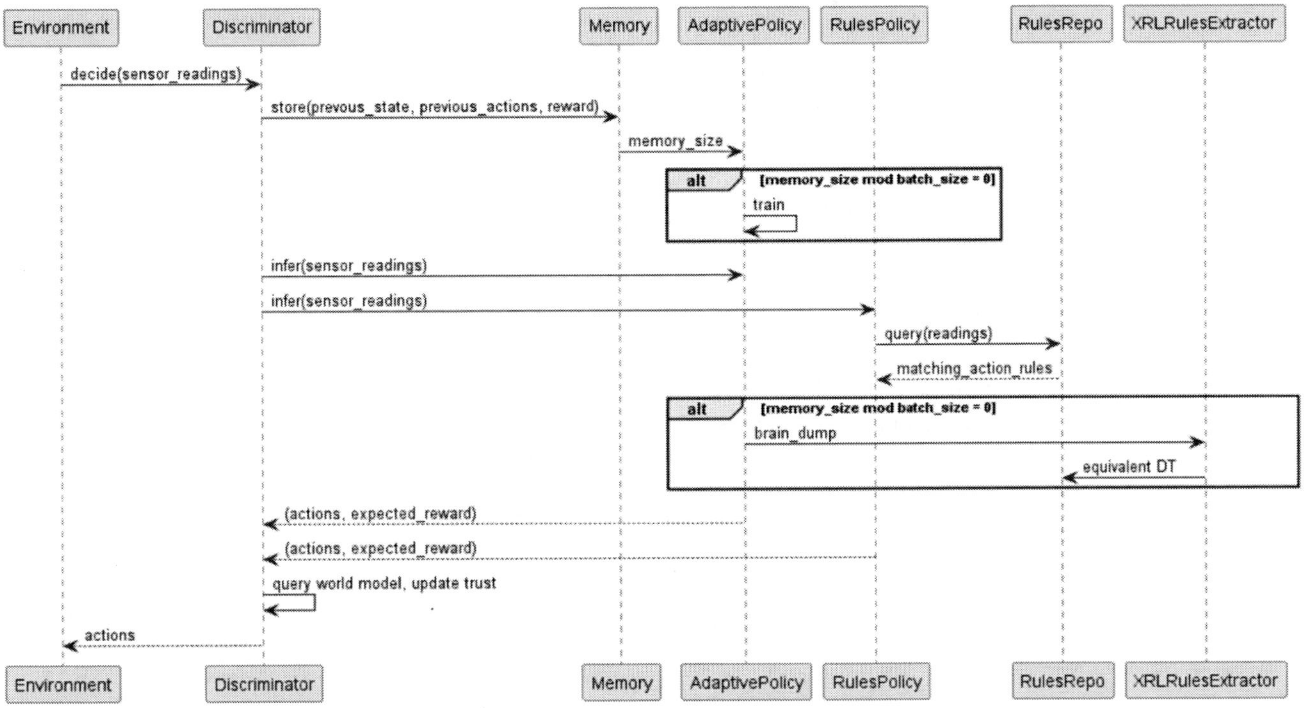

Figure 2. Activity diagram for training and self-explaining of an ARL agent.

$\hat{\boldsymbol{W}} = \boldsymbol{W}_0$
$\hat{\boldsymbol{B}} = \boldsymbol{B}_0^\top$
$rules$ = calc_rule_terms($\hat{\boldsymbol{W}}, \hat{\boldsymbol{B}}$)
T, new_SAT_leaves = create_initial_subtree($rules$)
set_hat_on_SAT_nodes(T, new_SAT_leaves, $\hat{\boldsymbol{W}}$, $\hat{\boldsymbol{B}}$)
for $i = 1, \ldots, n-1$ **do**
  SAT_paths = get_SAT_paths(T)
  for SAT_path in SAT_paths **do**
    $\boldsymbol{a}$ = compute_a_along(SAT_path)
    SAT_leave = SAT_path[−1]
    $\hat{\boldsymbol{W}}, \hat{\boldsymbol{B}}$ = get_last_hat_of_leave(T, SAT_leave)
    $\hat{\boldsymbol{W}} = (\boldsymbol{W}_i \odot [(\boldsymbol{a}^\top)_{\times k}])\hat{\boldsymbol{W}}$
    $\hat{\boldsymbol{B}} = (\boldsymbol{W}_i \odot [(\boldsymbol{a}^\top)_{\times k}])\hat{\boldsymbol{B}} + \boldsymbol{B}_i^\top$
    $rules$ = calc_rule_terms($\hat{\boldsymbol{W}}, \hat{\boldsymbol{B}}$)
    new_SAT_leaves = add_subtree(T, SAT_leave, $rules$, $invariants$)
    set_hat_on_SAT_nodes(T, new_SAT_leaves, $\hat{\boldsymbol{W}}, \hat{\boldsymbol{B}}$)
convert_final_rule_to_expr(T)
compress_tree(T)

Figure 3. NN2EQCDT algorithm for generating equivalent representation of DRL policy networks.

$$g\left(x = \frac{\sum_{i=1}^{|\boldsymbol{V}|} V_i}{|\boldsymbol{V}|}, A, \mu, C, \sigma\right) = A \cdot \exp\left(-\frac{(x-\mu)^2}{2\sigma^2} - C\right), \quad (2)$$

where $\boldsymbol{V}$ are voltages at the observed "victim buses" to which the hospital and the wind park are connected. The parameters

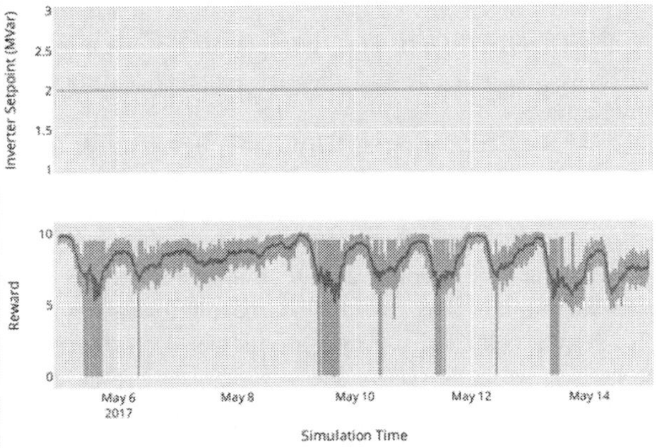

Figure 4. Setpoint and reward of the defender agent

A, μ, C, and σ shape the curve, so that we define:

$$\begin{aligned} reward_{attacker}\left(x = \frac{\sum_{i=1}^{|\boldsymbol{V}|} V_i}{|\boldsymbol{V}|}\right) = \\ g(x, A = -12.0, \mu = 1.0, C = -10.0, \sigma = -0.05) \\ + g(x, A = -12.0, \mu = 0.83, C = 0.0, \sigma = 0.01) \\ + g(x, A = -12.0, \mu = 1.16, C = 0.0, \sigma = 0.01) \quad (3) \end{aligned}$$

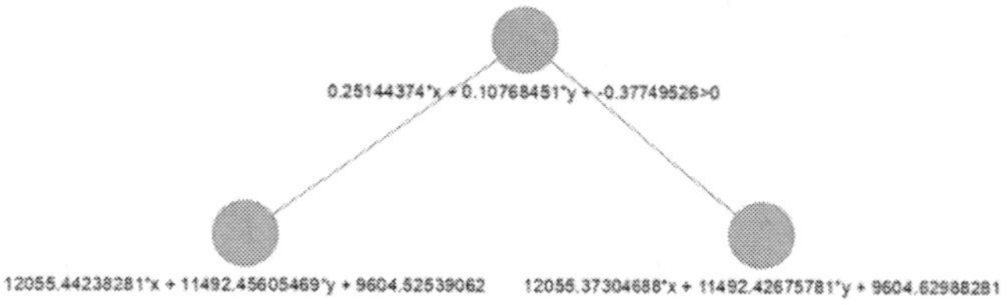

Figure 5. Decision tree as an equivalent representation of the agent's q-control policy

$$reward_{defender}\left(x = \frac{\sum_{i=1}^{|\boldsymbol{V}|} V_i}{|\boldsymbol{V}|}\right) = g(x, A = 10.0, \mu = 1.0, C = 0.0, \sigma = 0.032) \quad (4)$$

From Figure 4, we can see the setpoints and rewards of the defender agent. From these values alone, we can deduce that they have learned a very simple strategy (namely, one setpoint). This is expected in the simple scenario. We provided both agents with a larger-than-necessary policy network (a FF-DNN with $[2, 8, 8, 1]$ neurons).

IV. DISCUSSION

Even if the number of neurons in the policy network of the agents seems low compared to many Deep Neural Networks (DNNs), such a network would already suffer from co-adaptation. However, Figure 5 shows that the resulting DT contains only the single setpoint strategy over the range of perceived voltage levels. Moreover, when calculating the invariants of the DT and, thus, compressing it even further, it collapses to one node that exactly represents the simple learning strategy.

We can conclude that our NN2EQCDT algorithm is able to extract a reasonable representation even if the policy network is larger than needed. This is especially important considering that, as seen in Figure 1, the policy network is evolved through neuroevolution. We cannot assume that it is always of an appropriate minimal size, since the neuroevolutionary algorithm is not automatically fed size constraints based on the agent's memory.

All data of this experiment is available from [25].

V. CONCLUSION AND FUTURE WORK

In this work-in-progress paper, we presented preliminary results of our approach to explain learned strategies of agents in CNIs, which have been obtained in a autocurriculum setting.

In the future, we will expand our approach to more complex scenarios and a comprehensive experimentation regimen in order to show benefits and boundaries of our approach, especially focusing on scalability. We will present an extensive standard benchmarking scenario for our ARL methodology that will be based on a simulated power grid that includes a wide range of Distributed Energy Resources (DERs), consumers/prosumers, and assets the grid operator has access to. We will then show the benefits of the autocurriculum and, especially, our extended ARL agent architecture [24]. Through the steps outlined in this work-in-progress paper, as well our previous publications, we work towards making introspection of learned strategies in CNIs a default.

ACKNOWLEDGEMENTS

This work was funded by the German Federal Ministry for Education and Research (BMBF) under Grant No. 01IS22071.

REFERENCES

[1] E. M. Veith, *Universal Smart Grid Agent for Distributed Power Generation Management*. Logos Verlag Berlin GmbH, 2017.

[2] E. Frost, E. M. Veith, and L. Fischer, "Robust and deterministic scheduling of power grid actors," in *7th International Conference on Control, Decision and Information Technologies (CoDIT)*, IEEE, 2020, pp. 100–105.

[3] M. Sonnenschein and C. Hinrichs, "A distributed combinatorial optimisation heuristic for the scheduling of energy resources represented by self-interested agents," *International Journal of Bio-Inspired Computation*, pp. 69–78, 2017, ISSN: 1758-0366. DOI: 10.1504/IJBIC.2017.10004322.

[4] O. P. Mahela *et al.*, "Comprehensive overview of multi-agent systems for controlling smart grids," *CSEE Journal of Power and Energy Systems*, vol. 8, no. 1, pp. 115–131, Jan. 2022, Conference Name: CSEE Journal of Power and Energy Systems, ISSN: 2096-0042. DOI: 10.17775/CSEEJPES.2020.03390.

[5] S. Holly *et al.*, "Flexibility management and provision of balancing services with battery-electricautomated guided vehicles in the Hamburg container terminal Altenwerder," ser. Energy Informatics, SpringerOpen, 2020, pp. 1–20. DOI: https://doi.org/10.1186/s42162-020-00129-1.

[6] J. Styczynski and N. Beach-Westmoreland, "When the lights went out: Ukraine cybersecurity threat briefing," *Booz Allen Hamilton*, vol. 12, pp. 1–86, 2016.

[7] A. Aflaki, M. Gitizadeh, R. Razavi-Far, V. Palade, and A. A. Ghasemi, "A hybrid framework for detecting and eliminating cyber-attacks in power grids," *Energies*, vol. 14, no. 18, p. 5823, Jan. 2021, ISSN: 1996-1073. DOI: 10.3390/en14185823.

[8] T. Wolgast, E. M. Veith, and A. Nieße, "Towards reinforcement learning for vulnerability analysis in power-economic systems," in *DACH+ Energy Informatics 2021: The 10th DACH+ Conference on Energy Informatics*, Freiburg, Germany, Sep. 2021, pp. 1–20.

[9] E. M. Veith, N. Wenninghoff, S. Balduin, T. Wolgast, and S. Lehnhoff, *Learning to attack powergrids with DERs*, 2022. DOI: 10.48550/ARXIV.2204.11352. [Online]. Available: https://arxiv.org/abs/2204.11352.

[10] O. Hanseth and C. Ciborra, *Risk, complexity and ICT*. Cheltenham, UK: Edward Elgar Publishing, 2007.

[11] R. Diao *et al.*, "Autonomous voltage control for grid operation using deep reinforcement learning," in *2019 IEEE Power & Energy Society General Meeting (PESGM)*, Atlanta, GA, USA: IEEE, Aug. 2019, pp. 1–5, ISBN: 978-1-72811-981-6. DOI: 10.1109/PESGM40551.2019.8973924.

[12] L. Fischer, J. M. Memmen, E. M. Veith, and M. Tröschel, "Adversarial resilience learning—towards systemic vulnerability analysis for large and complex systems," in *ENERGY 2019, The Ninth International Conference on Smart Grids, Green Communications and IT Energy-aware Technologies*, Athens, Greece: IARIA XPS Press, 2019, pp. 24–32, ISBN: 978-1-61208-713-9.

[13] E. Veith, L. Fischer, M. Tröschel, and A. Nieße, "Analyzing cyber-physical systems from the perspective of artificial intelligence," in *Proceedings of the 2019 International Conference on Artificial Intelligence, Robotics and Control*, ACM, Dec. 2019, ISBN: 978-1-4503-7671-6.

[14] Y. Zheng *et al.*, "Vulnerability assessment of deep reinforcement learning models for power system topology optimization," *IEEE Transactions on Smart Grid*, vol. 12, no. 4, pp. 3613–3623, 2021. DOI: 10.1109/TSG.2021.3062700.

[15] T. T. Nguyen and V. J. Reddi, "Deep reinforcement learning for cyber security," *IEEE Transactions on Neural Networks and Learning Systems*, pp. 1–17, 2021. DOI: 10.1109/TNNLS.2021.3121870.

[16] C. Roberts *et al.*, "Deep reinforcement learning for der cyber-attack mitigation," in *2020 IEEE International Conference on Communications, Control, and Computing Technologies for Smart Grids (SmartGridComm)*, 2020, pp. 1–7. DOI: 10.1109/SmartGridComm47815.2020.9302997.

[17] J. Schrittwieser *et al.*, "Mastering Atari, Go, Chess and Shogi by planning with a learned model," pp. 1–21, 2019. arXiv: 1911.08265. [Online]. Available: http://arxiv.org/abs/1911.08265.

[18] S. Fujimoto, H. van Hoof, and D. Meger, "Addressing function approximation error in actor-critic methods," *arXiv:1802.09477 [cs, stat]*, Oct. 22, 2018. arXiv: 1802.09477. [Online]. Available: http://arxiv.org/abs/1802.09477 (visited on 08/07/2023).

[19] J. Schulman, F. Wolski, P. Dhariwal, A. Radford, and O. Klimov, "Proximal policy optimization algorithms," Jul. 19, 2017. arXiv: 1707.06347. [Online]. Available: http://arxiv.org/abs/1707.06347.

[20] T. Haarnoja, A. Zhou, P. Abbeel, and S. Levine, "Soft actor-critic: Off-policy maximum entropy deep reinforcement learning with a stochastic actor," *arXiv:1801.01290 [cs, stat]*, Aug. 8, 2018. arXiv: 1801.01290. [Online]. Available: http://arxiv.org/abs/1801.01290 (visited on 08/07/2023).

[21] E. Puiutta and E. M. S. P. Veith, "Explainable reinforcement learning: A survey," in *Machine Learning and Knowledge Extraction. CD-MAKE 2020*, Dublin, Ireland: Springer, Cham, 2020, pp. 77–95. DOI: 10.1007/978-3-030-57321-8_5.

[22] C. Aytekin, *Neural networks are decision trees*, Oct. 25, 2022. DOI: 10.48550/arXiv.2210.05189. arXiv: 2210.05189[cs]. [Online]. Available: http://arxiv.org/abs/2210.05189 (visited on 08/07/2023).

[23] T. Logemann and E. M. Veith, "NN2EQCDT: Quivalent transformation of feed-forward neural networks as DRL policies into compressed decision trees," in *Proceedings of the Fifteenth International Conference on Advanced Cognitive Technologies and Applications (COGNITIVE 2023)*, IARIA, IARIA XPS Press, Jun. 2023, pp. 94–100.

[24] E. M. Veith, "An architecture for reliable learning agents in power grids," in *Proceedings of the Thirteenth International Conference on Smart Grids, Green Communications and IT Energy-aware Technologies (ENERGY 2023)*, IARIA, IARIA XPS Press, Mar. 2023, pp. 13–16, ISBN: 978-1-68558-054-4.

[25] T. Logemann and E. Veith, *Towards explainable attacker-defender autocurricula in critical infrastructures: Source code to the paper*, Retrieved: 2023-09-18, 2023. [Online]. Available: https://gitlab.com/arl-experiments/simple-voltage-attack-explainability.

Next Generation Artificial Intelligence-Based Learning Platform for Personalized Cybersecurity and IT Awareness Training: A Conceptual Study

Michael Masssoth
Department of Computer Science, Hochschule Darmstadt (h_da)
University of Applied Sciences Darmstadt, member of European University of Technology (EUt+)
Darmstadt, Germany
e-mail: michael.massoth@h-da.de

Abstract- **The problem in cybersecurity and Information Technology (IT) awareness training is the inadequacy of traditional learning approaches in the field of computer science and cybersecurity education. These methods often struggle to provide personalized and adaptive learning experiences. Therefore, this conceptual study aims to explore the development of a next-generation learning platform for personalized cybersecurity and IT awareness training, focusing on the key aspects of content personalization and adaptive learning environments. The study explores the potential of using advanced technologies to enhance the learning experience and create adaptive environments that meet the individual needs of learners. In detail, we describe what constitutes a next-generation learning platform, the requirements and success factors, a possible architecture and system design, as well as the aspect of gamification and identification of player types for personalizing the learning environments.**

Keywords— Artificial Intelligence; next-generation learning platform; cybersecurit and IT awareness training.

I. INTRODUCTION

In today's rapidly evolving digital landscape, the demand for highly skilled computer scientists and cybersecurity professionals continues to grow. To meet this demand, it is critical to develop advanced learning platforms that effectively equip learners with the knowledge and skills they need. Traditional learning approaches often fall short when it comes to providing the personalized and adaptive learning experiences that are essential to meeting the diverse needs and learning preferences of individual learners. By harnessing the power of technology, there is an opportunity to create learning environments that can dynamically adapt to learners' needs, increase engagement, and maximize learning outcomes. This conceptual study seeks to explore the potential of such next-generation learning platforms and contribute to the advancement of cybersecurity education practices.

The field of computer science and cybersecurity is characterized by its fast-paced nature, requiring professionals to continuously update their knowledge and skills to stay ahead of emerging threats and technologies. Traditional education methods often struggle to keep up with the rapid changes in the field, making it imperative to explore innovative approaches to education and training. This study focuses on the development of next-generation learning platforms that leverage advances in technology, particularly in the areas of content personalization and adaptive learning environments. By tailoring the learning experience to the needs and preferences of individual learners, these platforms have the potential to significantly improve the effectiveness and efficiency of cybersecurity education and training. Through an in-depth review of existing literature, emerging trends, and best practices, this study aims to propose a conceptual framework for the design and implementation of such platforms, paving the way for future research and development in this critical area.

This paper is organized as follows. Section II reviews the specifications of a next-generation artificial intelligence-based learning platform. Section III describes the success factors and requirements for Artificial Intelligence (AI)-based learning. Section IV describes adaptive learning environments and personalization of learning content. Section V discusses a possible architecture and system design of a next-generation AI-based learning platform. Section VI deals with the addition of gamification elements according to predetermined player types. Section VII discusses cybersecurity and IT awareness training and a first version of a customizable learning environment prototype. Section VIII provides a summary and conclusion. Finally, Section IX provides an outlook on the next development steps.

II. SPECIFICATION OF A NEXT GENERATION ARTIFICIAL INTELLIGENCE-BASED LEARNING PLATFORM

Next-generation AI-based learning platforms are educational systems that use artificial intelligence technologies to enhance the learning experience for students. These platforms have several characteristics that set them apart from traditional learning environments. Here are some key features of next-generation AI-based learning platforms:

1. **Personalization of learning content:** AI enables these platforms to tailor learning content to each individual student's needs, abilities, and learning style. By analyzing data, about the student's past performance, preferences, and behavior, the platform can provide personalized recommendations, adaptive exercises, and targeted feedback. This personalized approach helps students learn at their own pace and focus on areas where they need improvement.

2. **Adaptive learning environments:** AI-based learning platforms create adaptive learning environments that dynamically adjust to the student's progress and provide appropriate challenges and support. The platform continuously analyzes the student's performance and adjusts the content, level of difficulty, and instructional strategies accordingly. This adaptivity ensures that each student receives an optimal learning experience, maximizing engagement and comprehension.

3. **Intelligent tutoring systems:** Next-generation learning platforms often include AI-powered intelligent tutoring systems. These systems can provide personalized guidance, answer student questions, and offer explanations tailored to individual needs. They can simulate one-on-one tutoring by understanding the student's strengths and weaknesses, diagnosing misconceptions, and providing targeted interventions to improve understanding.

4. **Data-driven insights:** AI-based learning platforms collect and analyze vast amounts of data about student performance, interactions, and learning patterns. This data can be used to gain insights into student progress, identify areas for improvement, and inform instructional decisions. Educators can use these insights to provide targeted support and interventions, track student progress over time, and make data-driven decisions to improve the learning experience.

III. SUCCESS FACTORS AND REQUIREMENTS OF AN AI-BASED LEARNING PLATFORM

We have scientifically identified the key success factors and requirements for an AI-enabled next-generation learning platform for cybersecurity and IT awareness training. These are:

Success Factor (SF) and requirement (Req) #1: High quality and trust in the information and data provided. Content quality at the highest expert level.

SF/Req #2: High user trust in data protection and in the handling of your personal data and information, as well as in the handling of your training and learning services. No blaming/shaming of users, but positive psychology and positive, inner motivational factors.

SF/Req #3: Highest effectiveness/efficiency/quality of didactics and teaching quality (learning gains, learning successes) for users and clients by using an AI-based next-generation learning platform for personalized learning and adaptive learning environments.

SF/Req #4: Relevance, Timeliness, and Timeliness. The content provided on the NG learning platform must be highly relevant to the needs of the user group and must be kept up-to-date on the latest threats, hazards, developments, and trends in cybersecurity and IT awareness on a daily basis.

SF/Req #5: Engaging and Interactive (UX-1). The platform should be engaging and interactive, using a variety of different learning formats and methods to best keep users interested and motivated.

SF/Req #6: Customization and Personalization (UX-2). The platform should be able to customize and personalize the learning experience based on the individual needs and preferences of each user.

SF/Req #7: Usability (UX-3). The platform should be easily accessible and user-friendly, with a user-friendly interface and a range of different learning formats and methods to accommodate different learning styles and player types.

SF/Req #8: Support and Resources: the platform should provide a range of support and resources to enable users to learn effectively, including guidance, gamification elements, feedback, and assessments.

SF/Req #9: Integration with other Systems: The platform should be able to integrate with other systems and tools, such as learning management systems, to provide a seamless learning experience.

IV. ADAPTIVE LEARNING ENVIRONMENTS AND PERSONALIZATION

In the context of adaptive learning environments and personalization of learning content, Artificial Intelligence (AI) can use various methods and techniques to customize the learning process for each individual learner. Below are some possible AI methods:

Adaptive Learning Paths: AI can be used to determine the optimal learning path for each learner based on their individual needs, prior knowledge, and learning styles. By analyzing data, such as learning history, test scores, and feedback, AI can provide personalized recommendations for the order and difficulty of learning content. This ensures that each learner learns at their own level and pace.

Adaptive content delivery: AI can help select and deliver the most relevant learning content for each learner. Based on the learner's interests, proficiency level, and preferred learning style, AI can apply algorithms to select appropriate content from a wide range of learning materials. This can increase learner motivation and engagement by providing them with content that is most relevant and interesting to them.

Automated assessment and feedback: AI techniques, such as machine learning and Natural Language Processing (NLP) can be used to automatically assess learning tasks, tests, or hands-on exercises. AI can analyze learners' responses and generate real-time feedback to identify errors, suggest improvements, and detect comprehension issues. This allows learners to receive immediate feedback and improve their performance.

Sentiment analysis and emotion detection: By analyzing user behavior, interactions, and communications on the platform, AI can use techniques, such as sentiment analysis and emotion recognition to understand the emotional state of learners. This information can be used to provide personalized support, such as targeted resources or activities to reduce frustration or maintain interest.

Chatbots and virtual assistants: AI-powered chatbots or virtual assistants can help learners with questions, problems, or for additional explanation. These systems can use natural language processing to provide human-like interactions and be available to learners 24/7 as needed.

It is important to note that these AI methods are not used in isolation but can be connected and integrated to create a comprehensive adaptive learning environment that meets learners' individual needs.

V. ARCHITECTURE AND SYTSEM DESIGN OF A NEXT GENERATION AI-BASED LEARNING PLATFORM

The architecture of a next-generation AI-based learning platform can vary depending on specific requirements and design choices. However, here is a high-level overview of the components typically found in such platforms:

Frontend: The frontend is responsible for the user interface and user experience. It provides the interface through which learners, instructors, and administrators interact with the platform. Common technologies used for frontend development include Hypertext Markup Language (HTML), Cascading Style Sheets (CSS), JavaScript, and frameworks, such as React, Angular, or Vue.js. These frameworks provide flexibility, responsiveness, and rich interactive features.

Backend: The backend handles the server-side logic, data management, and integration with external services. It typically consists of several components, including:

- Web Server: A web server, such as Apache or Nginx, handles Hypertext Transfer Protocol (HTTP) requests and serves web pages and resources.
- Application Server: The application server manages the core functionality of the learning platform, including user management, content delivery, and data processing. Popular choices for backend frameworks and languages include Django (Python), Ruby on Rails (Ruby), or Node.js (JavaScript).
- Database: A database system is used to store and manage user data, learning content, assessment results, and other relevant information. Common options include MySQL, PostgreSQL, or MongoDB.
- APIs and Integrations: APIs facilitate communication and integration with external services, such as authentication providers, Learning Management Systems (LMS), content repositories, or analytics platforms.

Artificial Intelligence (AI) Components: The AI capabilities in the learning platform can be implemented using various algorithms and techniques. Some commonly used AI algorithms and technologies in this context include:

- Machine Learning: Supervised and unsupervised machine learning algorithms can be used for tasks, such as learner profiling, content recommendation, and performance prediction.
- Natural Language Processing: NLP techniques enable language understanding, sentiment analysis, chatbots, and automated feedback systems.
- Deep Learning: Deep learning algorithms, particularly neural networks, can be applied to tasks, such as speech recognition, image recognition, or natural language understanding.
- Recommender Systems: Collaborative filtering and content-based recommendation algorithms can be utilized to suggest relevant learning resources based on learners' preferences, behavior, and past interactions.
- Data Analytics: Data analysis techniques, including statistical analysis, clustering, and visualization, can be employed to gain insights from the large amounts of data generated by learners' interactions and performance.

Regarding **open-source tools**, here are some popular options:

- Frontend: HTML, CSS, JavaScript, React, Angular, Vue.js
- Backend: Django (Python), Ruby on Rails (Ruby), Node.js (JavaScript)
- Database: MySQL, PostgreSQL, MongoDB
- AI Libraries/Frameworks: TensorFlow, PyTorch, scikit-learn, NLTK (Natural Language Toolkit), spaCy, Apache Mahout.

These are just a few examples, and the choice of tools and technologies may depend on factors, such as the specific requirements of the learning platform, the development team's expertise, and scalability considerations. Remember that this is just a high-level overview, and the actual architecture and tool choices may vary depending on the specific needs and goals of the learning platform being developed.

The system design of a Learning Management System (LMS) for **university courses in computer science** must consider the specific needs of students, instructors, and administrators. Here is a suggested architecture and system design for such an LMS:

User roles and access levels:

- Students: Access course materials, submit assignments, participate in discussions, view grades.
- Instructors: Create and manage courses, upload content, grade assignments, interact with students.
- Administrators: Manage system settings, user accounts, course enrollment, and general system administration.

Frontend:

- User Interface (UI): Develop an intuitive and user-friendly UI for easy navigation and seamless interaction with the LMS. Ensure responsive design for cross-device accessibility.
- Course Dashboard: Provide a centralized dashboard where students and instructors can access their respective courses, announcements, and notifications.
- Course Content: Display course materials, lecture slides, videos, code samples, and additional resources in an organized manner.
- Discussion forums: Enable students and instructors to engage in online discussions, ask questions, and share insights.
- Assignment submission: Provide an interface for students to submit assignments, view due dates, and receive feedback.
- Grading and Feedback: Allow instructors to grade assignments, provide comments, and share feedback with students.
- Progress Tracking: Include features to track student progress, completion of course modules, and overall performance.

Backend:

- User Management: Implement user authentication, registration, and profile management functionality.
- Course Management: Develop features for instructors to create, manage, and organize course content, modules, and assessments.
- Data storage: Set up a database system to store user profiles, course data, assignments, grades, and other relevant information.
- Content delivery: Efficiently deliver multimedia course content, such as videos and code samples, while ensuring scalability and performance.
- Collaboration tools: Implement features for collaborative project work, such as group creation, shared documents, and version control.
- Notifications: Enable automated notifications of important updates, deadlines, and announcements.
- Analytics and reporting: Incorporate data analytics to generate reports on student performance, course engagement, and learning outcomes.

Integration:

- External Tools and Services: Integrate with external tools, such as plagiarism detection systems, virtual lab environments, and online coding platforms.
- Learning Standards: Support integration with learning standards, such as Sharable Content Object Reference Model (SCOM) to import and export course content.

Security and privacy:

- Implement strong user authentication and data encryption mechanisms.
- Ensure role-based access control and privacy compliance.
- Regularly update and patch software to address security vulnerabilities.

Scalability and Performance:

- Design the system with scalability in mind to accommodate growing numbers of users and courses.
- Use caching mechanisms, load balancing, and efficient database design to ensure optimal performance.

It is important to note that the proposed architecture and system design are high-level guidelines. Actual implementation may require further analysis, considering factors, such as specific institutional requirements, technical constraints, and integration with existing systems.
Collaboration with stakeholders, faculty, and students throughout the design and development process can provide valuable insights to effectively tailor the LMS to their needs.

VI. GAMIFICATION AND 6 PLAYER TYPES

With the advent of gamification - the use of game elements in non-game contexts - the HEXAD model was developed by Marczewski [4]. The HEXAD model distinguishes six different types of gamers [4]:

Intrinsically Motivated Types: 4

Relatedness (Socialisers): Socialisers are motivated by relationships. They want to interact with others and create social connections.

Autonomy (Free Spirits): Free Spirits are motivated by autonomy and self-expression. They want to create and explore.

Mastery (Achievers): Achievers are motivated by excellence. They are out to learn new things and improve themselves. They seek challenges that they can overcome.

Purpose (Philanthropists): Philanthropists are motivated by purpose and meaning. This group is altruistic and wants to give to others and enrich the lives of others in some way without expecting a reward.

Extrinsically Motivated Types: 1

Players: Players are motivated by rewards. They do what is what they are asked to do, in order to collect rewards from a system. system. They are only in it for themselves.

Change-Oriented Types: 1

Disruptors: Disruptors are motivated by change. In general, they want to disrupt systems, either directly or with the other users to force positive or negative change. or negative changes.

The determination of HEXAD Gamification User Types is based on the use of a specially developed questionnaire, the HEXAD Gamification User Types Questionnaire [4]. This questionnaire was developed by Marczewski and his colleagues and is an important part of the HEXAD framework.

The HEXAD User Types Survey consists of a series of questions that address the specific characteristics and motivations of the six HEXAD player types. The questions are designed to be answered on a five-point Likert scale ranging from "strongly agree" to "strongly disagree."

The responses to these questions are then analyzed quantitatively to determine which HEXAD gamification user type a user is likely to be.

The work "The Gamification User Types HEXAD Scale" by Tondello et al. is an important addition to HEXAD theory and has contributed to the development and validation of the HEXAD User Types Survey [5]. The study strengthens the theoretical basis of the HEXAD model and provides empirical evidence of its validity. To validate the HEXAD User Types Scale, Tondello and his team conducted several studies [5]. The scale serves as a measurement tool to identify and quantify the six user types. The authors were able to show that their research results confirmed the existence of the six player types and demonstrated the effectiveness of the questionnaire in measuring them. The size of the questionnaire could be reduced from 30 to 24 questions, with comparable accuracy of the results.

In addition, the work provides valuable insight into the relationships between the different player types. For example, the results show that Philanthropists and Achievers often exhibit positive correlations, suggesting that users who are identified as one of these gamer types are also likely to exhibit characteristics of the other.

This is consistent with Marczewski's observations that people cannot be reduced to simple individual player types and exhibit these characteristics to varying degrees [4].

In April 2023, HEXAD-12, a shortened version of the original HEXAD-Scale questionnaire, was released [7].

HEXAD-12 addresses the challenges posed by the extensive 24-question questionnaire of the original scale, such as high dropout rates and participant fatigue. By reducing it to 12 questions, HEXAD-12 provides a more efficient and compact tool for assessing user types in gamification, particularly suited for limited interaction modalities, such as on mobile devices. Despite its brevity, HEXAD-12 retains a reliability and validity comparable to or better than the original HEXAD scale.

Importantly, a user's player type is not static. Marczewski emphasizes that users change between different player types depending on context, environment, and over time [4]. Therefore, determining user type should be viewed as a continuous process that requires regular iterations of the HEXAD User Types Survey requires.

An important finding is the practical applicability of the HEXAD Player types for the design of gamification applications. Through the player types of a user, designers can better understand what motivates their better understand what motivates their users, and create appropriate, individually tailored experiences. By knowing the dominant player type player type of a user, gamified features can be better tailored to individual needs and preferences better, leading to increased user engagement [6].

VII. CYBERSECURITY AND IT AWARENESS TRAINING

Cybersecurity and IT awareness [Definition]: IT and cybersecurity awareness mean problem awareness and secure behavior. In everyday dealings with IT systems, awareness is an elementary security measure. First, this means creating an awareness of the problem of cyber security attacks and threats. Building on this, it is possible to achieve a change in behavior toward secure digital use. Security awareness measures are successful if they empower the target groups and motivate individuals to improve their cyber security. It is important to develop awareness at eye level and in a practical manner [1].

As a first step towards a next-generation learning platform, we have implemented an IT Awareness Learning Platform with an AI chatbot as a demonstrator and prototype:

An AI-based learning chatbot is an intelligent, speech- or text-based dialog system that allows chatting with an artificial intelligence. Such an AI-based learning chatbot is to be used and tested for the first time as part of an IT awareness training for the basic sensitization of employees.

The AI chatbot delivers the most relevant IT awareness content to the learner in a simple and sometimes even playful dialog. The AI chatbot breaks down the knowledge into small "bites" and delivers them to the user one at a time.

The IT awareness learning platform with AI chatbots delivers expert knowledge on IT awareness and cybersecurity to specific target groups: Low-threshold, "in small bites", "for in between".

The user controls the AI learning chatbot through his questions, choices and selections.

The following topics are already included in the current IT Awareness Learning Platform with AI Chatbots and optimized for recognition rates above 75%:

TABLE I. SUBJECT MATERIALS

Malware	Phishing	Secure handling on the web	Good and secure passwords
Social engineering	Data protection on the web	Blackmail Trojan	Computer viruses
Spying on data	Botnets and DDoS attacks	Cyber and computer crime	Voice assistants
Hacking - my online bank data on the web	Industrial and commercial espionage	Cyberbullying and cyberstalking	Fake stores, fraud, subscription traps
Skimming	ICT criminal law	Sexting on the web	Catfishing

AI-based IT awareness training begins with a user self-assessment, placement and player type test based on the knowledge level of the individual participant. This takes into account the user's strengths and weaknesses, as well as their individual player type, and ensures that the training is tailored to the individual.

According to the player's type, the user is then offered suitable gamification elements so that the user receives a personalized offer. Thus, a first version of a customizable learning environment was prototypically realized for a cybersecurity and IT awareness training.

VIII. CONCLUSION

Individualized learning paths: In IT awareness and cybersecurity training, learners come from diverse backgrounds and have varying levels of technical knowledge. Our next-generation learning platform can personalize learning content based on each learner's existing skills and knowledge. This ensures that beginners receive basic concepts while advanced learners are exposed to more sophisticated cybersecurity topics, resulting in optimized learning outcomes.

Adaptive learning environment: Cybersecurity threats are constantly evolving, making adaptability a critical skill. Our learning platform uses adaptive learning environments that dynamically adjust the difficulty and complexity of content as learners progress. This approach ensures that cybersecurity professionals stay up-to-date on the latest threats and defense strategies, reducing the risk of cyber incidents.

Data-driven learning insights: The next generation learning platform generates rich data analytics and insights into learner progress and performance. In IT awareness and cybersecurity training, these analytics provide valuable information about learners' strengths and weaknesses, enabling trainers to effectively personalize their support and interventions, resulting in better skills development.

Gamified Learning Experience: Cybersecurity training can be complex and technical, which can disengage some learners. By incorporating gamification elements, such as points, badges, and leaderboards, our platform makes the learning process engaging and fun. Gamification encourages learners to stay motivated, track their progress, and strive for continuous improvement.

Flexibility and distance learning: In the fast-paced world of IT and cybersecurity, professionals may have limited time for training. Our platform offers flexible learning options that allow learners to access training materials anytime, anywhere, and at their own pace. This flexibility accommodates busy schedules and remote work arrangements, making it convenient for cybersecurity professionals to continually improve their skills.

In summary, a next-generation learning platform is uniquely suited for IT awareness and cybersecurity training due to its personalized content delivery, adaptive learning environment, and data-driven insights.

IX. OUTLOOK

In the future, other valuable additions to the Next Generation Learning Platform should include the following features:

The learning platform should include realistic threat simulations that allow students to engage in simulated cyberattacks in a safe environment. This hands-on experience strengthens their ability to effectively identify and respond to security threats, preparing them for real-world situations.

Certification and Recognition: In the IT and cybersecurity industry, certifications carry significant value and can enhance career opportunities. Our learning platform prepares learners for industry-standard certifications, giving them the knowledge and skills, they need to gain professional recognition and excel in their cybersecurity careers.

ACKNOWLEDGMENT

This work was supported by the Hessian Ministry of the Interior and Sports HMdIS, Government of the Federal State of Hessen; Research funding program: Cybersecurity. R&D project: "Awareness Training with AI chatbots".

REFERENCES

[1] Federal Office for Information Security (BSI), Germany, https://www.bsi.bund.de/EN/Home/home_node.html; [retrieved: 09, 2023].

[2] IBM Chatbots, https://www.ibm.com/cloud/learn/chatbots-explained; [retrieved: 09, 2023]

[3] A. D. S. Fernandes, " Implementation, evaluation and optimization of the user experience and IT security of an IT awareness learning platform with AI chatbots. ", Bachelor thesis 2021 at Darmstadt University of Applied Sciences at the Department of Computer Science.

[4] A. Marczewski, "User types." Even ninja monkeys like to play: Gamification, game thinking and motivational design, Volume 1, Edition 1: pp. 65-80, 2015.

[5] L. Diamond, G. Tondello, A. Marczewski, L. Nacke and M. Tscheligi, "The HEXAD Gamification User Types Questionnaire: Background and Development Process". October 2015. At: https://publications.ait.ac.at/en/publications/the-HEXAD-gamification-user-types-questionnaire-background-and-de; [retrieved: 09, 2023]

[6] G. Tondello, R. Wehbe, L. Diamond, M. Busch, A. Marczewski and L. Nacke, "The Gamification User Types HEXAD Scale". October 2016. doi: 10.1145/2967934.2968082.

[7] J. Krath, M. Altmeyer, G. Tondello and L. Nacke, "HEXAD-12: Developing and Validating a Short Version of the Gamification User Types HEXAD Scale". In: April 2023. doi: 10.1145/3544548.3580968

[8] D. Bahcecioglu, "Development and optimization of an IT awareness learning platform with AI chatbots with regard to quality assurance through UX testing.", Bachelor thesis 2022 at Darmstadt University of Applied Sciences at the Department of Computer Science.

[9] Y. C. Fung and L. K. Lee, "A Chatbot for Promoting Cybersecurity Awareness", Cyber Security, Privacy and Networking, 2022 – Springer.

[10] I. Hidayatulloh, S. Pambudi, H. D. Surjono and T. Sukardiyono, "Gamification on Chatbot-Based Learning Media: a Review and Challenges", ELINVO (Electronics, Informatics, and Vocational Education), May 2021; vol 6 (1):71-80, ISSN 2580-6424 (printed), ISSN 2477-2399 (online,) DOI: 10.21831/ elinvo.v6i1.4370

[11] F. Colace, M. D. Santo, M. Lombardi, F. Pascale and A. Pietrosanto, "Chatbot for E-Learning: A Case of Study", International Journal of Mechanical Engineering and Robotics Research Vol. 7, No. 5, September 2018.

Fusion or Fantasy

Is Cyber Fusion Living Up to the Dream?

Anne Coull
Flinders University
Sydney, Australia
email: anne.coull@proton.me

Abstract— The Cyber Fusion Centre has evolved from a military and antiterrorist intelligence gathering centre to become an intelligence focus for collating information and facilitating cyber incident management in organisations. Some benefit is being realised in Australia's larger banks as they manage the challenge of coordinating cyber response across disparate and siloed teams. These simple Cyber Fusion Centres provide basic, manual, reactive coordination of cyber incidents by generating open communication between response teams. This basic fusion model being implemented in Australian banks, and documented in the FS-ISAC whitepaper, is miles from the visionary Cyber Fusion Centre models described in the literature. These theoretical centres of response excellence incorporating strategic threat intelligence, orchestration, crisis simulations and ultimate real-time response-capability are well beyond the current reality. The answers for closing the gap between theory and practice can be found by looking into the original military fusion centres.

Keywords- Cyber Fusion Centre; Intelligence; Counterinsurgence Operations; Counterterrorism; Crisis Management.

I. INTRODUCTION

As the coordination centre for cyber intelligence and response within an organisation, the Cyber Fusion Centre would appear to be the logical place from whence to drive accelerated response to cyber security incidents. The literature describes the Cyber Fusion Centre as a collaboration between threat intelligence, incident response, threat hunting, and vulnerability management, with the purpose of accelerating identification and response to security threats. A fusion centre of this nature will enable an organisation to accelerate response by removing delays through orchestrating cyber response activities that span multiple departments and teams. By sharing strategic intelligence, it will allow the organization to be more proactive in their cyber response, pre-emptively preparing for and mitigating the emerging threats, rather than just responding to threats after the alerts have been generated, and the incidents have occurred.

The Cyber Fusion Centre emerging in Australian banks, and documented in a whitepaper by the Financial Services Information Sharing and Analysis Center (FS-ISAC), is a simple model of collaboration between security, service management, and customer service. The fusion centre team's role is to coordinate response activities involving these and other operations and technical support teams. This model is based on Cyber Fusion Centre capabilities operating in banks and organisations in the United States, Canada, Singapore, and Australia. Utilising fusion in this way reduces potential threat impact by decreasing time to identify complex and critical incidents and time to respond, but it does not deliver the scale of uplift nor the benefits anticipated in the literature.

Section 2 outlines the evolution of fusion centres from military coordination centres to intelligent Cyber Fusion Centres. Section 3 assesses the cyber fusion theory versus the reality. Section 4 looks at how Cyber Fusion Centres have been implemented in Australia and delves into a specific instance in a large Australian bank to highlight opportunities for improvement, and Section 5 provides insight into how the gap between the theory and reality can be closed.

II. CYBER FUSION EVOLUTION

Fusion centres have functioned as operations' response coordination centres since mankind participated in multi-domain warfare. Over time, the fusion centre model has evolved into a centre for intelligence, co-ordination, and information sharing, in response to terrorist incidents and the growth of cyber-crime.

A. *Military Fusion Centres*

For decades, fusion centres have operated in the military as Joint Operations Centres, to co-ordinate operations across the multiple domains of war: land, sea, air, and space, and more recently cyberspace [1][7][11][13][14] (see Figure 1).

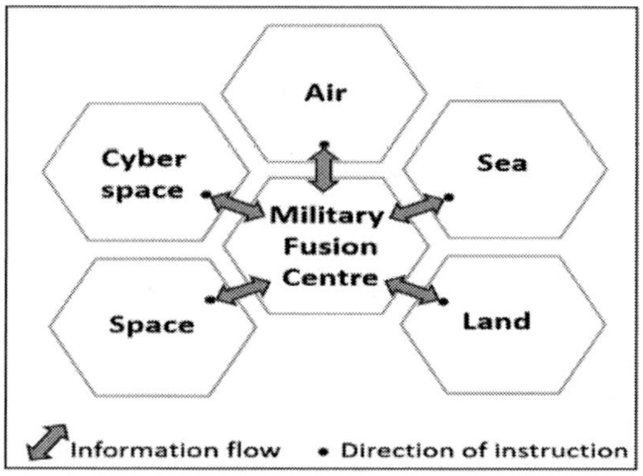

Figure 1. Military Fusion Centre.

Military fusion has enabled more efficient and effective offensive and defensive operations by providing broad situational awareness and facilitating coordination of activities across different regions, regiments, and domains.

B. *Counterinsurgency Operations' Intelligence Fusion and Flow*

Counterinsurgency operations (COINOPS) take this need for intelligence fusion and flow to a high level. To stay abreast of enemy movements, COINOPS need tangible real-time intelligence. This sensitivity is driven by COINOPS role working closely with both military and civilian populations. Insurgencies involve mixtures of conflict and tactics across multiple domains, topographies, and offensives. Information flow is critical during counterinsurgency operations' when this information needs to be disseminated from/to headquarters (HQ) and the front-line troops and commanders in real-time. Rather than having all the intelligence capabilities centralised in military HQ, the key is to have technology and personnel, with the necessary capabilities, implanted through all layers of the intelligence information flow, from front line platoons and commanders to HQ. These may be specialised language translators and intelligence analysts, or military personnel holding these skills [11] (See Figure 2).

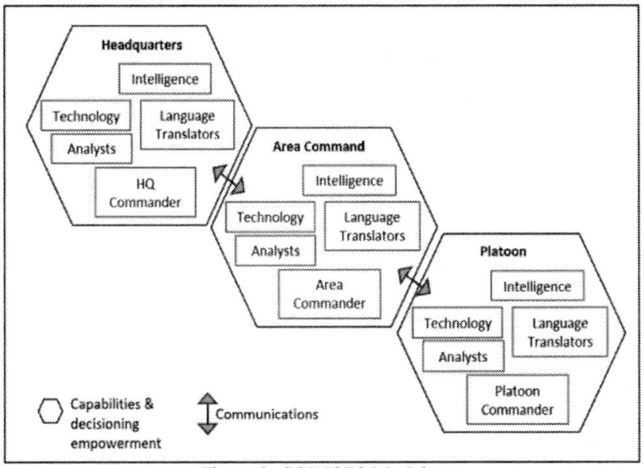

Figure 2. COINOPS Model.

C. *Counterterrorism Intelligence Fusion Centres*

Following the New York twin tower attacks on September 11, 2001, in the U.S., fusion centres evolved from wartime and operational co-ordination centres into centres for collating and correlating terrorist intelligence. In the U.S., the Department of Homeland Security (DHS) was created at the national level, to bring together intelligence and law enforcement. Correspondingly, law enforcement, public security, and emergency response were also centralised at the state level. Fusion centres were created to connect the local and state intelligence centres with federal intelligence organisations and services. This amalgamated model facilitates the flow of counterterrorism (CT) intelligence from/to local to/from federal [15] (See Figure 3). The purpose of creating a combined model of intelligence, law enforcement and emergency response was to drive more efficient and effective offensive and defensive intelligence-enabled security, public safety, and emergency response, through communications, collaboration, and coordination across these different capabilities at the state and national levels [15].

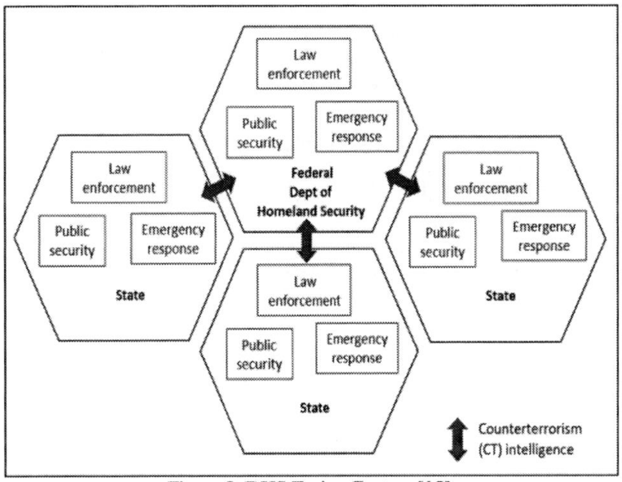

Figure 3. DHS Fusion Centres [15].

D. *Intelligent Cyber Fusion Centres*

As security leaders moved from roles in military defence into business, they saw the need, in their new organisations, for Intelligent Cyber Fusion Centres to drive more efficient and effective intelligence-enabled cyber response and incident management, through integrated intelligence and operations. As a result, Cyber Fusion Centres have been established in a number of larger organisations across the United States of America, and in some of the larger Australian Banks.

A Cyber Fusion Centre (CFC) is described in the literature as a physical or virtual entity created through collaboration between threat intelligence, incident response, threat hunting and vulnerability management, with the purpose of identifying, managing, and rapidly responding to security threats. This may be a separate team, a virtual team with representation from the local response teams, or a blend, with a small group of individuals facilitating and coordinating aggregation, collation, and distribution of information across the participating teams, and analysing this integrated information to identify themes and correlations [1][3][4][15][16]. The theoretical Cyber Fusion Centre accelerates threat response by bringing together:

1. Technical Threat Intelligence such as attack vectors, suspicious domains, malware hashes, and exploited vulnerabilities to assess the cyber threats facing the organization;

2. Strategic Threat Intelligence to map attack trends, motivations, and characteristics;
3. Analysis of this intelligence to generate insights about threats and adversary behaviours, Tactics, Techniques and Procedures (TTPs), and Indicators Of Compromise (IOC) [1]-[3].
4. Cyber incident management [6].

As it matures, the fusion centre will extend to deliver:

1. Security Orchestration, Automation and Response (SOAR), with automated operational workflows to facilitate incident triage, threat pattern analysis, and automated threat response capabilities;
2. Response plan testing and crisis simulations to prepare for major incidents; and
3. Short and long-term recovery planning [2][3][15] (See Figure 4).

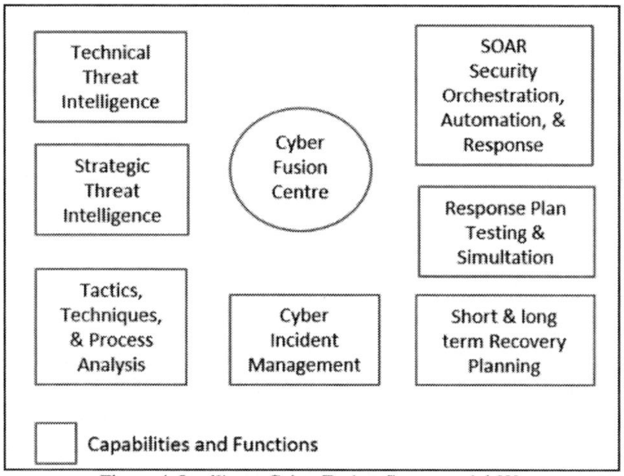

Figure 4. Intelligent Cyber Fusion Centre model [3].

III. Cyber Fusion Theory Versus Practice

The accelerated response enabled by Intelligent Cyber Fusion Centres should enable organisations to move towards proactive control and near real-time containment of cyber threats [1]-[6][10]. But Cyber Fusion Centres implemented in Australian businesses differ considerably from their theoretical counterparts.

A. *Objectives & Benefits*

Financial Services Information Sharing and Analysis Centre (FS-ISAC) is a collaborative not-for-profit venture whose mission is to "advance cybersecurity and resilience in the global financial system, protecting financial institutions and the people they serve" [8]. The 2023 whitepaper released by FS-ISAC and authored by a subcommittee of its members, provides recommendations for establishing and implementing a Cyber Fusion Centre in a bank. According to the FS-ISAC whitepaper, the CFC's primary benefit is derived from sharing information during an incident, by "synchronising response activities across different regions, business units, and other Fusion Centers." In addition, the whitepaper highlights that the CFC establishes a common language, streamlining communications between responders and leadership prior to and during security events, and improving c-suite risk reporting. The expected benefits revolve around the resultant uplift in response capability based on:

- "Standardised, repeatable, incident response and management processes;
- Enhanced transparency into tactical reactions to events;
- Dedicated, trained, and experienced incident commanders;
- Improved adherence to regulatory disclosure requirements;

  Demonstrated overall security posture to regulators/clients/and executives" [9].

B. *Fusion Centre Participants*

The FS-ISAC whitepaper on Cyber Fusion Centres (2023) describes a centralised, co-located or distributed, virtual model focused on response and incident management, where multiple areas in the business are impacted [9] (See Figure 5).

FS-ISAC recommends the core participants in the fusion centre include representatives from:

- Security Operations Centre (incl. Cyber & Technology)
- Incident & Crisis Management
- Fraud Management
- Physical Security
- Intelligence
- Third Party Management
- Communications
- Compliance, and
- Legal

A secondary group of participants are recommended to participate when an incident is relevant to their areas of responsibility. These secondary members include:

- Accounting
- Anti-Money Laundering (AML)
- Business Continuity
- Digital Protection & Forensics

- Data Privacy / Breach Incident Response
- Human Relations
- Group Insurance
- Internal Investigations (Insider Threat)
- Risk
- Public Relations
- Security Architecture
- Security Awareness
- Service Management (Eg Payments, Customer Service, Internet Banking), and
- Vulnerability Management [9].

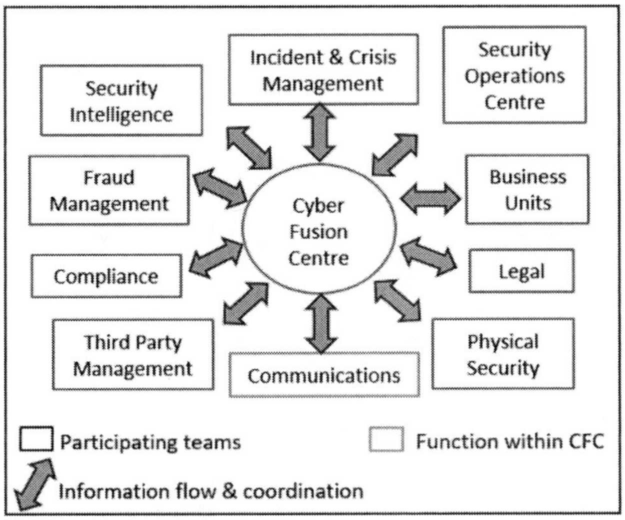

Figure 5. FS-ISAC Cyber Fusion Centre Model, based on [9].

C. *Implementation Model*

The FS-ISAC paper outlines the method for implementing a Cyber Fusion Centre starting with a daily check-in, where participants share observations and insights from the previous 24 hours. The purpose of the daily check-in is to facilitate collaboration between participating teams and capture the updates they provide. Participants raise items of interest, question one another, and look for common elements and themes. The coordinating CFC team documents and tracks items raised and actions involving multiple participating teams. As the CFC matures, trends and patterns may be identified and tracked [9].

IV. Implementation of Cyber Fusion Centres in Australia

The few fusion centres in Australia are concentrated in the larger banks. These organisations are highly complex, heavily regulated, and potentially lucrative targets for threat actors [4].

A. *Size and complexity matters*

Industry research indicates that only the big-4 banks in Australia are implementing or considering implementing Cyber Fusion Centres. In these large-scale organisations, the complexities of communicating between multiple teams who participate in cyber, fraud, and service management incident detection and response, with their different perspectives and priorities, can hamper fluid information flow. The large security departments that have evolved in these banks naturally segregate into silos, with each team focusing on their local accountabilities [2].

Two of the big-4 Australian Banks have attempted to implement cyber fusion centres. In these organisations, the CFC has played a role in bridging the gaps across disparate teams, facilitating open communications, and creating an integrated perspective for response activities. The first of the big 4 banks to implement Cyber Fusion, established a virtual capability where people from different teams across security came together to facilitate incident response. This virtual model was disbanded when the Chief Information Security Officer (CISO) who championed its creation, exited the organisation.

In another of the largest Australian banks, the CFC was established with an initial focus on facilitating information flow. The central fusion team coordinates daily communications forums each morning, with representatives from the different teams across cyber and physical security, fraud, IT service management priority incident response, crisis management, supplier management, and customer service (See Figure 6). These specialised teams have been functioning independently prior to the creation of the CFC. Coming together daily to share updates and insights on what they have seen in the previous 24 hours has facilitated greater cooperation between the teams. The CFC has been active in encouraging this cooperation, involving themselves when an incident spans multiple domains.

Beyond initial benefits elicited from the sharing of insights and improved cooperation, the value being derived from the CFC has been limited. While the non-cyber teams share their experiences openly, the core-cyber teams continue to show resistance to imparting any real information. The updates provided by these participants do not include detailed technical threat intelligence regarding the threats facing the bank, nor corresponding alerts, nor strategic threat intel showing trends, motivations and characteristics, and adversary behaviours. This is impacting the depth of situational awareness across the participants, which continues to be limited and localised. Further work is needed to develop trust and a sense of shared purpose for the cyber teams.

The expected benefits from the CFC, such as accelerating threat response, are not yet being seen. The CFC has not played a role in developing SOAR capabilities, nor have they made plans to facilitate practice sessions in preparation for major or significant incidents, nor are they involved in short- and long-term recovery planning. While the CFC team supports incident management spanning multiple domains, the majority of cyber incident management continues to be accomplished locally within the specialist teams.

Observational analysis indicates that, to a large degree, the development and success of the CFC is being hindered by the inexperience of the CFC leader and their lack of knowledge and understanding of cybersecurity, fraud, and/or financial crime. In addition, progress is stymied by the absence of a rousing vision, coupled with an inability to lead diverse teams and drive organisational change through inspirational leadership.

Without a clear vision and roadmap to propel them forward, in this instance, the CFC is falling prey to operating at the task level. Continued aversion to implementing performance measures, to focus their actions on outcomes, may make it challenging for them to justify their value over time.

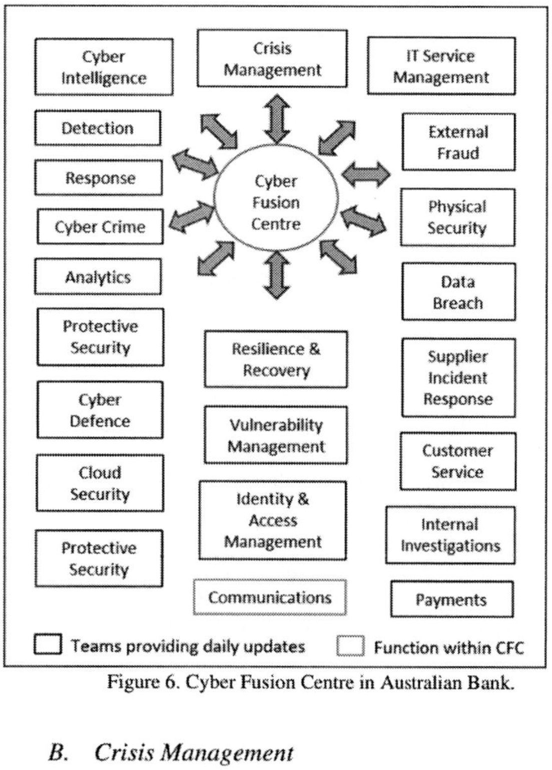

Figure 6. Cyber Fusion Centre in Australian Bank.

B. Crisis Management

In the Australian bank, where the CFC facilitates a daily standup with representatives from the areas illustrated in Figure 6, observations are discussed, insights are shared, and areas of overlap and interdependence are highlighted. Where interdependencies are more complex and broader-reaching incidents are revealed, the CFC team steps up to try to ensure an integrated response approach.

High Priority cyber incidents emerging from these collaborative sessions, whose scale of impact or potential impact exceeds an agreed threshold, are handed over to the Crisis Management Team (CMT). The CMT coordinates crisis management across IT support and operations, service management, suppliers, customer service, corporate communications, and business leaders to ensure a consistent approach. They receive tip offs from various sources, including the CFC daily standups. They have clear accountabilities and established, direct communication with senior management and the C-suite. The CFC team leans-in to provide day-to-day support to the Crisis Management Team during a crisis situation (See Figure 7).

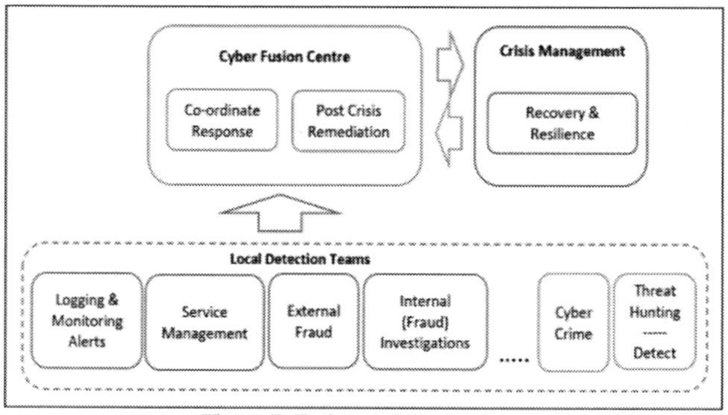

Figure 7. Fusion and Crisis Management in an Australian Bank.

C. Vulnerability Remediation

Vulnerabilities and remediation requirements identified through this bank's Crisis Management process are captured through the crisis management process. These vulnerabilities are prioritised, funded, and remediated to ensure similar situations are not repeated. Many of these vulnerabilities are known, reported and documented prior to the incident, but not prioritised or funded. These larger scale incidents, and the resultant crises, provide appropriate visibility and senior management focus to the potential risks, and the funding follows.

D. Small Scale

Smaller organisations can rely on open communications and close interpersonal relationships when coordinating their response efforts, but this is not scalable. The smaller scale organisations that were assessed in the energy and financial sectors did not see a need for a CFC, as communications and coordination during high priority incidents was straightforward. Analysis found that the communications within smaller organisations, such as those within the insurance and energy sectors, is naturally more open and less arduous. With only a handful of individuals involved in incident management and cyber response, it is easy for each participant to have a deep understanding of their own area of accountability, as well as visibility across the cyber and business landscape. In these smaller organisations, there is less opportunity for information to fall through the gaps.

V. ADDRESSING THE GAP

The lack of maturity observed in the existing Cyber Fusion Centres in Australia is reflected in the benefits they deliver. These fall far short of the goal. But the level of capability uplift described in the literature is attainable. The keys to addressing the gap between Cyber Fusion Centre theory and practice can be found in the fusion models that have been most successful in military operations; the COINOPS intelligence fusion and flow model. This model highlights the need for:

1. A Shared Vision

   The COINOPS commander in the field is clear on their direction, with a strong vision of the mission objectives. The vision of a cohesive mature CFC function, that brings together every aspect of cyber: intelligence; vulnerability management; detection; response; and recovery, with technology, and customer support, for complete situational awareness, is exciting. The CFS vision needs to be clearly and inspiringly communicated from the top echelons of leadership through the CFC leader, to the analysts and response teams working day-to-day with the CFC.

2. The Right Skills and Leadership Capability

   Cyber Fusion effectiveness relies on the right mix of skills and capabilities, in the same way the COINOPS effectiveness relies on the right mix of skills for intelligence fusion and flow. The effective COINOPS platoon in the field incorporates both military specialists and professionals who understand the environment, with language and technology specialists, and intelligence analysts who generate situation awareness [11]. The platoon commander's understanding of the civilian and military context, in that moment, in the field, is crucial. Their depth of experience and capability is reflected in their ability to lead a diverse team of specialists, through challenging situations; distilling intelligence, providing direction; and retaining grasp of the goal while flexing to fit with the constantly changing circumstances [11].

   The fusion centre leader requires an equivalent level of contextual appreciation, depth of leadership capability and experience, focus on outcomes, and the ability to distill information and lead diverse teams of specialists through potentially challenging situations.

3. Clear Information Flow and Accountabilities

   The DHS Counterterrorism Fusion model illustrates how different accountable teams can be brought together into fusion centres to work more collaboratively and to facilitate information flow from state to/from national level [15]. The COINOPS model has taken this to the next level, accelerating the flow of information and intelligence through the layers of command to enable and empower the platoon commanders in the field to make informed decisions, in the moment [11]. Similarly, the effectiveness and efficacy of Cyber Fusion and Incident Response in organisations relies on clear accountabilities and fluid flow of information and intelligence, vertically and horizontally.

4. Robust Strategy and Roadmap

   Turning the Cyber Fusion Centre vision into reality relies on having a roadmap that outlines the steps to get from the current, manual, reactive reality, to the proactive, informed real-time intelligent fusion analytics and integrated response capability. This roadmap needs to include all the relevant changes needed for policies, processes, technology and people.

   Significant performance uplift can be attained by strategically utilising existing technology and intelligence already available within the organization, to facilitate situational transparency and awareness across the response teams. As it matures, CFC will be required to leverage technology for timely information flow, integrated intelligence analytics, and orchestrated response capability.

5. Practice

   Regular simulated crises will build the skills to manage large scale and broad reaching incidents, uplifting response capability and building business readiness [12][16].

6. Collaborative Working

   Utilizing capable leadership to overcome resistance to the new ways of working is the most challenging aspect of building a fusion centre. The CFC is a shared responsibility with potential benefits that span the business. Effective organisational change management, with visible senior-leader sponsorship, and hands-on and capable leadership from the CFC, will inspire and encourage teams to participate, learn from one-another, build mutual trust, and share in the collective gain of fusion [3].

7. Performance Measures

Performance measures help team members to focus on the elements that make a difference. To demonstrate how the CFC can accelerate cyber threat response, performance metrics such as: the Mean Time To Detect (MTTD), Mean Time To Respond (MTTR), and Mean Time To Contain (MTTC) need to be baselined and tracked [6]. Improvements in these measures will highlight the CFC's value, as well as point to areas requiring their attention.

VII. Conclusion

The Cyber Fusion Centre holds great promise for organisations faced with coordinating multiple divisions and departments when responding to cyber incidents. The literature paints a picture of Cyber Fusion Centres as hubs of intelligence, knowledge, and response coordination excellence; where expertise comes together to problem solve and drive actionable outcomes. The reality is much simpler and more basic. The Cyber Fusion Centres described in the FS-ISAC whitepaper and being implemented in Australian banks, focus on basic manual and reactive response coordination through daily standups where representatives share their observations and insights with one another. While this has provided some benefit through open information sharing across teams, it is not delivering the anticipated improvements.

Building a mature intelligence-enabled cyber fusion capability and realising the associated benefits, requires visionary and strategic leadership, a broad appreciation of cyber security in all its aspects, an ability to engage and inspire cyber professionals to join-in, and a deep understand of the problems the fusion centre is addressing, along with the skills to make it happen.

References

[1] Anomali, What is a Cyber Fusion Centre, Available from: https://www.anomali.com/blog/what-is-a-cyber-fusion-center, accessed July 2023.

[2] Cyware, What is a Cyber Fusion Center Center and how is it different from Security Operations Center (SOC)?, August 2018, Available from: https://cyware.com/security-guides/cyber-fusion-and-threat-response/what-is-cyber-fusion-center-and-how-is-it-different-from-security-operations-center-soc-b13a, accessed June 2023.

[3] Cyware, Building a Cyber Fusion Center, November 2020, Available from: https://cyware.com/educational-guides/cyber-fusion-and-threat-response/building-a-cyber-fusion-center-ae08/, accessed June 2023.

[4] Cyware, Why are Financial Institutions Adopting Cyber Fusion Strategies, May 2022, Available from: https://cyware.com/security-guides/cyber-fusion-and-threat-response/why-are-financial-institutions-adopting-cyber-fusion-strategies-57b5, accessed June 2023.

[5] Cyware, How Can You Improve Your Security Posture with Cyber Fusion?, June 2022, Available from: https://cyware.com/security-guides/cyber-fusion-and-threat-response/how-can-you-improve-your-security-posture-with-cyber-fusion-3afb, accessed June 2023.

[6] Cyware, How Cyber Fusion Provides 360-degree Threat Visibility? July 2020, Available from: https://cyware.com/security-guides/cyber-fusion-and-threat-response/how-cyber-fusion-provides-360-degree-threat-visibility-8fda, accessed June 2023

[7] D. P. Fidler, Inter arma silent leges Redux? The law of armed conflict and cyber conflict, Cyberspace and national security threats, opportunities, and power in a virtual world, Georgetown University Press / Washington, DC 2012.

[8] FSISAC[1], Financial Services Information Sharing and Analysis Center, Available from https://www.fsisac.com/, accessed June 2023.

[9] FSISAC[2] Fusion Council, Considerations for Implementing a Fusion Operating Model in Financial Services– Whitepaper, Financial Services Information Sharing and Analysis Centre (FS-ISAC) May 2023. Available from https://www.fsisac.com/, accessed June 2023.

[10] K. L. Mclaughlin, Cybersecurity and fusion centers, The EDP Audit, Control, And Security Newsletter 2023, vol. 67, no. 4 2023, Available from: https://www.tandfonline.com/doi/pdf/10.1080/07366981.2023.2205689, accessed June 2023.

[11] A. Mishra, Synchronising Counterinsurgency Ops with Effective Intelligence, Available from: https://theforge.defence.gov.au/publications/synchronising-counterinsurgency-ops-effective-intelligence, accessed July 2023.

[12] A. Reeves and D. Ashenden, Understanding decision making in security operations centres: building the case for cyber deception technology, 2023. Available from: https://www.researchgate.net/search.Search.html?query=security+operations+centre&type=publication, accessed June 2023.

[13] S. Reveron, An introduction to National Security and Cyberspace, Cyberspace and national security threats, opportunities, and power in a virtual world, Georgetown University Press / Washington, DC 2012.

[14] J. B. Sheldon, Toward a theory of cyber power: Strategic purpose in peace and war, Cyberspace and national security threats, opportunities, and power in a virtual world, Georgetown University Press / Washington, DC 2012.

[15] J. E. Steiner, Needed: State-level, Integrated Intelligence Enterprises, Studies in Intelligence vol. 53, no. 3 (Extracts, September 2009), Available from: https://www.cia.gov/static/Needed-State-Level-Integrated.pdf, accessed June 2023.

[16] J. Steinke et al., Improving Cybersecurity Incident Response Team Effectiveness Using Teams-Based Research, Security and Privacy: building dependability, reliability, and trust, Multidisciplinary Security, July/August 2015, vol. 13, no.4, Available from: https://www.researchgate.net/publication/281467215_Improving_Cybersecurity_Incident_Response_Team_Effectiveness_Using_Teams-Based_Research, accessed September 2023.

Bespoke Sequence of Transformations for an Enhanced Entropic Wavelet Energy Spectrum Discernment for Higher Efficacy Detection of Metamorphic Malware

A Nonnegative Matrix Factorization, Multiresolution Matrix Factorization, and Continuous Wavelet Transform Amalgam

Steve Chan
Decision Engineering Analysis Laboratory, VTIRL, VT
Orlando, USA
e-mail: schan@dengineering.org

***Abstract*—A Robust Convex Relaxation (RCR) Long Short-Term Memory (LSTM) Deep Learning Neural Network (DLNN) can provide enhanced Entropic Wavelet Energy Spectrum (EWES) discernment regarding the potential use of packers, crypters, and protectors (it has been found that compressed or encrypted files have greater entropy values), which can be indicative of Metamorphic Malware (MM). The RCR-LSTM DLNN facilitates a more robust Recurrent Neural Network (RNN) to Feedforward Neural Network (FNN) progression via a bespoke Nonnegative Matrix Factorization (NMF) to Multiresolution Matrix Factorization (MMF) to Continuous Wavelet Transform (CWT) Sequence of Transformations (SOT). Preliminary experimentation pertaining to the RCR-LSTM DLNN framework indicates potential higher efficacy for an enhanced EWES discernment than traditional Machine Learning (ML) and DLNN methods. The potential impact includes the greater use of Industrial Internet of Things (IIOT) sensors, which have been beset by MM, for Industrial Control Systems (ICS), among others.**

Keywords-Industrial Systems; Industrial Control Systems; Distributed Control Systems; Operational Technology; Condition Monitoring Paradigm; Industrial Internet of Things; Metamorphic malware.

I. Introduction

The need for a greater volume and variety of sensors within the Operational Technology (OT) ecosystem — with higher resolution and enhanced edge analytics — has been steadily increasing over the past decade. As just one example, the involved Operation and Maintenance (O&M) Condition Monitoring Paradigm (CMP) is often established by policy in a top-down fashion and may be uniform throughout a region (without considering the greatly varied ambient factors affecting the locales); by way of example, Region A may be subject to seismic activity, Region B by high wind and salinity, Region C by heavy rainfall, high humidity, and lightning, and Region D by drought and high temperatures. Intuitively, the CMPs should be tailored to fit the regions accordingly, but quite frequently, this is not the case. As the equipment in these varied areas have experienced faster than anticipated degradation and failure rates, the introduction of specialty sensors to detect for aberrant conditions has become paramount. Yet, the use of such Industrial Internet of Things (IIOT) sensors are also beset by an array of potential cyber-related vulnerabilities, which has hindered their deployment and utilization. In particular, there has been a surge in polymorphic and metamorphic malware in this arena. If timely patching — which is often difficult in numerous OT environs that have high uptime requirements — is problematic, then alternative mitigation pathways are quite limited. Along this particular vein, the study space is still, comparatively, fairly nascent.

This paper posits that an amalgam of Nonnegative Matrix Factorization (NMF), Multiresolution Matrix Factorization (MMF), and Continuous Wavelet Transform (CWT) can be of some value-added proposition in MM discernment. This amalgam, particularly with regards to the Numerical Implementation (NI) of CWT, was operationalized via a particular class of Convolutional Neural Networks (CNNs) — a RCR-based Convolutional LSTM DLNN, which leverages deeper cascade learning (thereby nicely emulating CWTs). In addition to its value-added proposition of convex relaxation adversarial training, the RCR-LSTM DLNN framework also enhances the bounds tightening for the successive convolutional layers (which contain the cascading of ever-smaller "CWT-like" convolutional filters) for an Enhanced Discernment Accuracy or EDA capability, via support of the facilitation for an enhanced MM EWES Discernment (M2ED).

This paper is structured as follows. Section I provides a backdrop and introduces the problem space. Section II presents relevant background information and discusses the operating environment, as well as the state of the challenge. Section III provides some theoretical foundations and the posited/utilized approach. Section IV delineates a strategy for a Sequence of Transformations (SOT) and delineates some preliminary experimental forays regarding the referenced RCR-LSTM DLNN framework. Section V concludes with some preliminary reflections, puts forth envisioned future work, and the acknowledgements close the paper.

II. Background Information

Over the past several years, there has been a rapid convergence at the nexus of Information Technologies (IT) and OT, particularly in the realm of Industrial Systems (IS). As the requisite uptime and High Availability (HA) of various IS, such as Industrial Control Systems (ICS), Distributed Control Systems (DCS), etc. have increased, the need for an enhanced O&M CMP has also increased. This has involved the desire for a greater use of IIOT sensors, which can have higher resolution, greater reliability, and the potential for providing advance warning with regards to the potential failure of the involved devices (i.e., single item) and equipment (i.e., multiple items) within the CMP.

Legacy IS architecture has been, traditionally, bus topology-centric; this presumes that the involved devices/equipment are connected to the bus and have a common protocol. However, to leverage the wide array of specialized IIOT devices/sensors, which might not share the same protocol, REpresentational State Transfer (REST) Application Programming Interfaces (APIs) are often relied upon. IT/OT engineers have utilized REST APIs so as to obviate the need for protocol conversion, middleware, and/or gateways. These APIs are now heavily relied upon to detect issues, within IT/OT-related paradigms, such as that of unusually high temperatures, vibrations, etc. Yet, many other parameters are in need of monitoring as well. Unfortunately, many of the utilized APIs fall into the category of, among others, Open Worldwide Application Security Project (OWASP) API9:2023 and API10:2023; OWASP 9 (Improper Inventory Management) cites the use of deprecated API versions and exposed debug endpoints, and OWASP 10 (Unsafe Consumption of APIs) cites the use of potentially compromised third-party APIs.

According to a Dragos report, while 65% of advisories contain a patch to fix the cited vulnerability, it was challenging to implement the patch due to the downtime risk for the involved OT system [1]; in addition, there was no viable alternative mitigation, if patching was not an option. This paradigm is aggravated by the fact that, according a SysAdmin, Audit, Network, and Security (SANS) Institute survey, "Threat-Informed Operational Technology Defense: Securing Data vs. Enabling Physics," "47% of ICS organizations do not have internal dedicated 24/7 ICS security response resources to manage OT/ICS incidents" [2]. Furthermore, cyberattacks are occurring with high prevalence; the World Economic Forum's (WEF) Global Risk Report notes that these attacks on critical infrastructure operations (e.g., OT) are among the top five "currently manifesting risks" [3]. McKinsey & Company notes that OT cyberattacks have higher and more profound negative impacts, such as shutdowns, outages, and explosions [4].

Nevertheless, despite the fact that deprecated API versions and compromised third-party APIs are at play, advances in the area of mitigation have remained fairly nascent, if patching is not an option. Meanwhile, there has been an increase in the use of packers (i.e., self-extracting archives that unpack in memory upon execution of the packed file), crypters (i.e., a paradigm, wherein the use of obfuscation and/or encryption is at play), protectors (i.e., a paradigm, wherein a hybridization of both packing and encrypting is at play), etc. to obfuscate malicious intent from detectors. For example, packers greatly increase the complexity for the detectors to successfully perform statistical analysis (a prevalent approach by defenders). To aggravate matters, attackers are also anticipating the use of detection of the involved cryptor stub (i.e., a code segment or binary that accepts the malicious encrypted payload, decrypts, and executes it) signature and are now dividing the cryptor stub into multiple stages so as to obviate detection efforts. Along this vein, many attackers are now utilizing legitimate installers and supplanting the appended data with the crypter. They are also instantiating hollowed processes within trusted areas. Furthermore, they are often generating a unique binary for each compilation. Yet others utilize polymorphic code (i.e., code that utilizes a polymorphic engine to mutate its shape and signature while ensuring that the involved algorithm is preserved); indeed, the prevalence of polymorphic code is high, and researchers have noted that "94% of malicious executables are polymorphic" [5]. Compared to polymorphic malware, MM is even more complex, as it leverages numerous transformation techniques (successive and/or concurrent).

Researchers at Tripwire, among others, have posited that the rise in polymorphic or metamorphic malware is possibly tied to the current predominant signature-based security paradigm, wherein cyber threat intelligence-sharing has, to date, tended to be more heavily based upon the sharing of file hashes; hence, if the polymorphic or MM changes its file in each instance, potentially, "the effectiveness of defenses sharing threat intelligence about that piece of malware will drop drastically" [5].

III. THEORETICAL FOUNDATIONS AND APPROACH

The theoretical approach towards contending with metamorphic malware detection ranges from, by way of example, Ling et al., who focused upon leveraging NMF for detecting smaller subsets of the overarching set, via the utilization of structural entropy (which was deemed to exhibit greater promise than structural compression ratios) [6], to Begenholtz et al., who found that it is possible to accurately determine whether a file has been packed by a metamorphic packer "with an accuracy of up to 89.36% when trained on a single packer, even for samples packed by previously unseen packers" [7]; the latter study also focused upon leveraging Multilayered LSTM Networks for the involved detection. Along this vein, Ling et al. and many others have also focused upon structural entropy, such as via the use of Multilayer Perceptron (MLP) Neural Networks (NN) and other constructs, such as that of a Recurrent Neural Network (RNN) for behavioral feature extraction combined with a Feedforward Neural Network (FNN) (e.g., a Deep Feed Forward Concurrent Neural Network for classification, as put forth by Zhou [8]).

The premise is that when an executable file changes between states, such as from its native uncompressed state to a compressed, encrypted, etc. state, the file's representative structural entropy also changes. According to Lyda et al., compressed or encrypted files have greater entropy values [9]. Leveraging this heuristic, Wojnowicz et al. utilized wavelet decomposition (which can successfully decompose complex information/patterns into lower rank representations) on the representative structural entropy of files to obtain the associated EWES, which provides insight into the potential use of packers, crypters, and protectors [10]. Moreover, while Singular Value Decomposition (SVD) has been widely used to obtain low-rank matrix approximation, the advantage of NMF when contending with structural entropy is that it is a fairly robust unsupervised learning approach for the analysis of high-dimensional data, and it can facilitate feature extraction from very large sparse matrices [11], whereas other approaches are not as readily able to process very large matrices due to various issues, including, but not limited to, missing entries or prolonged convergence [12]. The classic example involves a very large matrix A being factorized into, let us say, matrices B and C. Ultimately, the desire is that all the involved matrices have no negative elements [13]. However, if a prototypical method of matrix factorization (e.g., SVD) is used, the resulting SVD-based lower rank representation leads to both positive and negative elements (which is the antithesis of the intent to have no negative elements), thereby making interpretation quite challenging due to the ensuing ambiguity. In contrast to SVD, because NMF has the inherent constraint that the factorized matrices be comprised of non-negative (i.e., positive) elements, it can facilitate a more robust interpretation of the original matrix data, as it segues to a more intuitive structural representation by parts; as previously discussed in [12], the involved approximation/representation as the sum of positive elements (e.g., matrices, vectors, integers) is more intuitive, logical, and naturalistic given the matrices of positive integers. By leveraging the advantage of NMF's non-negative element constraint, various high-level features are more readily discerned from the hidden layers of the involved NN. Hence, the more naturalistic NMF-based approach reduces the need for feature engineering (i.e., a coarser and less elegant approach of extraction). Consequently, when the posited SOT is utilized, which starts at NMF and ends at a CWT, it is indeed possible to extrapolate upon the works of Ling et al., Begenholtz et al, and Wojnowicz et al., among others.

IV. EXPERIMENTATION

A. Experimental Considerations

MM utilize various concealment/obfuscation methods while preserving the functionality of their intent. According to Borello et al., these methods can be classified as: data flow obfuscation (e.g., dead or junk code insertion, variable or register substition, instruction permutation or replacement, etc. [14]) and control flow obfuscation (e.g., code transposition, flattening — control flow flattening is a technique used not only to legitimately safeguard software from being reverse engineered, but is also illegitimately used by malware creators to obfuscate and hinder reverse engineering by cyber defenders, via the use of modification of the statement and loops in the code, layered obfuscation, etc. [15]). With regards to data flow obfuscation, Srdihara, et al. reported that by inserting a large amount of dead/junk code derived from benign files, the statistical properties of the ensuing MM morphed code could possibly be indistinguishable from benign codes [16]. With regards to control flow obfuscation, the transformed/obfuscated MM is semantically equivalent with regards to its original intent, but also immensely more difficult for detectors to analyze.

Various researchers have contributed to the detection of malware. For example, Ekhtoom et al. had classified MM families and obtained experimental results of 77% accuracy [17]. Bhattacharya et al. experimented with similarity measures and wavelet analysis and achieved an accuracy of 82.1% [18]. Bat-Erdene et al. experimented with entropy estimations and achieved an accuracy of 94.13% [19]. Alam et al. have asserted that they achieved a MM detection rate of 98.9% (with a false positive rate of 4.5%) [20].

B. Experimental Design & Implementation

Based upon the cited experimental consideration statistics, any posited MM detection should be in a similar range of detection efficacy to be of meaningful value-added proposition in the applied realm. This work chose to build upon the work of Ling et al., Begenholtz et al, and Wojnowicz et al., among others. An RNN paradigm was used for the behavioral feature extraction of the MM, and a FNN was utilized for the classification. However, one of the main contributions of this paper resided in the fact that an RCR-LSTM DLNN was utilized to support the RNN to FNN progression by facilitating a M2ED/output between the RNN and FNN; this would lead to improved discernment accuracy.

The RCR-LSTM DLNN accomplished its facilitation by operationalizing the posited SOT. The involved SOT in the experimentation for this paper progresses from NMF to MMF to Corresponding Wavelet Transform (CORWT) to an Enhanced CORWT (ECORWT), which was operationalized by way of a CWT PyWavelet Schema. The central aim of this approach was to arrive at a CWT paradigm, which does not substantively experience the energy leakage issues experienced by other commonly utilized transforms, such as Discrete Wavelet Transforms (DWT). For the involved experimentation, a particular NI of CWTs was utilized, via the referenced RCR-LSTM DLNN.

To successfully progress through the SOT, a non-conventional NMF approach is needed in the form of an Input Synthesis Model (ISM), which facilitates the MMF (the chosen method for ascertaining the involved multiscale structure and the delineation of the involved wavelets for a multi-resolution representation) [21] as well as, in turn, the determination of the MMF's CORWT, ECORWT, and the ensuing CWT. There is also a subtlety; certain operations are needed to fully transform the interim Gaussian

Composite Model (GCM) to a fully formed ISM, which then segues to the MMF. There is yet another subtlety. As illuminated in [12], the leveraging of a CWT PyWavelet schema (a Python-based open-source WT library) must be accompanied by the cognizance of the contained Mother Wavelets (i.e., families of Wavelets, which encompass both DWT and CWT); within each of these Wavelet families, there may be varied subordinate Wavelet subcategories, which are, generally speaking, differentiated by the number of coefficients (i.e., the number of vanishing moments, which refers to the state wherein the Wavelet coefficients are zero for those polynomials with a degree of at most $p-1$, and the scaling function alone can be utilized to represent the function) as well as the level of decomposition — as the number of vanishing moments increases, the polynomial degree of the wavelet also increases, the involved graph tends to become smoother, and it also turns out that the leveraging of CWT well enables the intricate structural characteristics of the NMF input, within the transform space, to be more amenable to the process of analysis and discernment [22][23]. The experimental design and implementation is summarized in Fig. 1 below.

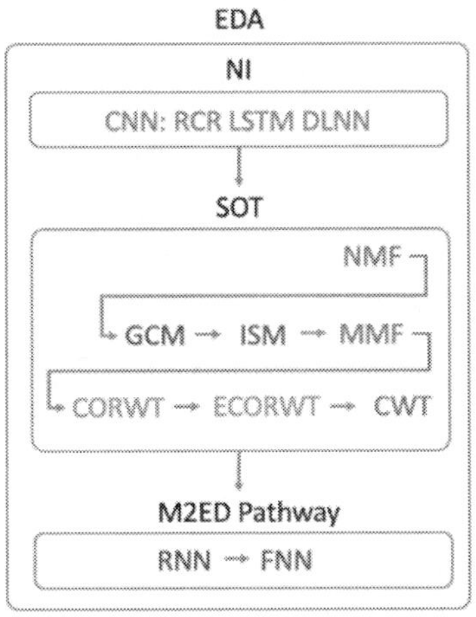

Figure 1. EDA Instantiation via an NI-enabled SOT for a M2ED Pathway

Ultimately, the experimental implementation involved three facets: utilization of an RNN for behavior feature extraction of the MM, utilization of a FNN for classification of the MM, and an RCR-LSTM DLNN-based NI to operationalize the SOT. The first facet addressed the static features (e.g., operation codes or opcodes, byte-level n-grams [extracted from, by way of example, Portable Executables or PEs], as a non-signature- based approach for detection, etc.) and dynamic features (e.g., recorded API calls) of the MM file. The feature vectors derived from the static and dynamic information were concatenated. The RCR-LSTM DLNN assisted the RNN in the conversion to a M2ED/output, which the FNN then utilized for classification; in other words, the RCR-LSTM DLNN facilitated the RNN to FNN progression.

C. *Experimental Results*

It should be noted that the utilized RNN was utilized for behavioral feature extraction. It should further be noted that the FNN was utilized for MM sample classification. While prototypical NNs have numerous layers, DLNN is a type of NN that is comprised of numerous hidden layers. Medina et al. had shown that the use of CNNs reduces the false positive rate [24]. Along this vein, Moradi et al. and others have described how the use of LSTMs addresses the gradient vanishing issue (a consequence of the derivative of the activation function used to instantiate the NN, which can be, by way of example, obviated by using an activation function, such as Rectified Linear Unit or ReLU instead of sigmoid), which besets RNNs [25]. The bespoke RCR-LSTM DLNN is one such CNN leveraging a LSTM. The RCR-LSTM DLNN was evaluated against other prototypical ML and DLNN methods. As just one indicator, the bespoke RCR-LSTM DLNN classification results are shown in Table I below. As a summary, a preliminary version of the posited bespoke RCR-LSTM DLNN method was able to achieve comparable ACC as other well-known methods, such as KNN, RNN, and RBF SVM; however, despite the fact that the posited bespoke method did not achieve the 98.9% rate (with a false positive rate of 4.5%) reported by Alam et al., it is hoped that future versions of the RCR-LSTM DLNN may possibly break the glass ceiling that is currently constraining the aforementioned methods. Future work will tell.

TABLE I. CLASSIFICATION RESULTS OF VARIOUS ML METHODS

Methods	Models	Accuracy (ACC)
Prototypical ML methods	Decision Tree (DT) [26]	82.4%
	Hidden Markov Models (HMM) [27]	87.3%
	Random Forest (RF) [28]	91.43%
	Sigmoid Support Vector Machine (SVM) [26]	95%
	k-Nearest Neighbor (KNN) [29]	97.6%
	Radial Basis Function (RBF) SVM [26]	97.9%
Prototypical DLNN methods	CNN [30]	96.96%
	RNN [31]	97.8%
Posited bespoke RCR-LSTM DLNN method	RCR-LSTM DLNN	97.9%

MM samples were obtained by using krmaxwell/maltrieve and jstrosch/malware-samples. The Cuckoo Sandbox was utilized to record the API calls and analyze the MM; however, while the use of API calls to unveil behavioral patterns was utilized to great effect by Hansen et al., Daeef et al., and others [32][33], it seems to have limited efficacy against potent MM. Prototypical ML libraries (e.g., Keras, Scikit-learn, etc.) were utilized. Experimental variations included PyTorch (PT), Tensorflow (TF), Caffe (CE), Caffe2 (CE2), and SciPy (SP). PT and TF were the favored implementations due to their prevalence and robust documentation. The choice of leveraging NMF, via the utilization of structural entropy (rather than structural compression ratios) seems to have been affirmed; after all, NMF's non-negative element constraint provides more ready discernment of high-level features from hidden layers. Likewise, the use of LSTM for the detection (to mitigate against the RNN deficiency of the gradient vanishing issue), seems to have been prudent; in addition, although Begenholtz et al., had experimented with multi-layer LSTM models, Catak et al. and others found that single-layer and multi-layer LSTM models attained similar classification outcomes [26]. For the experiment discussed in this paper, a single-layer LSTM was utilized, per Catak's findings.

On the entropy front, generally speaking, entropy refers to the measure of uncertainty pertaining to the data of an involved file, and the measurement value ranges between 0 to 8. The lower the value, the lower the probability that the code has been obfuscated, encrypted, etc. The higher the value, the higher the probability that the code has been obfuscated, encrypted, etc. [9]. A M2ED/output (associated with an enhanced wavelet decomposition) will segue to more accurate values for the involved measurement values. As an additional heuristic, MM coefficient scores tend to condense close to 1.0, whereas the substantive portion of benign files tend to have "smaller similarity coefficient scores as they are relatively far from 1.0" [34]. Preliminary experimentation has shown that the posited bespoke RCR-LSTM DLNN method does segue to enhanced measurement values, and the determination of entropy values is enhanced (i.e., M2ED), thereby providing greater confidence in utilizing the heuristic of "compressed or encrypted files have greater entropy values" [9].

A prototypical confusion matrix (utilized to depict the classification performance) was utilized for evaluation. True Positive Rate (TPR) equates to True Positive (TP)/Positive (P), wherein P = TP + False Negative (FN). Along this vein, False Positive Rate (FPR) equates to False Positive (FP)/Negative (N), wherein N= FP + True Negative (TN). Furthermore, Accuracy Rate (AR) equates to (TP + TN)/(P + N). The Receiver Operating Characteristic (ROC) curve was utilized to depict the classification performance at various classification thresholds with the two parameters of TPR and FPR. Following the lead of Zhou and others [8], Area Under the [ROC] Curve (AUC) was utilized for the measure of separability (i.e., classification performance). The performance of the nine classifiers cited in Table 1 was also supported by the utilization of N-fold cross-validation, via Waikato Environment for Knowledge Analysis (WEKA). As our posited approach is predicated upon an Adaptive Weighting System (AWS) [35], the subtle intent of cross-validation is somewhat obviated. For example, if all data samples were utilized to train the involved NN, the ensuing weights and bias values would tend to overfit (thereby setting the stage for poor performance again new, previously unseen data). To mitigate again overfitting, the convention is to separate the data into training data (e.g., 80%) and test data (e.g., 20%) so as to find an apropos balance. With an AWS, the mechanics of N-fold cross-validation become evidently more trite. The prototypical number of folds utilized is 10, and the involved experimentation uses this figure. The n-fold cross-validation provides a measure of quality (i.e., classification error) of each fold; axiomatically, the smaller the ensuing value, the better the performance. It was prudent to adhere to the standard of utilizing an artifically suppressed number of training iterations (a high number yields will result in higher performance) to provide a more realistic sense of performance. Generally, the performance at the first fold is better than that at the last fold. As noted in the next section, more experimentation will be conducted for augmenting the training data and studying classification performance [36].

V. Conclusion

The increase in cyber threat information feeds has provided an expanding corpus of malware samples to analyze. The discussed corpuses include, among others, krmaxwell/maltrieve and jstrosch/malware-samples. Meanwhile, as ML approaches have become more robust and sophisticated, ML-based MM detection approaches have improved as well. This is opportune due to a convergence of factors: (1) the required uptime and HA of ICS and DCS, among others, have increased, the necessity of IIOT sensors for an enhanced O&M CMP has also risen, (2) the necessity for higher resolution and greater reliability IIOT sensors, (3) the dependence upon APIs to detect for CMP-related issues, (4) the range of cyber-related vulnerabilities, particularly MM, which have plagued the APIs of IIOT sensors, (5) the dramatic rise and prevalence of MM, (6) the fact that strategic/critical infrastructure IIOT sensors and OT are part of the top five "currently manifesting risks," as noted by the WEF.

The theoretical approach utilized, to operationalize the discussed M2ED/output for an improved MM detection paradigm, involved non-conventional NMF and MMF (used in conjunction so as to facilitate the capture of the structure and content of the involved matrices so as to attain higher resolution and EDA) to more elegantly segue to CWT (via the intermediary steps of CORWT and ECORWT). This NMF-MMF-CWT paradigm, operationalized by the discussed RCR-LSTM DLNN (which supported the RNN to FNN progression), was the key SOT for EDA (i.e., M2ED) and one of the main contributions of this paper. The RCR LSTM DLNN amalgam brings several value-added propositions to bear: (1) the CNN amalgam construct itself reduces the false positive rate, (2) the RCR construct facilitates more robust bounds tightening, and (3) the LSTM mitigates against the RNN deficiency of the gradient vanishing issue. The operationalization of the SOT (the leveraging of wavelet decomposition on the representative structural entropy to ascertain the associated EWES) for an enhanced EWES, which was referenced as M2ED, provided a form of Indications and Warnings (I&W) for the potential use of packers, crypters, and protectors. Future work will involve more quantitative experimentation in this area.

Overall, the paper discussed the theoretical foundations and approaches utilized within this ecosystem, various experimental designs, and results related to MM detection. The paper also explored various pertinent techniques and methods, including leveraging RCR, LSTM, DLNN, NMF, MMF, CORWT, ECORWT, CWT, RNN, and FNN. The paper further details an experimental design using a bespoke RCR-LSTM DLNN method and presents the results, comparing them with other ML methods. The paper's focus on MM detection should be of relevance to the current cybersecurity landscape, particularly as attacks on OT for strategic/critical infrastructure operations are among the top currently manifesting risks.

ACKNOWLEDGMENT

This research is supported by the Decision Engineering Analysis Laboratory (DEAL), an Underwatch initiative of VTIRL, VT. This is part of an ongoing VTIRL technical series, on behalf of the Quality Assurance/Quality Control (QA/QC) unit, to advance the involved TRLs.

REFERENCES

[1] A. Waldman, "Dragos: Ransomware topped ICS and OT threats in 2021," Tech Target, Feb 23, 2022, Accessed: July 28, 2023. [Online]. Available from: https://www.techtarget.com/searchsecurity/news/252513714/Dragos-Ransomware-topped-ICS-and-OT-threats.

[2] I. Bramson, "Vulnerable Today, Hacked Tomorrow: How a Lack of OT Cybersecurity Affects Critical Infrastructure," Cyber Defense Magazine, May 6, 2022, Accessed: July 28, 2023. [Online]. Available from: https://www.cyberdefensemagazine.com/vulnerable-today/

[3] World Economic Forum, Marsh McLennan, and Zurich Insurance Group, "Global Risks Report 2023," World Economic Forum, January 11, 2023, Accessed: July 28, 2023. [Online]. Available from: https://www.weforum.org/reports/global-risks-report-2023/in-full/1-global-risks-2023-today-s-crisis/.

[4] McKinsey & Company, "How to Enhance the Cybersecurity of Operational Technology Environments," March 23, 2023, Accessed: July 28, 2023. [Online]. Available from: https://www.mckinsey.com/capabilities/risk-and-resilience/our-insights/cybersecurity/how-to-enhance-the-cybersecurity-of-operational-technology-environments.

[5] SSL, "Polymorphic Malware and Metamorphic Malware: What You Need to Know," March 25, 2021, Accessed: July 28, 2023. [Online]. Available from: https://www.thesslstore.com/blog/polymorphic-malware-and-metamorphic-malware-what-you-need-to-know/.

[6] Y. Ling, N. Sani, and M. Abdullah, "Nonnegative Matrix Factorization and Metamorphic Malware Detection. J Comput Virol Hack Tech 15, 2019, pp. 195–208, doi: 10.1007/s11416-019-00331-0

[7] E. Bergenholtz, E. Casalicchio, D. Ilie, and A. Moss, "Detection of Metamorphic Malware Packers Using Multilayered LSTM Networks," Information and Communications Security. Lecture Notes in Computer Science vol 12282, Springer, Cham, doi: 10.1007/978-3-030-61078-4_3

[8] H. Zhou, "Malware Detection with Neural Network Using Combined Features," Communications in Computer and Information Science, vol 970, 2019, pp 96–106, doi: 10.1007/978-981-13-6621-5_8

[9] R. Lyda and J. Hamrock, J, "Using Entropy Analysis to Find Encrypted and Packed Malware," IEEE Secur. Priv. 5(2), 2007, pp. 40–45, doi: 10.1109/MSP.2007.48.

[10] M. Wojnowicz, G. Chisholm, M. Wolff, and X. Zhao, "Wavelet Decomposition of Software Entropy Reveals Symptoms of Malicious Code," J. Innov. Digit. Ecosyst. 3(2), 2016, pp. 130–140, doi: 10.48550/arXiv.1607.04950.

[11] N. Gillis, "The Why and How of Nonnegative Matrix Factorization," Regularization, Optimization, Kernels, and Support Vector Machines, Jan 2014, pp. 257-291, doi: 10.48550/arXiv.1401.5226.

[12] S. Chan, M. Krunz and B. Griffin, "Adaptive Time-Frequency Synthesis for Waveform Discernment in Wireless Communications," 2021 IEEE 12th Annual Information Technology, Electronics and Mobile Communication Conference (IEMCON), Vancouver, BC, Canada, 2021, pp. 0988-0996, doi: 10.1109/IEMCON53756.2021.9623140.

[13] A. Zaeemzadeh, M. Joneidi, B. Shahrasbi, and N. Rahnavard, "Missing Spectrum-Data Recovery in Cognitive Radio Networks Using Piecewise Constant Nonnegative Matrix Factorization," MILCOM 2015 - 2015 IEEE Military Communications Conference, 2015, pp. 238-243, doi: 10.1109/MILCOM.2015.7357449.

[14] J. Borello and L. Mé, "Code Obfuscation Techniques for Metamorphic Viruses," J. Comput. Virol. 4(3), 2008, pp. 211–220, doi: 10.1007/s11416-008-0084-2.

[15] H. Xu, Y. Zhou, and J. Ming, "Layered Obfuscation: A Taxonomy of Software Obfuscation Techniques for Layered Security," Cybersecurity 3(1):9, 2020, pp. 1-18, doi: 10.1186/s42400-020-00049-3.

[16] S. Sridhara and M. Stamp, "Metamorphic Worm That Carries Its Own Morphing Engine," J Comput. Virol. Hacking Tech. 9(2), 2013, pp. 49-58, doi: 10.1007/s11416-012-0174-z.

[17] D. Ekhtoom, M. Al-Ayyoub, M. Al-Saleh, M. Alsmirat, and I. Hmeidi, "A Compression-Based Technique to Classify Metamorphic Malware," 2016 IEEE/ACS 13th International Conference of Computer Systems and Applications (AICCSA), 2016, pp. 1–6, doi: 10.1109/AICCSA.2016.794580.

[18] A. Bhattacharya and R. Goswami, "Data Mining Based Detection of Android Malware," Proceedings of the First International Conference on Intelligent Computing and Communication. Advances in Intelligent Systems and Computing, v 458, 2016, pp 187–194, doi: 10.1007/978-981-10-2035-3_20.

[19] M. Bat-Erdene, H. Park, H. Li, H. Lee, M. Choi, "Entropy Analysis to Classify Unknown Packing Algorithms for Malware Detection," Int J Inf Secur 16(3), 2017, pp. 227–248. doi: 10.1007/s10207-016-0330-4.

[20] S. Alam, I. Traore, and I. Sogukpinar, "Annotated Control Flow Graph for Metamorphic Malware Detection," The Computer Journal, vol. 58, no. 10, Oct. 2015, pp. 2608-2621, doi: 10.1093/comjnl/bxu148.

[21] R. Kondor, N. Teneva, and P. Mudrakarta, "Parallel MMF: A Multiresolution Approach to Matrix Computation," Arxiv, 2015, Accessed: July 28, 2023. [Online]. Available from: https://arxiv.org/abs/1507.04396.

[22] P. Addison, "Introduction to Redundancy Rules: The Continuous Wavelet Transform Comes of Age," Philosophical Transaction of the Royal Society A., 2018, pp. 1-38, doi: https://doi.org/10.1098/rsta.2017.0258.

[23] A. Levinskis, "Convolution Neural Network Feature Reduction Using Wavelet Transform," Electronics and Electrical Engineering, vol. 19, 2013, pp. 61-64, doi: 10.5755/j01.eee.19.3.3698.

[24] E. Medina, M. Petraglia, J. Gomes, and A. Petraglia, "Comparison of CNN and MLP classifiers for Algae Detection in Underwater Pipelines," Seventh International Conference on Image Processing Theory, Tools and Applications (IPTA), 2017, pp. 1-6, doi: 10.1109/IPTA.2017.8310098.

[25] M. Mahvash, S. Sadrossadat, and V. Derhamit, "Long Short-Term Memory Neural Networks for Modeling Nonlinear Electronic Components," IEEE Transactions on Components, vol 11 Issue 5, doi: 10.1109/TCPMT.2021.3071351.

[26] C. Ferhat, Y. Ahmet, E. Ogerta, and A Javed, "Deep Learning Based Sequential Model for Malware Analysis using Windows exe API calls," PeerJ Comput Sci vol 6, 2020, doi: 10.7717/peerj-cs.285.

[27] C. Annachhatre, T. Austin, and M. Stamp, "Hidden Markov Models for Malware Classification," J. Comput. Virol. Hack. Tech. 11(2), 2014, pp. 59–73, doi: 10.1007/s11416-014-0215-x.

[28] B. Khamma, "Ransomware Detection Using Random Forest Technique," ICT Express, Vol 6, Issue 4, December 2020, pp. 325-331, doi: 10.1016/j.icte.2020.11.001.

[29] G. Dahl, J. Stokes, and L. Deng, "Large-scale Malware Classification Using Random Projections and Neural Networks," IEEE International Conference on Acoustics, Speech and Signal Processing (ICASSP), 2013, pp. 3422-3426, doi: 10.1109/ICASSP.2013.6638293.

[30] S. Lad and A. Adamuthe, "Malware Classification with Improved Convolutional Neural Network Model," I.J. Computer Network and Information Security, 2020 pp. 30-43. doi: 10.5815/ijcnis.2020.06.03.

[31] H. Madani, N. Ouerdi, A. Boumesaoud, and A. Azizi, "Classification of Ransomware Using Different Types of Neural Networks," Sci Rep. 12(1), March 19, 2022, pp. 4770. doi: 10.1038/s41598-022-08504-6.

[32] S. Hansen, T. Larsen, M. Stevanovic, and J. Pedersen, "An Approach for Detection and Family Classification of Malware Based on Behavioral Analysis," Proceedings of the 2016 International Conference on Computing, Networking, and Communications (ICNC), 2016, pp. 1-5, doi: 10.1109/ICCNC.2016.7440587.

[33] A. Daeef and A. Al-Najii, "Features Engineering for Malware Family Classification Based API Call," Computers 11(11), 2022, doi: 10.3390/computers11110160.

[34] L. Yeong, N. Sani, M. Abdullah, N. Hamid, "Nonnegative Matrix Factorization and Metamorphic Malware Detection," Journal of Computer Virology and Hacking Techniques 15, 2019, pp. 195-208, doi: 10.1007/s11416-019-00331-0.

[35] S. Chan and P. Nopphawan, "Accelerant Facilitation for an Adaptive Weighting-Based Multi-Index Assessment of Cyber Physical Power Systems," 2023 IEEE 3rd International Conference in Power Engineering Applications (ICPEA), 2023, pp. 156-162, doi: 10.1109/ICPEA56918.2023.10093212.

[36] K. O. Babaagba, Z. Tan and E. Hart, "Improving Classification of Metamorphic Malware by Augmenting Training Data with a Diverse Set of Evolved Mutant Samples," 2020 IEEE Congress on Evolutionary Computation (CEC), 2020, pp. 1-7, doi: 10.1109/CEC48606.2020.9185668.

Cyber Situational Awareness of Critical Infrastructure Security Threats

Fatemeh Movafagh
School of Computing Science
Simon Fraser University
British Columbia, Canada
email: fma44@sfu.ca

Uwe Glässer
School of Computing Science
Simon Fraser University
British Columbia, Canada
email: glaesser@sfu.ca

Abstract—**The rising frequency and sophistication of cyber-attacks pose a notorious threat to critical infrastructures, heavily reliant on industrial control systems for advanced automation. To explore this evolving challenge systematically, a robust cyber situational awareness framework is essential. Our paper adopts a dual approach, focusing on both the broader scope of threat mitigation and remediation to understand the breadth of the problem and on online intrusion detection applied to supervisory control data to comprehend its depth. The methodical framework and analytic model we propose here are tailored to cyber-physical systems used for industrial control and operational technology. By acknowledging transitional vulnerabilities in these systems, we stress the necessity of proactive measures to mitigate the risk of widespread cascading and escalating infrastructure failures. At the core of our contribution lies GenericAttackTracker, a novel analytic framework for online anomaly detection, which combines dynamic attack scoring with Bayesian inference to fuse results from supervisory control data analysis with real-time contextual information into actionable threat intelligence. By leveraging the abstract semantic properties of Heterogeneous Information Network Analysis for structural analysis and of Abstract State Machines for deriving executable abstract models of complex distributed systems, our framework supports a system of systems view of critical infrastructures and facilitates the daunting task of dynamically analyzing their intricate interdependencies.**

Keywords*—*Cyber-physical systems; supervisory control systems; online threat detection; infrastructure interdependencies; machine learning; anomaly detection; dynamic attack scoring.

I. Introduction

Increasingly frequent and sophisticated cyberattacks have become a severe threat. Responding to the evolving cyber threat landscape, security technology is advancing, but not fast enough to keep pace with the threat. Security breaches frequently compromise the protection of sensitive information, exposing personal identities, intellectual property and financial assets. This trend means mounting damages in the hundreds of billions of dollars, erosion of trust in conducting business and collaboration in cyberspace and mounting fears of catastrophic events triggered by attacks that can physically cripple Critical Infrastructure (CI). Such attacks aim at indefinite disruptions of services that are essential for the functioning of our society and economy. In times of escalating political tensions and rising financial rewards from cybercrime, CI is at high risk from global cyber threat activity [1]–[3].

Critical infrastructures rely on Industrial Control Systems (ICS) as principal components of Operational Technology (OT) used for advanced automation of industrial processes. This includes different types of devices, systems, and networks to monitor and control physical processes, machinery, and other infrastructure components. Two standard control system architectures widely used for CI facilities are Supervisory Control and Data Acquisition (SCADA) and Distributed Control Systems (DCS) [4]. ICS technology offers robust and reliable solutions for advanced automation used in a variety of industries including manufacturing, oil and gas, electric energy generation and distribution, aviation, maritime, rail, and utilities, among many other CI sectors [5].

With progressive automation of critical industrial processes, the attack surface for sophisticated cyber threats expands, intensifying the risk of cascading and escalating failures [1][6]. When directly or indirectly connected to the Internet, ICS hardware and software can get exposed to illicit online access in attempts to exploit OT system vulnerabilities through various adversarial scenarios. A well-orchestrated cyberattack on a facility's integrated process control system may cause lasting and widespread disruptions and extensive physical damage by overloading vital system components [7]–[10]. Despite the many diverse uses, ICS architectures frequently build on the same core technologies, mostly SCADA, DCS, and Programmable Logic Controllers (PLC), for lower-level control tasks. SCADA systems and DCS are often networked together. Homogenous core architectures and tight coupling make them more vulnerable to cyberattacks because a single discovered vulnerability can potentially be exploited across several different systems [4].

This paper explores emerging threats to OT used in various critical sectors [5] and analyzes why CI security is a matter of growing concern that calls for enhanced resilience against the most aggressive threats. When vital components, systems, or networks get compromised, the incapacitation or destruction of CI assets could result in catastrophic loss of life, adverse economic effects and significant harm to public confidence [11]. The research presented here aims at a holistic methodical framework for devising a novel generic analytic model for cyber situational awareness of critical infrastructure threats. A central focus is on distributed online anomaly detection and interpretation of abnormal activity patterns in supervisory control data streamed from the operation of CI; i.e., patterns that deviate from the expected normal behavior beyond what could be explained by the presence of regular noise in the control data. The scope of our analytic model is not limited to single infrastructure entities but rather takes into account that multiple infrastructures are often interconnected as a system of systems with complex interdependencies [4]. "What happens to one infrastructure can, directly and indirectly, affect other infrastructures, impact large geographic regions, and send ripples throughout the national and global economy." [12]

The broader intent of our methodical framework is to also serve as a "lens" for gauging CI security and resilience against evermore advanced adversarial scenarios. Considering that network technology may never be completely secure, cybersecurity is about risk mitigation at the end of the day [13]. A holistic understanding of cybersecurity risks is crucial for making informed decisions on rational grounds. Risk mitigation strategies call for a complete assessment of vulnerabilities and consequential security risks to effectively enhance CI resilience. This fact was also stressed by the U.S. Government Accountability Office in their 2022 report on the U.S. electric grid security status: "DOE has developed plans to implement a national cybersecurity strategy for protecting the grid. However, we found that DOE's plans do not fully incorporate the key characteristics of an effective national strategy. For example, the strategy does not include a complete assessment of all the cybersecurity risks to the grid. Addressing this vulnerability is so important that we made it a priority recommendation for DOE to address." [14]–[16].

Besides the methodical framework, our main contribution is GenericAttackTracker, a distributed analytic framework for online detection and interpretation of anomalous activity patterns in supervisory control data. Building in part on our previous work, AttackTracker [17], the novel features of GenericAttackTracker significantly advance the core analytic model and expand the scope of AttackTracker to: (1) integrate contextual real-time threat intelligence and apply Bayesian inference to offer a broader decision basis and more reliable decision-making process; and (2) directly support a "system of systems" view for situational awareness of the cybersecurity status of multiple interdependent CI entities [18].

The remainder of this paper is organized as follows. Section II describes the broader scope of the problem in light of a multidimensional problem space. Next, Section III provides some background on industrial automation and the notorious challenges of online analysis and interpretation of supervisory process control data. Section IV introduces our methodical framework and generic analytic model. Building on AttackTracker, the generic model, GenericAttackTracker, expands the scope of the basic model in two principal ways. Finally, Section V concludes the paper.

II. Problem Scope

The evolving threat landscape underscores the critical necessity for a robust cyber situational awareness framework. Such a framework should provide a comprehensive overview of a system's cyber environment, enabling quicker identification, understanding, and assessment of potential or existing threats, and mitigation approaches for such threats. This is particularly pertinent to OT and ICS, which oversee the functioning of CIs. Given their pivotal role in operating facilities such as electrical utilities, oil and gas pipelines, water utilities, chemical plants, and rail systems, among others [19], any compromise of these systems may result in serious disruptions and severe damage.

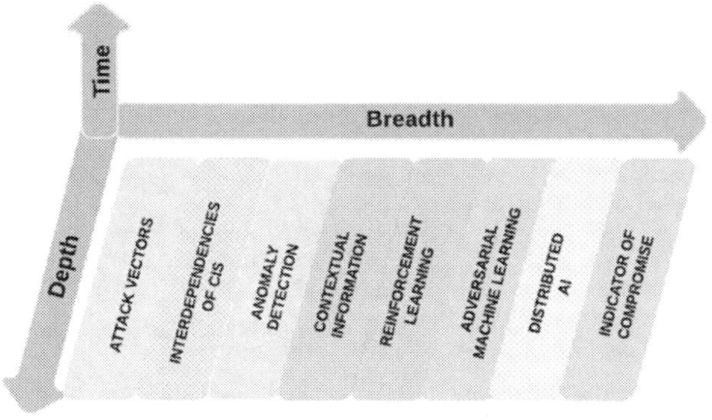

Figure 1. Multidimensional problem of security threats.

A. Cyber Situational Awareness Framework

The multidimensional problem of security threats calls for a multifaceted solution, where multiple layers of defence mechanisms and strategies must be put in place to safeguard systems. Hence, to effectively tackle this intricate challenge, we propose a cyber situational awareness framework characterized by three dimensions: breadth, depth and time. This framework offers a holistic view of essential approaches for protecting ICS from escalating cyber threats, illustrated in Figure 1. As much as one must consider various aspects of defense breadth, one must also consider defense depth at the same time and routinely reassess both breadth and depth [1]. In fact, it is inadequate to defend in one dimension only. Defense that lacks depth despite breadth leaves vulnerabilities, while depth without breadth still allows attackers to find alternate entry points. Routine reassessment is critical to ensure that defense mechanisms remain fully intact and newly discovered vulnerabilities and exposures get patched in a timely manner. In the remainder of this section, we explore briefly some aspects of the breadth that also need to be taken care of in other dimensions.

1) Attack Vector, Indicator of Compromise (IOCs): OT is critical for industrial processes but exposes systems to cyberattacks through various attack vectors, including network-based and physical process attacks [20]. Attackers employ advanced multi-vector strategies, targeting multiple entry points to exploit system vulnerabilities [21], emphasizing the need for a comprehensive and multifaceted defense approach to protect ICS. On the other hand, IOCs are forensic data logs that offer evidence of malicious activity on a system or network. Monitoring IOCs enables incident responders to detect signs of malicious actions and respond promptly to similar intrusions in their early stages [22].

2) Interdependencies of CIs: Due to the complex interdependencies between different infrastructures, a disturbance in one system can trigger cascading failures, leading to far-reaching and severe impacts. Thus, it becomes essential to leverage the data from one CI as a potential alert trigger for others. By doing so, we can anticipate and address the risk of cascading failures, strengthening the overall resilience of our critical systems. This part will be explored in depth in Sections III and IV.

3) Anomaly Detection, Machine Learning, Reinforcement Learning, Contextual Information: Anomaly detection particularly focused on time series data prevalent in ICS [23], forms a crucial aspect of the cyber situational awareness framework. Identifying temporal deviations in data patterns can be the key to uncovering potential threats or system malfunctions. Behavior-based and process-based anomaly detection are two approaches to safeguard ICS. The former uses machine learning to monitor system behavior and detect deviations, while the latter focuses on monitoring physical processes controlled by the ICS. These methods, augmented by reinforcement learning, address the limitations of traditional signature-based detection against novel and complex cyber-attacks such as zero-day attacks [24]. In addition, by integrating Bayesian inference, which utilizes probabilistic models, the detection process can dynamically update the likelihood of ongoing attacks based on incoming contextual data, and detect anomalous attack-based events accurately [25].

4) Adversarial Machine Learning (AML): The use of Machine Learning (ML), DL (Deep Learning), and RL (Reinforcement Learning) techniques in cybersecurity has improved threat detection. However, it also introduces vulnerabilities through AML attacks. These attacks can manipulate input data or the model itself to cause false positives and false negatives in anomaly detectors, weakening security system performance by exposing it to evasion and poisoning attacks [26]. The goal is to make ML, DL and RL in security a strength, and to enhance the resilience of OT and ICS security, not to be an exploitable vulnerability. Therefore, working on the robustness of anomaly detectors against AML such as what has been done in [27] is a must. This also demonstrates that staying ahead of threats requires constant situational awareness and readiness to respond to emerging cyber threats.

III. Industrial Process Control

Automation is essential for the steady operation of critical infrastructure to continuously monitor and control machinery, systems, and processes; it enhances efficiency, productivity, quality of service delivery and safe operation of critical assets. We have thus become inexorably dependent on automated services and will be even more so with future smart industrial process control applications. An apt example to epitomize this ongoing trend is smart manufacturing in the fourth industrial revolution, tagged Industry 4.0 [28]. Under the cyber-physical system (CPS) paradigm, this situation is further exacerbated through the increasing integration of embedded computing with sensor networks (and other IoT devices) to monitor and control processes in the physical environment.

1) Cascading and Escalating Failures: While achieving great efficiencies through seamless interoperability of software and networking components with dynamics of physical processes, CPS technology intensifies fragility. When exploited by advanced threats, fragility amplifies the risk of cascading and escalating failures. Cascading events occur when local equipment failure or other disruptions trigger subsequent failures or disruptions on a larger scale.

Although triggered by "natural" causes, the phenomenon occurred in August 2003 for the Eastern Interconnection, one of the three major electric power grids in North America. A local fault of a high-voltage transmission line went unnoticed due to an alarm system malfunction, which in turn tripped a cascade of failures throughout southeastern Canada and eight northeastern U.S. states. In total, 50 million people lost power for up to two days in the biggest blackout in North American history [29]. In February 2021, the U.S. state of Texas suffered a major power crisis after severe winter storms, resulting in at least 246 deaths and property damages in excess of $195B. Cascading failures propagated across multiple interdependent infrastructures causing insufficient power generation capacity online, which resulted in insufficient natural gas supply to the power plants. When power was cut, it disabled compressors that push gas through pipelines, knocking out further gas plants due to lack of supply [8].

2) Abnormal Activity Patterns: Critical processes require constant supervisory control of their operational status to issue alerts and initiate an emergency shutdown when abnormal activity patterns approach defined safety margins. Supervisory control data is temporal data interpreted as streamed sequences of real-value measurements taken at regular time intervals, referred to as time series data. Any observed activity patterns that do not conform to the expected behavior but seem to occur "out of place" are denoted as anomalies or outliers. An intuitive definition of the meaning of outlier is offered by Hawkins [30]: "an observation that deviates so much from other observations as to arouse suspicion that it was generated by a different mechanism."

3) Anomaly Detection Challenges: Real-world processes are notoriously prone to uncertainties caused by "external" factors such as communication errors, fluctuations in demand and supply, and technical instabilities resulting in inevitable variance in the data, characterized as noise. A number of factors make online anomaly detection in time series data streamed from the operation of a supervisory control system a challenging problem:

- Identifying anomalous activity patterns that often remain hidden to the human eye requires learning normal activity to train a robust model that not only fits previously observed data but also carries over to unobserved data; naturally, developing such a model is not a trivial task.
- Anomalies occur for various reasons, thus an even more intricate problem often is to differentiate the typically few anomalies of interest—above all, suspicious anomalous behavior indicating a potential security threat—from the vast majority of anomalies caused by noise, seasonality or other trends irrelevant to security.

Figure 2 illustrates common variance due to noise observed in time series data for electricity power consumption recorded at one datapoint per minute over four consecutive days. While

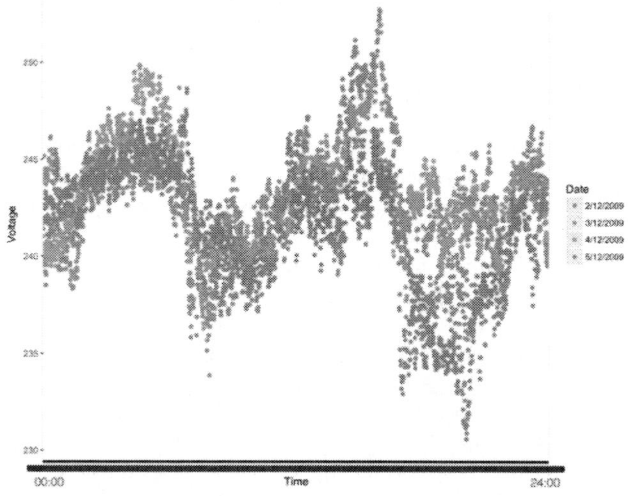

Figure 2. Electricity power consumption data for households over four 24-hour periods on consecutive weekdays show changes in voltage due to fluctuating demand and supply.

the exact power consumption behavior over a 24-hour time period differs on any given day, a recognizable overall pattern emerges; however, the boundaries for what constitutes normal variations of routine activity remain blurry. This phenomenon is persistent and not just due to the small sample size.

IV. Methodological Framework

Online analysis of supervisory control data streamed from the operation of mission-critical systems is the basis for early threat activity detection. Finding suspicious and potentially harmful behavior anomalies without delay is key for swift mitigation and remediation to reduce the impact of an attack by launching countermeasures containing security breaches locally before they spread laterally across wider networks.

We first discuss AttackTracker, a distributed analytic model using dynamic attack scoring for online cyber threat activity detection for single infrastructure entities [17]. Building on this model, we then propose GenericAttackTracker, expanding the scope of the basic model to: (1) integrate contextual real-time threat intelligence and apply Bayesian inference for a broader and more reliable decision-making basis; and (2) support a "system of systems" view for situational awareness of multiple interdependent critical infrastructures [18].

A. Attack Tracker

AttackTracker offers a robust and scalable framework based on a distributed analytical model for online tracing of threat activity patterns in supervisory control data by orchestrating a hierarchical network of threat activity detectors. This way, evidence of threat activity observed anywhere in the system is aggregated across control system architecture levels. Utilizing dynamic attack scoring boosts the analytic performance and reduces the false alarm rate by ignoring potential contextual noise and errors in the behavior prediction phase [17].

AttackTracker produces highly encouraging results [31] when applied to the Secure Water Treatment (SWaT) testbed created by Singapore University of Technology [32]. SWaT serves as a control signal source for data collected from a scaled-down version of an industrial water purification plant targeted by a variety of realistic attacks on different parts of the system. Figure 3 illustrates the basic AttackTracker architecture and its hierarchical organization.

A hierarchy of linked attack detectors continuously monitors the operation of controllers at different levels of a supervisory control system. (l_1)-detectors monitor peripheral controllers such as PLC units at the local level. At higher levels, (l_i), for $i = 2, 3, \ldots$, detectors monitor the output of multiple detectors at level (l_{i-1}). At the top level, a single detector determines the global operational status of the whole system and reports attacks in progress in any one of the subsystems.

In other words, local detectors analyze the operation of a local subsystem as mirrored by the state of its sensors and actuators to spot abnormal patterns in the control data stream indicating a collective anomaly associated with an attack on this subsystem. Each local detector uses a Behavior Predictor module feeding the 'expected' next observation values into an Inference Engine. The Inference Engine module processes and labels observations, assigns attack scores, and raises red flags based on the deviation of observed values from predicted ones relative to a dynamically adjusted threshold. For $i \geq 2$, (l_i)-detectors aggregate data and information received from their lower-level detectors to determine the attack scope in the underlying levels. This way, detectors operating at higher levels are able to distinguish distributed threat activities in addition to centralized attacks.

For illustration, we consider a simple example in a SCADA-based testbed with three subsystems (A, B, C). Subsystem A has detected an unusual water pressure spike, while subsystem C observed a decline in the water flow rate; no anomalies were found in subsystem B. Two secondary l_2-detectors overseeing pairs of these subsystems recognized the irregularities in A and C. A top-level detector, consolidating findings from the l_2-detectors, identified anomalies in two out of the three subsystems and signaled a system-wide alert. The top-level detector's Inference Engine deduced that the concurrent abnormalities in A and C might indicate a coordinated attack, recommending prompt action. This layered detection system ensures complex anomalies do not go unnoticed even when overlooked locally.

1) Behavior Predictor: Behavior Predictor is a core component that learns the normal behavior of a subsystem and forecasts the next local feature values based on previous observations. It uses a Multivariate Temporal Convolutional Network (MTCN) model to learn hidden patterns from a history of discrete observations in the form of a multivariate stochastic time series. Behavior Predictor is implemented to detect potential drifts in the stream data and adapt itself to not to be fooled by attacks.

2) Inference Engine: Inference Engine is the other component that decides based on a multi-modal view provided by its associated Behavior Predictor and the underlying detectors. It

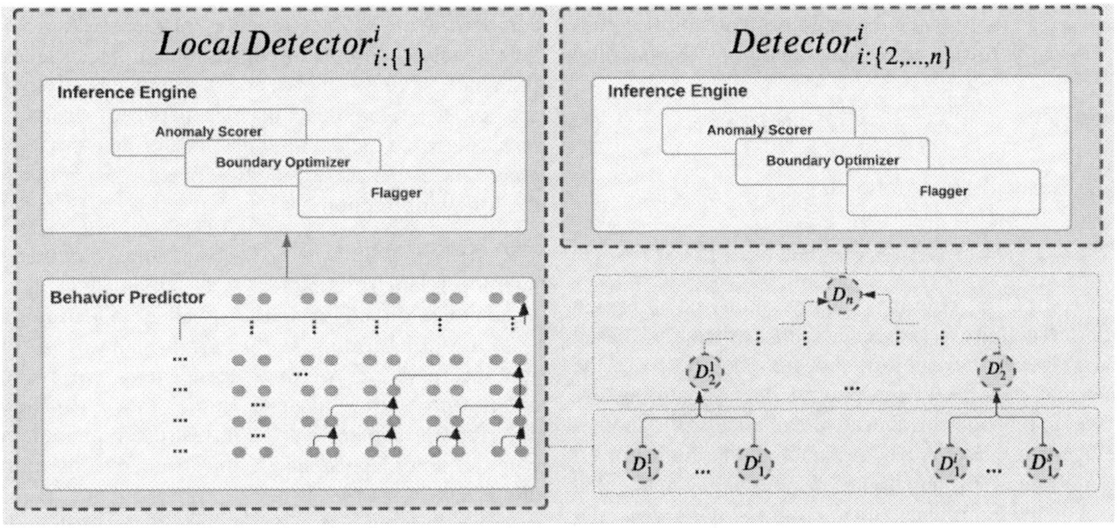

Figure 3. AttackTracker Framework Architecture: Local detectors operate at Level 1; regular detectors operate at all levels higher than Level 1.

enhances higher-level detectors by utilizing Behavior Predictor to trace the collective behavior of their underlying subsystems. Inference Engine is responsible for making decisions based on the information provided by the Behavior Predictor components and detectors, and it can help the end-user to choose the best mitigative action by highlighting the attack target and its potential cascading influences.

The Inference Engine component of the AttackTracker framework utilizes individual scoring and system-wide scoring as part of its anomaly detection process. The individual scoring phase involves offline and online steps, where a model is trained to detect anomalies based on transformed feature vectors. This phase focuses on detecting local subsystem anomalies. The system-wide scoring phase aggregates results from individual detectors to identify system-wide attacks, which individual detectors may miss due to the distributed nature of the network. Simultaneous anomalies and global log-based anomaly scores are considered in this phase.

The combination of individual and system-wide scoring enhances attack detection accuracy and reduces false alarms. This combination happens through the "moving average" strategy in the Inference Engine component. It helps to identify collective and correlated anomalies as one single attack. This decision-making strategy is based on the trade-off between deviation and persistence, where a persistent anomalous interval is more suspicious of being an attack than a single strike caused by sensor noise or predictor faults.

3) Dynamic Scoring: The dynamic scoring method is based on a sliding window approach that considers the current observation and the previous observations to calculate the anomaly score. The anomaly score is then compared to a threshold value to determine whether an attack has occurred. The threshold value is dynamically adjusted based on the current state of the system and the historical data. The dynamic scoring method is designed to ignore potential contextual noise and errors in the Behavior Predictor components and to handle regular spikes of observed "anomalies" in cases where they have not captured all the patterns of normal data.

B. Generic Attack Tracker

Our GenericAttackTracker framework advances the analytic model and expands the scope of AttackTracker significantly by encompassing two principal novel features called: Bayesian View and System of Systems View (see below). Please note that this paper emphasizes the principles of GenericAttack-Tracker and their application, not the detailed implementation.

1) Bayesian View: A problematic aspect of time series anomaly detection in control data streamed from a mission-critical system is the rate of false positives: even when the relative rate is low, the absolute number of false positives may still be intolerable for high data volumes depending on a system's critical mission. One way to mitigate the problem is fusing the results from control data analysis with contextual information from other potential sources of actionable threat intelligence to be used in the decision-making process. This leads to Bayesian methods. The strength of the Bayesian approach is its ability to combine information from multiple sources, thereby allowing greater 'objectivity' in final conclusions [33]. The result is a broader foundation for making more reliable decisions [34], whereas ignoring actionable threat intelligence originating from supplementary sources may come at the expense of missing out on the bigger picture.

A holistic view of threat activities calls for integrating data- with knowledge-driven threat analysis as a basis for applying Bayesian inference [35]. Assuming an evidential interpretation of probability, Bayes' rule is used to update the probability for a hypothesis H as more evidence or information E becomes available. Formally, this is stated as a conditional probability:

$$P(H|E) = \frac{P(E|H) \cdot P(H)}{P(E)}, \text{ for } P(E) > 0, \quad (1)$$

where $P(E)$ is calculated as follows:

$$P(E) = P(H) \cdot P(E|H) + P(\neg H) \cdot P(E|\neg H) \quad (2)$$

In our case, $P(H|E)$ describes the probability of observing actual malicious activity as associated with a cyberattack based on prior knowledge of conditions that may be related to the event (abnormal patterns in the control data stream) before and after accounting for corroborative evidence from another threat intelligence source. A basic example is the Indicator Of Attack (IOA) status [36]: any digital or physical evidence that a cyberattack is likely imminent or in progress. IOAs generally focus on the intent of what an attacker is trying to accomplish, regardless of the malware or exploit used in an attack [37]. Events indicative of suspicious activity include: HTTP/HTTPS connections via non-standard ports (rather than port 80 or port 443); unusual network traffic; multiple user logins from different regions; internal hosts communicating with countries outside of the business range, among many others.

The following example illustrates the idea using numbers are not based on real-world or experimental data but are solely meant for the sake of explanation.

- Prior belief, $P(H)$: The value is determined by the Inference Engine component. Based on control data patterns, the anomaly detector estimates there's a 30% chance an attack is occurring: $P(H) = 0.30$.
- Evidence, E: The value is based on contextual information, for instance, an external threat intelligence feed that alerts us to an ongoing global cyber attack campaign.
- Likelihood, $P(E|H)$: This is the probability of receiving an external threat alert given that an attack is in progress. From past data, a value of $P(E|H) = 0.70$ is assumed.
- Probability of evidence, $P(E|\neg H)$: The probability of receiving an alert even when there is no attack is assumed to be $P(E|\neg H) = 0.10$ based on past data.

First, the probability of getting the external alert is calculated using Equation 2:

$$P(E) = 0.30 \times 0.70 + 0.70 \times 0.10 = 0.28$$

Next, the posterior (updated) probability of being under attack given the alert is calculated using Equation 1:

$$P(H|E) = \frac{0.70 \times 0.30}{0.28} \approx 0.75$$

Given the alert from the external threat intelligence feed, our updated belief that we're under attack went up from 30% (based solely on anomaly detection) to 75% (after accounting for the external threat intelligence).

Feeding supplementary IOA status information or threat intelligence from other alternative sources into the inference component of detector modules of GenericAttackTracker requires only a limited modification of AttackTracker's basic Inference Engine component. An example is threat intelligence derived from interdependencies between separate CIs. This reveals how an incident in one CI can ripple through and affect other CIs. A deeper exploration of this concept is provided in the following section.

2) System of Systems View: Generally, CI entities are highly interdependent in complex ways; an incident in one infrastructure can directly or indirectly affect related infrastructures, resulting in cascading and escalating failures [4]. The nature and reverberations of interdependencies are a complex and difficult problem to analyze. In their work, Rinaldi et al. [12] describe six dimensions of infrastructure interdependencies: types of interdependencies, infrastructure environment, coupling and response behavior, infrastructure characteristics, types of failures and state of operations. Although each has distinct characteristics, these classes of interdependencies are not mutually exclusive. Understanding these dimensions and applying them to the analysis of interdependencies among different CIs is crucial for maintaining a resilient system of systems. Incidents like the ransomware attack on the Colonial Pipeline in 2021 [38], or the large-scale electric grid failures cited in Section I, are vivid reminders that the impact due to interdependencies is very real.

Many studies of individual CI systems overlook their interconnection and mutual dependency [12]; only a few take interdependencies into account. However, these works either use simplified simulation platforms to analyze interdependencies among a limited type of CI entities, e.g., in [18], or they only measure risk based on interdependencies [39][40]. In contrast, GenericAttackTracker is designed to facilitate the modeling of CI systems with complex relations between their constituent entities. Our model abstractly identifies linked infrastructure entities as populations of interacting agents, in accordance with [12]. Nowadays, complex technical systems frequently comprise a large number of interacting, multi-typed components interconnected through communication and control networks. The information infrastructure of many such systems can abstractly be viewed as Heterogeneous Information Networks (HINs) [41] and be analyzed through Heterogenous Information Network Analysis (HINA) [42]. The HINA paradigm has gained wide attention from researchers in data mining and information retrieval fields; especially, it is used to mine hidden patterns through mining link relations from networked data [43].

The concepts of HIN/HINA align with our situation where multiple linked CIs with different interdependencies with each other are using GenericAttackTracker for online anomaly detection. GenericAttackTracker enhances our methodological framework by utilizing HINA [44][43]. This way, we model and analyze static representations of CI interdependencies for a more realistic approach to anomaly detection. With this objective, we define the following sets as interdependency categorises [12]:

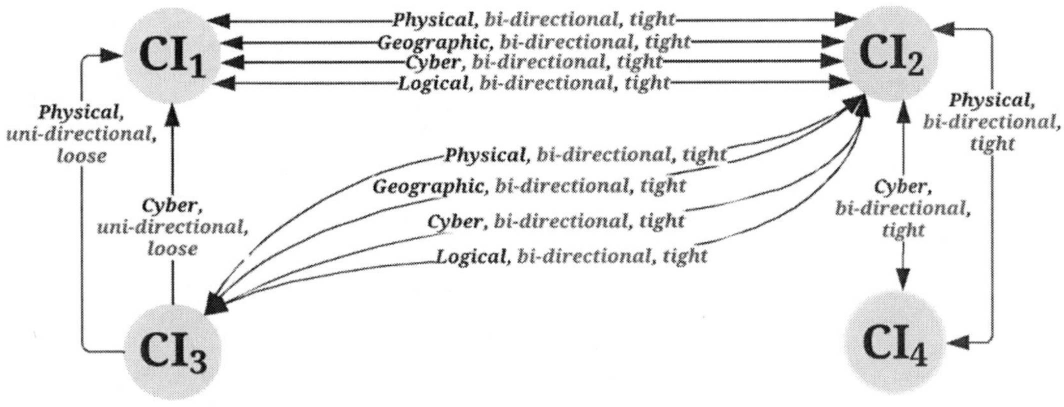

Figure 4. The Network schema NS_G comprises four different infrastructure types; directional links between the various node types state constraints on CI interdependencies.

$Class = \{Physical, Cyber, Geographic, Logical\}$
$Direction = \{uni - directional, bi - directional\}$
$Degree = \{loose, tight\}$

We build on the HIN definition in [43]: A heterogeneous information network $G(V, E, A, R)$ is composed of an object set $V = \{n_1, n_2, ..., n_n\}$ with object types $A = \{a_1, a_2, ..., a_m\}$, and a set of links $E = \{e_1, e_2, ..., e_k\}$ with relation types $R = \{r_1, r_2, ..., r_l\}$, where $|A| > 1$ or $|R| > 1$ (to differentiate HINs from regular graphs). Two surjective function mappings assign object types to objects and relation types to links. If two links belong to the same relation type, the two links share the same starting object type as well as the ending object type.

For a better understanding of the composition of a complex HIN G, the network schema NS_G is a template that describes the meta network structure of G by specifying type constraints on the sets of objects and links of G. The result is a directed graph defined over object types A, with edges that are relation types from R. An HIN that conforms with a network schema is called a network instance of the schema. For a link type R connecting object type S to object type T, denoted by $S \xrightarrow{R} T$, S and T are the source and target object type of link type R.

A meta path $\mathcal{P}$ is a path defined on a schema $S_G = (\mathcal{A}, \mathcal{R})$, and is denoted in the form of $A_1 \xrightarrow{R_1} A_2 \xrightarrow{R_2} ... \xrightarrow{R_l} A_{l+1}$, which defines a composite relation $R = R_1 \circ R_2 \circ ... \circ R_l$ between objects $A_1, A_2, ..., A_l$, where $\circ$ denotes the composition operator on relations. The rich semantics of meta path is an important characteristic of HIN. Based on different meta paths, objects have different connection relations with diverse path semantics, which may affect many data mining tasks including clustering, classification, link prediction, ranking, and information fusion [43].

Figure 4 is an example of a HIN graph, G, that shows a network schema, NS_G, of four SCADA-based CI entities and their interdependencies derived from the NIST guide to ICS security [4]. These CIs are natural gas pipelines, electric power grids, water distribution systems, and railway transportation systems. Natural gas pipelines need electric power for their compressors, storage and control systems. On the other hand, electric power generation needs natural gas as a main or backup fuel for its generators. Thus, the physical interdependencies between these two CI types are bidirectional. Natural gas pipelines also might need water from case to case for cooling or emission reduction. So this is a unidirectional and loose physical interdependency.

Not only is electric power supply essential for the operation of railway transportation and water distribution systems but these two CI types are essential for power generation. Hence, the physical interdependencies between them are bidirectional. Within the GenericAttackTracker framework, each of these CI types acts as an agent that interacts with other CI entities. Bi-directional cyber interdependencies must be considered for all interdependent CIs. Building upon the graph in Figure 4, it is plausible that a disruption in the natural gas infrastructure can cause power disruptions, and electric power failures may lead to disruptions in other infrastructures.

In Figure 5, we delve deeper into a specific instance of the NS_G of Figure 4, where the CIs are not just represented in their general form. Indeed, by identifying and analyzing different meta paths $\mathcal{P}$ within this schema graph, we can undertake a range of data mining tasks. Each unique meta path reveals distinct insights into the intricate interdependencies existing among the CIs.

Finally, it is not necessary to manually produce complex HIN graph structures as these can be generated automatically through the use of representation learning methods [45]. The details are beyond the scope of this paper.

Going beyond identifying and understanding normally static interdependencies, the final challenge is how to operationalize the cyber situational awareness framework and analytic model as needed for determining the broader impact of dynamically cascading and escalating failure scenarios in a timely manner. The state of operation of an infrastructure can be thought of

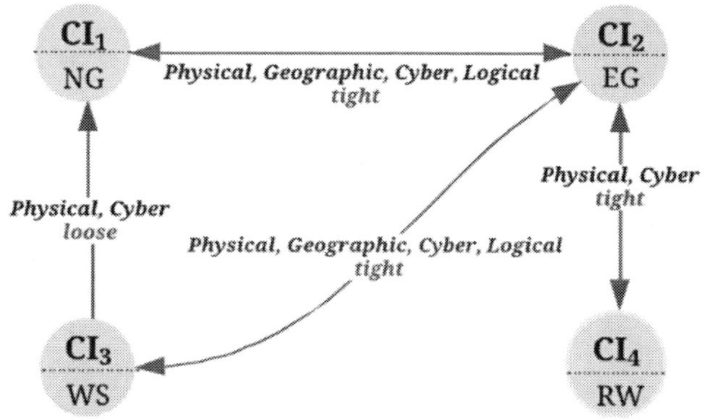

Figure 5. Network instance of schema NS_G: i) Natural gas pipeline (NG), ii) Electric grid (EG), iii) Water distribution systems (WS), iv) Railway transportation systems (RW).

as a continuum that exhibits different behaviors during normal operation conditions, times of severe stress or disruption, or repair and restoration activities. At any point in the continuum, the state of operation is a function of interrelated factors and system conditions [12]. This may be the hardest task after all.

Any viable solution does require continual reassessment of the security status of complex CIs and their constituent entities to account for emerging cyber threat events and incidents. By viewing linked infrastructure entities as interacting agents, the impact of threat activities on the operational status of related entities is modeled in terms of a distributed abstract machine. The model computes the situational awareness status of a complex CI based on the combined status of the component CI entities. The underlying formal model for developing the abstract machine builds on the operational modeling paradigm of Abstract State Machines (ASM) [46] and its method for stepwise refinement [47].

A distributed ASM, by definition, is a collection of asynchronously interacting ASM agents that collectively update a distributed global state. In previous work, we have successfully used the ASM paradigm as formal semantic foundation for modeling a complicated distributed situation analysis framework for maritime security [48] and also designed and developed a computational platform for making such models executable [49]. The design of the CI abstract machine model exceeds the scope of this paper but will be the subject of a separate paper.

Finally, in a system-of-systems context, the dynamic analysis of the operational status of interacting CI entities can also generate threat intelligence as input for the Inference Engine of GenericAttackTracker to enhance anomaly detection accuracy and overall system resilience. An attack on one entity may also spell trouble for other interdependent entities downstream.

V. Conclusion and Future Work

With evermore sophisticated and damaging threats targeting critical infrastructure, cyber risks are intensifying and security breaches are more and more inevitable. In light of expanding the attack surface for advanced threats and zero-day exploits, enhancing the resilience of operational technology against the most serious threats is critical. Risk mitigation strategies call for a complete assessment of vulnerabilities and consequential risks to make informed decisions for effective risk mitigation and remediation on rational grounds.

Our main technical contribution, GenericAttackTracker, is a distributed and scalable analytic framework for detection of threat activity patterns in supervisory control data; its novel features significantly advance and expand the scope of the analytic core of the basic AttackTracker model in two principal ways: 1) fusing results from control data analysis with contextual threat intelligence from IOA sources into actionable insights yields a broader, more reliable decision basis, expected to further reduce false positive rates; 2) modeling infrastructures as interacting agents linked in complex ways—both physically and through ICT, i.e., what happens to one infrastructure can directly or indirectly affect other infrastructures—supports a "system of systems" view for situational awareness of the security status of multiple interdependent infrastructure entities.

Handling CI security is a complex and challenging task. In our research, we tackle this problem by combining advanced analytic methods with intuitive modeling paradigms to manage complexities. The ultimate goal is a coherent and consistent integration in an abstract methodical framework that facilitates a holistic view of the full scale problem scope.

While putting a spotlight on SCADA, a prevalent industry standard for monitoring and control of vital services not only in North America, the strategies we discuss here do likely apply to a much broader range of industrial process control systems. By exploring the feasibility of our approach for SCADA architectures, we aim to show the practical relevance of our analytic framework for ICS/OT at large.

Our future work, will continue the research to model and analyze complex network schemas of linked infrastructures to extract and interpret more intricate interdependencies. We believe HIN/HINA provides the expressiveness needed to tackle these tasks. Further, we will build upon our previous work on modeling distributed situation analysis processes as Abstract State Machine models, focussing on dynamically evaluating the status of complex CIs in near real-time.

Acknowledgment

The research project for the work presented here was funded by the Natural Sciences and Engineering Research Council of Canada (NSERC) and by Innovation, Science and Economic Development Canada (ISED).

References

[1] O. S. Saydjari, "Engineering trustworthy systems: a principled approach to cybersecurity," *Communications of the ACM*, vol. 62, pp. 63–69, May 2019.

[2] CrowdStrike, "CrowdStrike 2023 Global Threat Report." Available upon online request: https://go.crowdstrike.com/2023-global-threat-report. Accessed: 2023.08.31.

[3] Canadian Center for Cyber Security, "National Cyber Threat Assessment 2023–2024," *Communications Security Establishment*, 2022.

[4] K. Stouffer, V. Pillitteri, S. Lightman, M. Abrams, and A. Hahn, "Guide to Industrial Control Systems (ICS) Security," Tech. Rep. NIST SP 800-82r2, National Institute of Standards and Technology, June 2015.

[5] Cybersecurity & Infrastructure Security Agency, U.S. Department of Homeland Security, "Critical Infrastructure Sectors." Online: https://www.cisa.gov/topics/critical-infrastructure-security-and-resilience/critical-infrastructure-sectors. Accessed: 2023.08.01.

[6] D. W. Hubbard and R. Seiersen, "How to Measure Anything in Cybersecurity Risk," *John Wiley & Sons*, 2016.

[7] T. Tsvetanov and S. Slaria, "The effect of the colonial pipeline shutdown on gasoline prices," *Economics Letters*, vol. 209, p. 110122, 2021.

[8] K. Madhavan and D. Rajamani, "2021 Texas Electricity Black-out Crisis: Root-cause Analysis and Recommendations," *Journal of Student Research*, vol. 11, no. 1, pp. 1–10, 2022.

[9] A. Matrosov, E. Rodionov, D. Harley, and J. Malcho, "Stuxnet under the microscope," *ESET LLC (September 2010)*, vol. 6, pp. 1–85, 2010.

[10] I. Thomson, "Everything you need to know about the petya, er, notpetya nasty trashing pcs worldwide." Online: https://www.theregister.com/2017/06/28/petya_notpetya_ransomware/, 2017. Accessed: 2023.08.31.

[11] Public Safety Canada, "Canada's Critical Infrastructure." Online: https://www.publicsafety.gc.ca/cnt/ntnl-scrt/crtcl-nfrstrctr/cci-iec-en.aspx, 2022. Accessed: 2023.08.01.

[12] S. M. Rinaldi, J. P. Peerenboom, and T. K. Kelly, "Identifying, understanding, and analyzing critical infrastructure interdependencies," *IEEE control systems magazine*, vol. 21, no. 6, pp. 11–25, 2001.

[13] T. Bossert and U.S. Department of Homeland Security, "Presentation at Cyber Week 2017," *Blavatnik Interdisciplinary Cyber Research Center, Tel Aviv University, Israel*, 2017.

[14] U.S. Government Accountability Office, "Securing the U.S. Electricity Grid from Cyberattacks." Online: https://www.gao.gov/blog/securing-u.s.-electricity-grid-cyberattacks, Oct. 2022. Accessed: 2023.08.31.

[15] U.S. Government Accountability Office, "ElectricityL Grid Cybersecurity: DOE Needs to Ensure Its Plans Fully Address Risks to Distribution Systems." Online: https://www.gao.gov/assets/720/713257.pdf, Mar. 2021. Accessed: 2023.08.31.

[16] U.S. Government Accountability Office, "Critical Infrastructure Protection: Actions Needed to Address Significant Cybersecurity Risks Facing the Electric Grid." Online: https://www.gao.gov/assets/710/701114.pdf, Aug 2019. Accessed: 2023.08.31.

[17] Z. Zohrevand and U. Glässer, "Dynamic attack scoring using distributed local detectors," in *ICASSP 2020-IEEE International Conference on Acoustics, Speech and Signal Processing*, pp. 2892–2896, 2020.

[18] I. Eusgeld, C. Nan, and S. Dietz, "System-of-Systems Approach for Interdependent Critical Infrastructures," *Reliability Engineering & System Safety*, vol. 96, no. 6, pp. 679–686, 2011.

[19] M. Conti, D. Donadel, and F. Turrin, "A Survey on Industrial Control System Testbeds and Datasets for Security Research," *IEEE Communications Surveys & Tutorials*, vol. 23, no. 4, pp. 2248–2294, 2021.

[20] T. Mason and B. Zhou, "Digital forensics process of an attack vector in ics environment," in *2021 IEEE International Conference on Big Data (Big Data)*, pp. 2532–2541, IEEE, 2021.

[21] E. Irmak and İ. Erkek, "An overview of cyber-attack vectors on scada systems," in *2018 6th international symposium on digital forensic and security (ISDFS)*, pp. 1–5, IEEE, 2018.

[22] M. Asiri, N. Saxena, R. Gjomemo, and P. Burnap, "Understanding indicators of compromise against cyber-attacks in industrial control systems: a security perspective," *ACM transactions on cyber-physical systems*, vol. 7, no. 2, pp. 1–33, 2023.

[23] B. Kim et al., "A comparative study of time series anomaly detection models for industrial control systems," *Sensors*, vol. 23, no. 3, p. 1310, 2023.

[24] MR. Gauthama Raman, C. M. Ahmed, and A. Math, "Machine learning for intrusion detection in industrial control systems: challenges and lessons from experimental evaluation," *Cybersecurity*, vol. 4, pp. 1–12, 2021.

[25] C. Wang et al., "Robust intrusion detection for industrial control systems using improved autoencoder and bayesian gaussian mixture model," *Mathematics*, vol. 11, no. 9, p. 2048, 2023.

[26] S. Zhou et al., "Adversarial attacks and defenses in deep learning: From a perspective of cybersecurity," *ACM Computing Surveys*, vol. 55, no. 8, pp. 1–39, 2022.

[27] Y. Jia et al., "Adversarial attacks and mitigation for anomaly detectors of cyber-physical systems," *International Journal of Critical Infrastructure Protection*, vol. 34, p. 100452, 2021.

[28] L. Thames and D. Schaefer, "Industry 4.0: An overview of key benefits, technologies, and challenges," *Cybersecurity for Industry 4.0: Analysis for Design and Manufacturing*, pp. 1–33, 2017.

[29] J. Minkel, "The 2003 northeast blackout–five years later," *Scientific American*, vol. 13, pp. 1–3, 2008.

[30] D. M. Hawkins, *Identification of outliers*, vol. 11. Springer, 1980.

[31] Z. Zohrevand, *End-to-end anomaly detection in stream data*. PhD thesis, School of Computing Science, Simon Fraser University, 2021.

[32] J. Goh et al., "A dataset to support research in the design of secure water treatment systems," in *Critical Information Infrastructures Security: 11th International Conference, CRITIS 2016, Paris, France, October 10–12, 2016, Revised Selected Papers 11*, pp. 88–99, Springer, 2017.

[33] A. Gelman et al., *Bayesian Data Analysis (3rd Edition)*. CRC Press, 2014.

[34] N. Silver, *The signal and the noise: the art and science of prediction*. Penguin UK, 2012.

[35] R. Kelter, "Statistical Rethinking: A Bayesian Course with Examples in R and STAN," 2020.

[36] E. Kost, "What are IOAs? How they differ from IOCs." Online: https://www.upguard.com/blog/what-are-indicators-of-attack, April 2023. Accessed: 2023.08.31.

[37] CrowdStrike, "IOA VS IOC." Online: https://www.crowdstrike.com/cybersecurity-101/indicators-of-compromise/ioa-vs-ioc/, October 2022. Accessed: 2023.08.31.

[38] C. Wilkie, "Colonial Pipeline paid $5 million ransomware one day after cyberattack, CEO tells Senate." Online: https://www.cnbc.com/2021/06/08/colonial-pipeline-ceo-testifies-on-first-hours-of-ransomware-attack.html, 2021. Accessed: 2023.08.01.

[39] A. O. Adetoye, M. Goldsmith, and S. Creese, "Analysis of dependencies in critical infrastructures," in *Critical Information Infrastructure Security: 6th International Workshop, 2011, Lucerne, Switzerland, September 8-9, 2011, Revised Selected Papers 6*, pp. 18–29, Springer, 2013.

[40] P. Kotzanikolaou, M. Theoharidou, and D. Gritzalis, "Interdependencies between critical infrastructures: Analyzing the risk of cascading effects," in *Critical Information Infrastructure Security: 6th International Workshop, CRITIS 2011, Lucerne, Switzerland, September 8-9, 2011, Revised Selected Papers 6*, pp. 104–115, Springer, 2013.

[41] J. Han, "Mining heterogeneous information networks by exploring the power of links," in *International conference on discovery science*, pp. 13–30, Springer, 2009.

[42] Y. Sun and J. Han, "Mining heterogeneous information networks: a structural analysis approach," *Acm Sigkdd Explorations Newsletter*, vol. 14, no. 2, pp. 20–28, 2013.

[43] C. Shi, Y. Li, J. Zhang, Y. Sun, and S. Y. Philip, "A survey of heterogeneous information network analysis," *IEEE Transactions on Knowledge and Data Engineering*, vol. 29, no. 1, pp. 17–37, 2016.

[44] C. Shi, SY. Philip, *Heterogeneous Information Network Analysis and Applications*. Springer, 2017.

[45] Y. Lei, L. Chen, Y. Li, R. Xiao, and Z. Liu, "Robust and fast representation learning for heterogeneous information networks," *Frontiers in Physics*, vol. 11, p. 1196294, 2023.

[46] E. Börger and R. Stärk, *Abstract State Machines: A Method for High-Level System Design and Analysis*. Springer, 2003.

[47] E. Börger, "The ASM refinement method," *Formal Aspects of Computing*, vol. 15, no. 2, pp. 237–257.

[48] N. Nalbandyan, U. Glässer, H. Y. Shahir, and H. Wehn, "Distributed situation analysis: A formal semantic framework," in *Abstract State Machines, Alloy, B, TLA, VDM, and Z: 4th International Conference, ABZ 2014, Toulouse, France, June 2-6, 2014. Proceedings 4*, pp. 158–173, Springer, 2014.

[49] R. Farahbod, V. Gervasi, and U. Glässer, "Executable formal specifications of complex distributed systems with CoreASM," *Science of Computer Programming*, vol. 79, pp. 23–38, 2014.

Raising Awareness in the Industry on Secure Code Review Practices

Andrei-Cristian Iosif
Siemens AG
Munich, Germany
email: andrei-cristian.iosif@siemens.com

Tiago Espinha Gasiba
Siemens AG
Munich, Germany
email: tiago.gasiba@siemens.com

Ulrike Lechner
Universität der Bundeswehr München
Munich, Germany
email: ulrike.lechner@unibw.de

Maria Pinto-Albuquerque
Instituto Universitário de Lisboa (ISCTE-IUL), ISTAR
Lisboa, Portugal
email: maria.albuquerque@iscte-iul.pt

***Abstract*—As products and services become increasingly digital and software increasingly complex, all aspects of an industrial software development lifecycle must contribute to quality. Code review serves as a means to address software quality and fosters knowledge exchange across teams. Nonetheless, code review practices require resources and often require more resources than planned, while the benefit of a code review to code quality is less tangible. In our work, we address the effectiveness and efficiency of code review practices and develop an understanding of what is a good and valuable code review practice as part of a software development lifecycle. Our focus is code reviews meant to identify and address security weaknesses in an industrial context. This work presents a design study on how to design a workshop on code review. We conducted and evaluated three workshops with 37 industrial software developers. The findings of our work reveal that presenting constructive code review practices can contribute to raising awareness of secure coding and software lifecycle practices among software development professionals. This contributes to the quality and, in particular, security of software.**

***Index Terms*—code review, cybersecurity, compliance, development lifecycle, quality, standards**

I. Introduction

As more of the modern world relies on digital infrastructure, ensuring software quality is paramount. To address this issue in a tangible and standardized way, the ISO/IEC 25000 series [1] has been created as an international standard that provides guidelines and frameworks for assessing quality in software, encompassing various characteristics, such as functionality, reliability, usability, efficiency, maintainability, and portability. Among these quality aspects, security is a critical domain, as it ensures the protection of sensitive data and prevention and protection against potential cyber threats. The ISO 27000 series explicitly addresses information security management systems, with ISO/IEC 27001 [2] playing an essential role in establishing and maintaining a comprehensive security framework within organizations.

Cybersecurity threats are constantly evolving, and the security of critical infrastructures is at risk. In developing software for Operational Technology, security is an essential requirement. Code reviews are one of the measures to detect weaknesses in the code and address other quality aspects, such as adhering to standards or policies. In contemporary software development practices, industry practitioners are tasked with creating functioning code, adhering to established standards, and integrating their work within the company's adopted software development lifecycle pipeline without considerable overhead. There is a growing push for standardized processes within companies to ensure consistent and efficient practices in the software industry. Compliance with established standards is crucial for maintaining code quality and security. One way of easing this goal is by employing code review focusing on software security.

To achieve this, exposing practitioners to the concepts and principles behind the code review process is imperative. By providing practitioners with a clear understanding of methodologies, organizations can foster a culture of compliance, enhance code quality, and promote a cohesive approach to software development that adheres to industry best practices. This endeavor requires disseminating knowledge across all organizational levels, ensuring a shared understanding of best practices and methodologies. Interactive workshops serve as effective communication channels for achieving this goal, as participants can engage with theoretical concepts and solidify their understanding through hands-on exercises. By fostering a collaborative learning environment, such workshops empower industry practitioners to enhance their technical skills, align with organizational standards, and contribute to the overall betterment of the software development process.

On the other hand, automation technologies and especially DevSecOps, are promising methods in reducing the human load in auxiliary programming tasks, such as software testing, according to Sánchez-Gordón et al. [3]. Nonetheless, according to Mao et al., [4], these emerging fields come with limitations – Static Code Analysis Tools (SAST), for example, produce reports that often include many false positives that need human attention for filtering. The perceived gain in testing coverage and less human involvement may therefore be lost through manual filtration and, more concerning, distract developers from the false negatives, which are not included in the output of SAST tools, and often require deep insight into the code. Manual code review should, therefore, not be disregarded in security-critical applications, as a professional's scrutiny can catch architecture-level bugs and vulnerabilities, whereas tools often fail, as shown by Kupsch et al. [5].

According to our experience, decision-supporting and process tools must be enriched with human insight to ensure that the software development lifecycle benefits from the team's expertise behind the software products being developed and delivered. For this purpose, our current work aims toward developing and evaluating an educational medium suitable for the industry in which knowledge about code review, including current standards and practical takeaways, can be disseminated effectively.

This paper presents the initial design of a workshop to train industrial software developers in code review. We also present empirical results on the workshop's evaluation and the participants' awareness of software development. The present work poses and systematically addresses the following research questions:

RQ1 What elements of the workshop contribute to raising awareness on security when performing code review, and are important and helpful for the participants when conducting a workshop on code review?

RQ2 How can code review in practice be improved?

RQ3 How do practitioners receiving training on security awareness compare against SAST tools?

Our work follows Action Design Research (ADR) methodology principles, and the present results shall serve as the first step of ADR, with further refinement to be carried out in the following, future design iterations.

The article is organized as follows: Section II provides an overview of related work on code review and the standards that may govern it. Section III follows by presenting the employed methodology. The intervention is then presented in Section IV. Based on the collected results, a discussion is presented in Section V. Finally, Section VI reiterates our work and presents further potential research directions based on the conclusions reached in the present work.

II. Related Work

The foundations of this work rely on established code review standards and workflows, as well as the international standards that govern code review and software security. To elaborate on the workshop's contents, a literature survey was conducted on these two topics, and each of the two shall be discussed in the remainder of this section.

A. Code Review

Code review is a practice that is well established within the software development lifecycle, with one of the first works on formalizing this process being formulated by Fagan [6], [7] – where the author highlights code inspections in mitigating errors during program development. The research emphasizes how early identification and rectification of defects through inspection processes leads to improved software quality and increased productivity.

More recent research in the industry indicates that practitioners consider a review beneficial primarily if the review comments lead to improved code quality, as per Bosu et al. [8]. In another study, MacLeod et al. [9] looked at the defining characteristics of a code review that is perceived as useful by the individuals that changed the code. Their findings highlight the challenges of code review, e.g., the improper focus of the review, uncertainty about the process, and lack of formal training. The authors also provide recommendations for best practices for all stakeholders – reviewers, change authors, and the organization itself.

In his research, W. Charoenwet [10] conducted work on integrating automated program security analysis into the code review workflow. The work acknowledges the limitations of automated findings and plans to design a review-assisting framework based on tool findings. While similar in focus, the research does not account for security standards and is not explicitly targeted at the industrial work practices.

As previously mentioned, the studies serve as a consistent foundation of insights into the benefits and pitfalls of code review, pointing towards the potential trade-offs that need to be considered when opting to integrate code review in an industrial software development context. Though comprehensive, the studies point to a gap in providing the necessary knowledge for developers to perform a code review that is considered beneficial within their teams.

Our work complements the existing body of knowledge on code review by specifically focusing on reviews that aim predominantly at reducing security flaws in code and which follow the current standards. To the best of our knowledge, there is no other ongoing research on raising industrial practitioners' awareness of cybersecurity-focused and standard-compliant code reviews. We aim to heighten practitioners' security awareness without having them rely on decision-supporting tools.

B. Standards

The three standards we broadly covered as part of the workshop presented in this work will be introduced in the remainder of this section.

The ISO/IEC 62443 is an international series of standards that address cybersecurity for Industrial Automation Control Systems (IACS). The standard is divided into sections and describes technical and process-related aspects of automation and control systems cybersecurity. Furthermore, the standard divides the cybersecurity topics by stakeholder category and roles (e.g., operator, service providers, component and system manufacturers). The different roles each follow a risk-based approach to prevent and manage security risks in their activities. This standard includes code review as part of its Secure Development Lifecycle (SDL) requirements for products intended for use in the industrial automation and control systems environment. Specifically, the IEC 62443-4-1 [11] outlines process requirements for the secure development of products used in IACS. One important aspect is that the standard mentions that the people performing the review should have specialized knowledge. This requirement leads to the need for training and awareness, not only for software developers but also for the parties involved in code review. The IEC 62443-4-2 [12] details low-level technical requirements that need to be fulfilled when implementing software for IACS. These requirements must also be taken into consideration during code review.

The ISO/IEC 20246 [13] standard establishes a generic framework for work product reviews. It can be referenced and used by all organizations managing, developing, testing, and maintaining systems and software. The standard contains a generic process, activities, tasks, review techniques, and documentation templates applied during the review of a work product, i.e., any artifact produced by a process. This document defines work product reviews that can be used during any phase of the life cycle of any work product. It is intended for parties involved across all levels – i.e., project managers, development managers, quality managers, test managers, business analysts, developers, testers, customers, and others involved in developing, testing, and maintaining systems and software. Following a code review standard is vital during the SDL process, audits, and accreditation.

From a programming-language perspective, the ISO/IEC TR 24772-1 [14] standard provides low-level guidance to avoiding vulnerabilities in programming. This standard is programming-language agnostic. It specifies vulnerabilities to be avoided in developing systems where assured behavior is required for security, safety, mission-critical, and business-critical software. Another broad secure coding standard is provided by MITRE [15] through the Common Weakness Enumeration (CWE). Our work is based on the 2023 release of this standard. The Open Web Application Security Project (OWASP) releases the OWASP Top 10 [16] standard on a regular basis that is specific to software developed for the web. Our work is based on the 2021 release of this standard.

III. Methodology

The research design is guided by the Action Design Research (ADR) method. As stated by Sein et al. [17], ADR is a research method for generating prescriptive design knowledge through building and evaluating ensemble IT artifacts in an organizational setting. It deals with (1) addressing a problem encountered in a specific organizational setting by intervening and evaluating and (2) constructing and evaluating an IT artifact that addresses the class of problems typified by the encountered situation. ADR is done in close collaboration between researchers and practitioners in an iterative way in which problem understanding, action-taking, and evaluation are closely intertwined.

This research is situated in an industrial software development context in which cybersecurity is paramount. We aim to generate knowledge on code review practices to increase code review effectiveness and to raise awareness for security and code review. Designing and evaluating instruments for training industrial software developers are critical activities in our research design. Two researchers are embedded in an industrial software development context and dispose of several years of experience in industrial software development and secure coding. This industrial context is open to collaborating with academia to bring in new ideas for individual and organizational learning and rigorous evaluation of current practices. In this article, we describe the results from activities undertaken in industrial practice to design a workshop format and content to raise awareness for code review as a practice in the software lifecycle. We report on three workshops and the evaluation of data from the workshops.

The first step in our research process was identifying relevant scholarly literature and findings, de-facto standards and norms on code reviews, software quality, and the software lifecycle. Then, relevant content was selected and tailored to the organization's needs, and a workshop was designed. We developed original code review exercises to be part of this workshop to activate workshop participants and foster transfer from the workshop practice to the everyday job situation.

We conducted three workshops as three separate events with 37 participants between May and June 2023. These workshops included semi-structured interviews for evaluation of the code review training. We analyze data from the interviews, together with the participatory observations. The intervention was conducted in the context of industrial training aimed at professionals in software development for operational technology that are not specialized in cybersecurity.

The three workshops had between 7 and 16 participants. Workshop participants aged between 21 and 63, each with a technical background. The professional functions varied – each of the three workshops included representatives for software developers, project managers, and product owners.

Following the workshop, we conducted semi-structured interviews. All the participants were informed clearly about the purpose of the study. Moreover, it was noted that participation in the review was optional, and the collected results shall be collected anonymously. In total, 20 individual feedbacks were collected. The survey was conducted online via Microsoft Forms, with the participants being granted indefinite access to the questionnaire at the end of the workshop. The interviews conducted in our work follow a semi-structured methodology, as per Wilson et al. [18] – the questions delivered to the participants were aimed towards assessing the workshop's content in terms of balance between the topics it spanned across. The questions are not directly addressing security but rather the workshop design itself. Following the principles of action design research, the initial phase of workshop planning is meant mainly to collect information for further design steps.

IV. Intervention – The Code Review Workshops

A. Design of the Code-Review Training Workshop

The workshop was designed to last a day with a target group of software developers and people holding managerial positions. The delivery method was designed to be suitable for both on-site and remote settings. A vital element of the workshop was an exercise consisting of Python code which contained several security vulnerabilities. The goal of the exercise was for the participants to spot these vulnerabilities through code review. The exercise allowed the participants to put to practice the theoretical concepts that were learned during the workshop.

The covered topics included: a taxonomy of common software vulnerabilities, code review standards, and available security and review tooling, as well as practical examples of exploitation, mitigation, and reviewing methodology. The designed workshop was conducted three times in an industrial setting. Table I summarizes the three interventions. A questionnaire followed each intervention, the contents of which can be observed in Table II.

TABLE I
INDUSTRY INTERVENTIONS

IN	Date	NP	No. CWEs	Delivery	Participants from
1	3.05.2023	14	21	Online	Germany, India
2	25.05.2023	7	21	Online	Germany
3	12.06.2023	16	21	On-site	United Kingdom

IN - Intervention Number, **NP** - Number of Participants

The first two interventions took place online through Microsoft Teams with participants mainly from Germany. During the first workshop, four participants joined the online meeting from India. The third workshop took place on-site in the United Kingdom. We conducted a small survey at the end to evaluate the workshop design. Additional details on the survey are provided in Section IV-C.

B. Design of the Exercise

The exercise was developed to engage participants, as these were tasked to work as a group, with a time limit of 15 minutes, and spot as many potential flaws in the code as possible. Participants were also asked to use the SAST tool *Bandit* [19] to enhance their code review. A discussion based on their findings accompanied the exercise, with opinions being exchanged about what lessons could be drawn.

As this workshop is taking part in an industrial context, a requirement for the delivery was to traverse the contents of the training in a manner with adequate pacing for the given time constraints given for disseminating information to participants.

We, therefore, opted for a compact code snippet with a high density of defects per Line of Code (LoC) - see Appendix. As the participant's programming background was polyglot, we opted for a Python Flask Web Application to serve as a snippet. This choice is due to the popularity and readability of the Python language [20], as well as the rising prevalence of web applications overall – see Collins [21]. Nonetheless, a codebase's security is a quality metric that is considered non-negotiable, according to our experience in the industry as security researchers, irrespective of the type or scope of application – no application meant for an end-customer can be insecure and standards-compliant at the same time.

The specially crafted code, although relatively small, contains a high number of vulnerabilities (22) - this is meant to cover as much of OWASP Top 10 [16] and CWE [15] through the breadth of exposure. Excluding blank lines, `include` statements, and rewrapping a multi-line statements, the snippet comprises thirty-six lines of code. Of the thirty-six LoC, expert security professionals managed to uncover 20 vulnerabilities. This observation translates into an average of 0.55 vulnerabilities per LoC. The annotated snippet is provided as an Appendix to the paper. The exercise targets code defects rather than architectural defects, as the architecture design and planning should be carried out earlier in the lifecycle of an application, and the majority of industry reviews mostly concern themselves with code rather than the underlying architecture.

The exercise under scrutiny serves as a way of quantifying the *behavior* aspect from Hänsch et al. [22] in the broader context of the workshop. In the context of the present study, *Perception* refers to disseminating knowledge of possible issues, *Protection* addresses knowledge of possible countermeasures, and *behavior* describes the observed performance of the participants during practical exercises. Gaining insight into the proposed **RQ**s is intended to lead to a well-designed workshop, such that *Perception*, *Protection*, and *Behavior* of the practitioners can be improved.

C. Empirical Evaluation

The evaluation is done in a semi-structured interview. In the evaluation of the workshop content and perceived usefulness of the workshops to the participants, we refer to the definition of awareness as given by Hänsch et al. [22], who structure awareness into three constituent components: perception (knowledge of issues), protection (available countermeasures) and behavior (individuals actively employing countermeasures).

We group the questions into four distinct categories, as per Table II: keep factors (**K**), reject (discard) factors (**R**), delivery of the content (**D**), and perceived value (**V**). All questions were delivered via Microsoft Forms, with the answering options consisting of freeform text, except for questions **Q11** and **Q12**, which employed a 5-point Likert [23] scale that spanned between "Very unlikely" to "Very likely" and "Very dissatisfying" to "Very satisfying" respectively.

Refering to our driving research questions, answering **RQ1** can be done by observing the answers to the questions pertaining to the keep factors (**K**), as well as the discard factors (**R**) serving as counter-examples.

Observing what participants rank as valuable from the training can provide insight into **RQ2**, with their answers serving as tangible measures of what can be done to improve code review in practice.

V. EVALUATION RESULTS

In total, 20 individual feedback results were collected from the structured interviews across the three interventions.

Regarding keep factors, practical examples were the most mentioned among the participants' answers, with seven mentions across the 20 collected answers.

In terms of discard factors, participants consistently mentioned the medium of delivery for the exercise, as usage of the platform sometimes hindered the intended goal of the exercises. The employed medium for conducting the exercise was Microsoft Conceptboard, a generic collaboration and

TABLE II
SURVEY QUESTIONS

QN	Category	Question
Q1	K	What would you keep from this training?
Q2	R	What would you discard from this training?
Q3	K	What did you find most useful/valuable in this presentation/training?
Q4	D	Was the content presented clearly and effectively?
Q5	R	Were there any parts of the presentation/training that you found confusing or difficult to understand?
Q6	K & R	Did the presentation/training meet your expectations? If not, what could have been improved?
Q7	K	Were there any specific examples or case studies that resonated with you?
Q8	D	Did you feel the presentation/training was engaging and interactive enough?
Q9	V	Did the presentation/training meet your learning objectives?
Q10	K	Were there any additional topics or areas you would have liked to see covered in this presentation/training?
Q11	V	How likely are you to recommend this presentation/training to others?
Q12	V	Overall, how would you rate the quality of the presentation/training?

QN - Question Number, **K** - Keep, **R** - Reject, **D** - Delivery, **V** - Value

brainstorming platform. Approximately half of the participants also expressed a lack of familiarity with the platform, which might influence the perception in this regard. Other negatively received aspects of the training were advanced concepts that were mentioned, but not sufficiently addressed, specifically formal verification and advanced pentesting techniques as supplementary means of code testing. Furthermore, through answers on **Q10**, participants expressed interest in the following additional topics/aspects: receiving supplementary practical guidance, such as a sample code review report and strategies in finding issues.

Focusing on the answers to question **Q3**, which inquires about the most useful part of the presentation, the participants' answers can be clustered into two main categories: practical examples and standards. This clustering is in line with the expectations considering their demographic, as the audience consisted of a balanced crowd of developers and managerial and organizational professionals.

The positive results collected from **Q11** and **Q12** encourage the pursuit of further design cycles – Recommending the training to others was responded to with 50% *Very likely*, 41% *Likely* and 9% *Neutral*; The quality of the training was considered by 58% of the participants to be *Very Satisfying*, 25% reported it as *Satisfying*, and 17% *Neutral*.

In terms of delivery, the participants considered the overall format adequate, sans the delivery method for the exercises. The workshop also contained a dedicated section of *Do's* and *Don't* regarding code review comments, where best practices were suggested. As coding style is often highly a matter of personal preference, some debate was expected. This discussion occurred organically across all three interventions, initiated from the participants' side, and denotes a high degree of implication and opinion, which proved valuable in opening up the workshop for fruitful open discussion concerning what affects and does not affect code security. Through open dialogue, a consensus was reached that coding style does not impact security as long as readability is not negatively impacted.

In addition to the questions from Table II, participants were encouraged to provide additional thoughts they considered worth sharing. This free-form feedback was observed to be more brief and sparse than its semi-structured counterpart.

Some examples of replies from the participants include:

- *"Thank you, I really liked it and am happy to get the slides as a reference for later."*
- *"Consider adapting the exercises to the Conceptboard."*
- *"Keep up the great work. Thanks."*

In order to do a preliminary exploration of **RQ3**, we introduce the metrics collected from the practical exercise in Table III.

TABLE III
NUMBER OF IDENTIFIED VULNERABILITIES

IN	PF	EF	TF
1	11	22	5
2	12	22	5
3	14	22	5

IN - Intervention Number, **PF** - Participant Findings
EF - Expert Findings, **TF** - Tool Findings (SAST tool Bandit)

None of the participants had cybersecurity knowledge or familiarity with Python Flask applications for all three intervention runs. Referring to the discussion following the exercise, participants were positively impressed to see how they outperformed the SAST tool provided to them, considering the group's cumulative experience and the exercise's time limit. Observing the limitation of automated security testing was beneficial to the participants' general awareness of vulnerabilities and the threat of false negatives from tools.

It is interesting to point out that the participants' findings constantly ranked, across all interventions, at approximately the halfway point between the number of findings from the tools and the number of findings from security experts. This indicates that any party involved in the software development lifecycle may positively impact the security of the work product, even after just minimal training.

Furthermore, based on the discussion following the exercise, the participants reached an intended conclusion: deep familiarity with the technology under review (programming language and libraries) is necessary to uncover all underlying security issues fully.

A. Threats to validity

The results of this work rely on data interpreted from the collected from surveying a total of 37 working professionals. The limited number of participants and variance in their backgrounds may introduce bias in the conclusions. Preliminary results are positive for the most part, which could partly be influenced by the voluntary nature of the survey and participant number – a negative reviewer may opt out of feedback submission, and it is typical for participants that are aware of the purpose of a study's purpose to display positive bias.

Nevertheless, the results of this work are in line with previous and related work in the field of security awareness conducted in the industry. This fact, together with the inherent limitation of design science studies carried out in an industrial context, leads us to regard that the formulated conclusions of the present study would not be subject to significant variation if the participant number had been higher.

According to the design science paradigm by Hevner et al., [24], we are dealing with a *wicked problem* – the requirements dealt with in the industry and in practice are unstable and changing, as conducting the interventions cannot be done with respect to a control group, and the demographics of the participants and their capabilities are changing from one run to the other. In this case, conducting a quantitative measurement would constitute a tedious endeavor, and we, therefore, employ the active design methodology laid out by Hevner et al.

As ADR employs iteration across multiple design cycles, the authors would like to expand the participant pool through industrial interventions to gain more refined insight and validate the current results.

B. Lessons Learned

Through investigating **RQ3**, we conclude that SAST tools do not cover all the aspects of code review. Coding guidelines contain both decidable and non-decidable problems – this translates into automated assessment being a helpful decision-supporting mechanism but not a final solution for the adherence to standards.

The false sense of security provided by the tools also translates into a more relaxed attitude during manual code review – practitioners have been observed to sometimes overlook the *banal* security malpractices that are reported by SAST tools while focusing on the more subtle defects introduced in the snippet presented in the exercises.

The series of industrial interventions was conducted together with audiences that were heterogeneous in terms of knowledge and professional role. We have found that our generalist approach to the content of the workshop was suitable for this context, as focus and time could be reallocated dynamically throughout the workshop to suit better the gaps in each of the audience's awareness.

VI. Conclusions and Further Work

As experience in the industry includes adhering to rigorous standards, practitioners at all layers of the software development lifecycle must be made aware of the aspects governing processes that are part of adhering to current standards. In our study, we have observed that, though code review has been established, it is not yet widespread. Although the ISO 20246 standard on code review found its roots in 2008, through IEEE 1028, general awareness of its practice was lacking in our study group. With the inclusion and actualization of formalized code reviews within ISO 62443, companies are sure to include more code reviews in their internal processes. Raising awareness concerning this standard is therefore needed in the industry.

To address this issue, we propose raising awareness of security issues through code review by means of an interactive workshop. In our training, the participants are given a snippet of vulnerable code and are tasked with finding issues within it, similar to a real-life review.

Our work contributes to understanding how to structure a workshop in the industry to address the participants' needs. We evaluated the workshop through semi-structured interviews spanning three separate interventions, throughout which 37 practitioners participated, and feedback from 20 individuals was collected. Preliminary results indicate that the workshop's content, with emphasis on the practical side, was well received. Having the participants formulate some of the workshop's intended takeaway points during follow-up discussions of the hands-on parts of the training serves as substantial validation that the exercises contained in the workshop are fulfilling their purpose of building and raising awareness on code review in the context of software security.

In further work, the authors would like to refine the implementation of the practical exercises toward a serious game. Based on the feedback, the new iteration shall cover elements that would steer the participant's information toward the content while keeping interface and interaction elements at a minimum necessary. Accounting for the current studies' participants, future content may be added in the direction of an appendix of tailored code review checklists based on the intended objective of the review (e.g., audit, release). Furthermore, the authors would like to assess practitioners' current awareness of the interplay between code review and software security by employing a representative survey.

Acknowledgments

This work is partially financed by Portuguese national funds through FCT–Fundação para a Ciência e Tecnologia, I.P., under the projects FCT UIDB/04466/2020 and FCT UIDP/04466/2020. Furthermore, Maria Pinto-Albuquerque thanks the Instituto Universitário de Lisboa and ISTAR, for their support. We acknowledge funding for project CONTAIN by the Federal Ministry of Education and Research under project numbers 13N16581 and 13N16585.

The authors would like to thank Anton Bartl for the useful discussions and provision of the original starting idea for the vulnerable code snippet used in the study.

References

[1] ISO/IEC 25000:2014, "Systems and software engineering – systems and software quality requirements and evaluation (square) – guide to square," International Organization for Standardization, Geneva, CH, Standard, 2014.

[2] ISO/IEC 27001:2013, "Information technology – Security techniques – Information security management systems – Requirements," International Organization for Standardization, Geneva, CH, Standard, 2013.

[3] M. Sánchez-Gordón and R. Colomo-Palacios, "Security as culture: A systematic literature review of DevSecOps," in *Proceedings of the IEEE/ACM 42nd International Conference on Software Engineering Workshops*, ser. ICSEW'20. New York, NY, USA: ACM, 2020, p. 266–269. [Online]. Available: https://doi.org/10.1145/3387940.3392233

[4] R. Mao, H. Zhang, Q. Dai, H. Huang, G. Rong, H. Shen, L. Chen, and K. Lu, "Preliminary Findings about DevSecOps from Grey Literature," in *2020 IEEE 20th International Conference on Software Quality, Reliability and Security (QRS)*, 2020, pp. 450–457.

[5] J. A. Kupsch and B. P. Miller, "Manual vs. Automated Vulnerability Assessment: A Case Study," in *First International Workshop on Managing Insider Security Threats (MIST)*, 06 2009, pp. 83–97. [Online]. Available: pages.cs.wisc.edu/~kupsch/va/ManVsAutoVulnAssessment.pdf

[6] M. Fagan, "Design and code inspections to reduce errors in program development," *IBM Systems Journal*, vol. 38, no. 2.3, pp. 258–287, 1999.

[7] M. Fagan, "A History of Software Inspections," in *Software Pioneers*. Springer Berlin Heidelberg, 2002, pp. 562–573.

[8] A. Bosu, M. Greiler, and C. Bird, "Characteristics of Useful Code Reviews: An Empirical Study at Microsoft," in *2015 IEEE/ACM 12th Working Conference on Mining Software Repositories*, 2015, pp. 146–156.

[9] L. MacLeod, M. Greiler, M.-A. Storey, C. Bird, and J. Czerwonka, "Code reviewing in the trenches: Challenges and best practices," *IEEE Software*, vol. 35, no. 4, pp. 34–42, 2017.

[10] W. Charoenwet, "Complementing Secure Code Review with Automated Program Analysis," in *Proceedings of the 45th International Conference on Software Engineering: Companion Proceedings*, ser. ICSE '23. IEEE Press, 2023, p. 189–191.

[11] ISO/IEC 64223-4-1:2018-1, "ISO/IEC 62443-4-1:2018 Security for industrial automation and control systems - Part 4-1: Secure product development lifecycle requirements," International Organization for Standardization, Geneva, CH, Standard, 1 2018.

[12] ISO/IEC 64223-4-2:2019-12, "Security for Industrial Automation and Control Systems - Part 4-2: Technical Security Requirements for IACS Components," International Electrical Commission, Geneva, CH, Standard, 1 2019, ISBN 978-2-8322-6597-0.

[13] ISO/IEC 20246:2017, "Software and systems engineering – Work product reviews," International Organization for Standardization, Geneva, CH, Standard, 2017.

[14] ISO/IEC TR 24772-1:2019, "Programming languages – Guidance to avoiding vulnerabilities in programming languages – Part 1: Language-independent guidance," International Organization for Standardization, Geneva, CH, Standard, 2019.

[15] "CWE Top 25 Most Dangerous Software Weaknesses," https://cwe.mitre.org/top25/archive/2023/2023_top25_list.html, MITRE Corporation, 2023, online, accessed 2023.07.24.

[16] "OWASP Top 10 - 2021," https://owasp.org/Top10/, OWASP Foundation, 2021, online, accessed 2023.07.24.

[17] M. K. Sein, O. Henfridsson, S. Purao, M. Rossi, and R. Lindgren, "Action Design Research," *MIS Quarterly*, vol. 35, pp. 37–56, 2011.

[18] C. Wilson, "Semi-Structured Interviews," in *Interview Techniques for UX Practitioners*. Burlington, Massachusetts, USA: Elsevier, 2014, pp. 23–41. [Online]. Available: https://doi.org/10.1016/b978-0-12-410393-1.00002-8

[19] "Bandit," https://pypi.org/project/bandit, PyCQA, 2023, online, accessed 2023.07.24.

[20] GitHub, "Why Python Keeps Growing, Explained," https://github.blog/2023-03-02-why-python-keeps-growing-explained/, March 2023, online, accessed 2023.07.24.

[21] V. Collins, "Why You Don't Need to Make an App: A Guide for Startups Who Want to Make an App," https://www.forbes.com/sites/victoriacollins/2019/04/05/why-you-dont-need-to-make-an-app-a-guide-for-startups-who-want-to-make-an-app/, April 2019, online, accessed 2023.07.24.

[22] N. Hänsch and Z. Benenson, "Specifying IT Security Awareness," in *Proceedings - International Workshop on Database and Expert Systems Applications, DEXA*. Munich, Germany: IEEE, 12 2014, pp. 326–330.

[23] R. Likert, "A Technique for the Measurement of Attitudes." *Archives of psychology*, vol. 22, no. 140, pp. 1–55, 6 1932, . [Online]. Available: https://legacy.voteview.com/pdf/Likert_1932.pdf

[24] A. Hevner, S. March, J. Park, and S. Ram, "Design Science in Information Systems Research," *Management Information Systems Quarterly*, vol. 28, pp. 75–, 03 2004.

APPENDIX - VULNERABLE FLASK APP

Listing 1. Code snippet used for manual review

```
import sqlite3, random
from flask import Flask, abort, request, jsonify
from flask_cors import CORS

app = Flask(__name__)
CORS(app)
database = './login.db'

def create_response(message):
    response = jsonify({'message': message})
    response.headers.add('Access-Control-Allow-
        Origin', '*')
    # TODO Ticket: id91263
    return response

@app.route('/setup', methods=['POST'])
def setup():
    connection = sqlite3.connect(database)
    SECRET_PASSWORD = "letMeIn!";
    THIS_IS_A_VARIABLE = "WBneKJwlfHch8Qd3XFUS";
    print("Super Secret Password SSH Server Password
         to 10.10.10.1:22: " + SECRET_PASSWORD)
    connection.executescript('CREATE TABLE IF NOT
        EXISTS login(username TEXT NOT NULL UNIQUE,
        password TEXT NOT NULL);INSERT OR IGNORE
        INTO login VALUES("user_1","123456");')
    return create_response('Setup done!')

@app.route('/login', methods=['POST'])
def login():
    username = request.json['username']
    password = request.json['password']
    connection = sqlite3.connect(database)
    cursor = connection.cursor()
    cursor.execute('SELECT * FROM login WHERE
        username = "%s" AND password = "%s"' % (
        username, password))
    user = cursor.fetchone()
    if user:
        response = create_response('Login successful
            !')
        response.set_cookie('SESSIONID', str(random.
            randint(1,9999999999999999999999)),
            httponly=False,secure=False)
        response.set_cookie('TESTID1', str("
            TESTSTRING1"), httponly=True,secure=True
            )
        response.set_cookie('TESTID2', str("
            TESTSTRING2"))
        return response
    else:
        response = create_response('Login failed!')
        response.delete_cookie('username')
        return response, 401

if __name__ == "__main__":
    app.run(host='0.0.0.0', port=8080, debug=True)
```

Challenges in Medical Device Communication: A Review of Security and Privacy Concerns in Bluetooth Low Energy (BLE)

Michail Terzidis
CERTH - ITI
Thessaloniki, Greece
email : terzmich@iti.gr

Notis Mengidis
CERTH - ITI
Thessaloniki, Greece
email : nmengidis@iti.gr

Georgios Rizos
CERTH - ITI
Thessaloniki, Greece
email : grizos@iti.gr

Mariana S. Mazi
CERTH - ITI
Thessaloniki, Greece
email : msmazi@iti.gr

Konstantina Milousi
CERTH - ITI
Thessaloniki, Greece
email : kmilousi@iti.gr

Antonis Voulgaridis
CERTH - ITI
Thessaloniki, Greece
email : antonismv@iti.gr

Konstantinos Votis
CERTH - ITI
Thessaloniki, Greece
email : kvotis@iti.gr

***Abstract*—The employment of medical devices and sensors in healthcare is growing rapidly each year, as their contribution in diagnosis and treatment is immeasurable. Given the paramount importance of security and privacy in the healthcare sector, the increasing number of devices in the industry also brings a rise in potential targets for exploitation and security misconfigurations. Most of these devices communicate using Bluetooth Low Energy (BLE), and despite BLE's advantage in providing a communication protocol characterized by low energy consumption, an indispensable requirement for medical applications, its simplified protocol stack and general architecture render it susceptible to various security and privacy flaws. Consequently, a comprehensive analysis of the BLE protocol becomes imperative in order to assess the security aspects of medical devices thoroughly. Furthermore, this analysis aims to identify the most critical vulnerabilities and specific attacks targeting the Bluetooth protocol that necessitate mitigation and remediation.**

***Keywords*-Bluetooth; BLE; Internet of Things; IoT; Cybersecurity; Medical Devices.**

I. Introduction

The development and widespread adoption of the Internet of Things (IoT) have given rise to a significant proliferation of smart medical devices and sensors designed to record, store, and transmit data. These technological advancements find diverse applications, with a notable emphasis on their integration into the medical field. Within the healthcare sector, such medical devices and sensors are deployed to enhance the quality of patient care, encompassing a range of examples such as heart rate monitors, blood pressure monitors, blood glucose monitors, insulin pumps, and implantable cardiac devices.

In order to achieve seamless interoperability, many of these medical devices and sensors rely on wireless communication protocols. Among the key considerations in choosing a communication technology that enables interconnection in IoT applications is low power consumption, making Bluetooth Low Energy (BLE) an increasingly favored option, as stated in the Bluetooth Marker Research report of 2020 [4]. However, as mentioned in [9], [13] and [14] the simplicity of Bluetooth's protocol stack also gives rise to certain inherent security and privacy vulnerabilities.

The issue of medical device security has garnered significant concern within the healthcare sector, particularly in the wake of several incidents involving malicious attacks. R. Horton in [1] shared his research, which uncovered plenty of cases where, Bluetooth was the reason for the recall of thousands of medical devices, which raised a lot of concerns in the patients that were in need of these devices. BLE, has potential security risks, which in turn can impact the security of the interconnected devices. Consequently, a more robust security and vulnerability assessment process becomes imperative to identify flaws in BLE's security architecture, delineate specific Bluetooth-related attack vectors, and propose effective mitigation strategies. These measures are essential to uphold security and privacy standards within healthcare IoT environments.

In Section 2, we provide a background for medical devices and the Bluetooth protocol followed by a presentation of the security issues of the BLE protocol and an overview of various attacks against it in Section 3. In the concluding section, a detailed examination of Bluetooth attack incidents in healthcare is presented along with an analysis of pertinent mitigation techniques.

II. Background

Medical devices have changed from the once non-networked and isolated equipment to devices with one-way vendor monitoring, to fully networked equipment with bi-directional communications, remote access, wireless connectivity, and software. Thus, with software increasingly embedded into medical devices, the transition to Software-as-a-Medical-Device (SaMD) has occurred [2]. The global wearable medical devices market size was estimated at USD 28.15 billion in 2022 and is expected to hit over USD 169.58 billion by 2030 with a registered Compound Annual Growth Rate (CAGR) of 25.6% from 2022 to 2030 [3]. Further accentuating the expansion of wearable medical devices, the 2020 Bluetooth Market Research report highlights the significant impact of the COVID-19 pandemic on this sector. Consequently, the healthcare wearable market, encompassing connected blood pressure monitors, continuous glucose monitors, pulse oximeters, and electrocardiogram monitors, witnessed a surge in demand, resulting in 12 million shipments in 2020 alone. This upward trajectory is anticipated to continue, with projected shipments reaching 52 million in 2025 [4]. BLE is currently used in many types of medical devices that have been approved and cleared by the Food and Drug Administration (FDA), including Blood pressure, Blood Glucose Meter, Continuous Glucose Meter, Pulse oximeter, Thermometer, Weight scale, Insulin pump, Cardiac implant, Electrocardiogram and Prosthetics [12].

A. *Security and privacy in healthcare*

Many consumers and clinicians are eager to adopt and use medical devices and health-related technologies to promote health and well-being. Nevertheless, despite the potential benefits in terms of enhanced efficiency and cost, the integration of such technologies also necessitates the careful examination and resolution of concerns pertaining to security and privacy.

Vulnerabilities identified in the Bluetooth protocol have rendered certain Bluetooth-enabled medical devices susceptible to exploitation. This concern has been further underscored by reported incidents of Bluetooth attacks against defibrillators, according to a recent report by WIRED [5]. The study, conducted by security experts affiliated with a Midwestern medical facility chain over a span of two years, revealed critical security weaknesses in medical devices utilizing Bluetooth technology. Despite the fact that Bluetooth technology has given diabetes patients a more efficient and effective way to manage their diabetes by providing them with the ability to easily monitor their blood glucose levels, it is crucial to acknowledge the potential risks associated with its usage. As presented in [6], individuals in close proximity can potentially exploit this technology through Man-in-the-Middle and eavesdropping attacks. Notably, even seemingly innocuous wearable devices like smartwatches and smart bracelets, which also employ Bluetooth communication channels, are not exempt from vulnerability to Bluetooth-based attacks, as demonstrated by the findings of Bitdefender experts [7], [8].

B. *Basic architecture of Bluetooth Low Energy protocol*

BLE was first introduced in the Bluetooth 4.x version, released in June 2010. Bluetooth, specifically BLE, has become the preferred technology for IoT devices [9]. Bluetooth Low Energy is regarded as a different technology that specifically targets markets where the demand is for ultra-low power rather than high throughput [48]. This low energy version of Bluetooth could positively affect IoT technology, by giving devices the ability to exist and successfully function in a wide variety of application scenarios [9].

The main building blocks of the BLE protocol stack [13] are the controller, which includes the hardware to transmit and receive data and the host, which enables applications to scan, discover, connect, and exchange information with peer devices. The communication between those two parts is done through the Host Controller Interface (HCI). The BLE Protocol Stack has the following functionalities [48]:

- ATT (Attribute Control Protocol) : is a client-server-based stateless low-level protocol that defines data exchange between a client and a server.
- GAP (Generic Access Profile): specifies device roles, modes and procedures for the discovery of devices and services, the management of connection establishment and security.
- SM (Security Manager): controls the pairing mechanism, key distribution and key management of a device. It is also responsible to encrypt and decrypt data.
- GATT (Generic Attribute Profile): defines a framework that uses the ATT for the discovery of services, and the exchange of characteristics from one device to another.

The security properties of a BLE connection are defined primarily through the selected security mode, security level and the used pairing method. BLE protocol was introduced in version 4.0 and was later developed through versions 4.1, 4.2, and 5.0x.

III. PROBLEM STATEMENT

A. *Inherent security issues of the BLE protocol*

The pairing process in Bluetooth and BLE has been identified as a significant contributor to security issues, as highlighted in [14]. Attacks can be executed at various stages, both prior to its completion and after successful device pairing.

Notably, the authentication challenge requests during pairing are unrestricted in number, thereby providing a potential attack surface for adversaries to accumulate challenge responses, which may reveal information about the secret link key [14].

Furthermore, if the storage of link keys is poorly implemented, then an adversary can view or even modify them. An additional vulnerability derives from the encryption key's minimum length, which can be as short as a single byte. This relatively limited key length could undermine the overall security of the system. Additionally, it is crucial to acknowledge that the Bluetooth standard incorporates only device authentication, lacking the additional layer of user authentication. Finally, another vulnerability lies in the indefinite duration of a device's discoverable/connectable mode. This opens a window of opportunity for potential attackers to exploit the device's accessibility over an extended period [14].

B. *BLE attacks*

In this section, we describe attacks like Man in The Middle (MiTM), Denial of Service (DOS), Eavesdropping and how to implement them against the BLE protocol, but also some BLE-specific attacks like the treacherous attacks, distortion and others that can be implemented because of specific BLE vulnerabilities.

Passive Eavesdropping attacks

This type of attack as mentioned in [15], refers to the unauthorized access and monitoring of Bluetooth communications and involves the use of specialized software and hardware tools capable of intercepting and analyzing Bluetooth traffic. Within this context, attackers can execute a passive sniffing attack, wherein they position themselves along the data transmission path. The susceptibility of BLE to this attack is particularly pronounced due to its simplified and predictable channel hopping design.

Active Eavesdropping attacks

In addition to the previous type of attack, where an attacker monitors Bluetooth communication, in this attack he also tries to steal sensitive data. MiTM and Replay are two variations of active eavesdropping attacks.

- In the context of BLE, a conventional MiTM approach faces a limitation, as it cannot establish simultaneous connections to both communication endpoints. Hence, executing a BLE MiTM attack necessitates the utilization of two components with the capability to act in unison. For instance, in a scenario involving a mobile app attempting to communicate with a smart device, one of the components can be employed to establish a connection with the mobile app while posing as the smart device, while the other component simultaneously connects to the smart device while posing as the mobile app. This dual-component approach enables the MiTM attacker to intercept and manipulate the data being exchanged between the communication parties [8].
- Replay attack is a common form of attack for wireless communications where the attacker captures legit communication packets and then re-transmits those packets at a later time. After intercepting the packets, the attacker can simply re-transmit the whole intercepted packet; an example of such attack, performed on a smart lock, is described in [16].

Device Cloning

In this type of attack, the attacker tries to deceive the target by assuming the identity of a trusted device, thereby misleading them into establishing a connection. Afterwards, in the case of successful connection, he tries to actively steal the victim's data and cause notable damage to the victim's devices. To perform this type of attack, an attacker should spoof his MAC address, name, and GATT characteristics to confuse the victim.

- MAC spoofing : The attacker spoofs the MAC address as well as GATT services. By employing specialized software tools like Gattacker, the attacker effectively replicates the GATT services of the original peripheral device, thereby assuming the role of a counterfeit peripheral entity [17].
- Forced Repairing : BLE devices, upon their initial connection, undergo a process of pairing and bonding, wherein a Long-Term Key (LTK) is generated. In this attack, the attacker tricks the paired devices to undergo the unpairing process and initiate a new connection. Unpairing two connected devices itself is not an inherently malicious act, however after successfully carrying out this attack, the malicious actor has the ability to launch more severe attacks such as eavesdropping passively or even actively performing a MiTM attack.

Cryptographic Vulnerabilities

In these type of attacks, the attackers try to compromise the encryption of the communication protocol, exploiting inherent cryptographic weaknesses and flawed key exchange mechanisms within the BLE protocol. Some of the most prominent attacks in the aforementioned category are the following:

- Offline PIN cracking attack : PIN Cracking attack can be done in many ways, such as using brute force to crack the PIN, another way is to use a dictionary with a set of possible given PINs, also known as dictionary attack. The security vulnerability of BLE is that the length of the Temporary Key (TK) to generate the encryption key is too short, as described in [18].
- Device Authentication attack : This attack is feasible because of a cryptographic weakness of the passkey-based pairing of BLE. The authors of [19] describe how an active fraudulent Responder can bypass passkey authentication, despite it being based on a one-time generated PIN.
- BlueMirror attacks : BlueMirror is a collection of seven attacks published in May 2021 [29] of which three affect BLE pairing. During a reflection attack an intruder collects a message in the authentication protocol, then sends it without modification to the original sender.
- BLUR attacks : The Bluetooth standard (v4.2) introduced Cross-Transport Key Derivation (CTKD). CTKD allows establishing BT and BLE pairing keys just by pairing over one of the two transports. The authors in [30] present the first complete description of CTKD obtained by merging the information from the Bluetooth standard with the results from their reverse-engineering experiments. These attacks allow to impersonate, MiTM, and establish connectins with arbitrary devices.

Denial of Service

Similarly to traditional DoS attacks, the goal is to make the resources of the system unavailable to the intended users. In BLE, the attacker primarily targets the master, so that the slave cannot get proper services in the BLE mesh network. Some of the most prominent attacks in the literature are:

- Battery Exhaustion Attack : One of the main features of BLE is its brief wake period, during which it facilitates data transfers before returning to its sleep mode once more. [20]. This attack targets this unique feature of BLE by keeping the device awake. Bluetooth piconet is subject to this form of attack [21].
- Denial of Sleep : When data from the base sensing layer is provided by low power technologies, such as BLE, a

class of vulnerabilities called Denial of Sleep attacks can be especially damaging to the network. These attacks can reduce the lifespan of the sensing nodes by several orders of magnitude, rendering the network unusable [22].

- Jamming : Jamming describes the deliberate blocking, and therefore suppression of specific parts of a communication or the target medium as a whole [13]. By jamming only packets sent by the peripheral to the central device, an attacker can trigger the timeout in the central device. Since the timeout was triggered only in the central device the attacker can step in as central device and hijack the BLE connection. This attack was published in 2018 by Damien Cauquil and implemented in the tool BtleJack [23].

Treacherous

The authors of [36] describe the treacherous attacks, as the type of attacks that are based on establishing a trusted relation between the devices and then breaking the trust. That way, the attacker can gain full access to the system and exploit it. There are two different attacks mentioned:

- The Backdoor Attack is the method of gaining trust of the victim device through the pairing mechanism. It ensures that the attacker's device does not appear on the victims list of paired devices. In this way, the attacker can monitor the activities of the victim device.
- Blue-Bump is a social engineering technique [47]. First, the attacker sends a file and gains the trust of the victim. Then the attacker persuades the victim to delete the link key that was established during the transaction by keeping the connection open. While the victim is unaware of the open connection, the attacker requests the victim to initiate another link-key. Now, the attacker device remains concealed in the paired list of the victim device and remains connected with the victim. To the victim the attacker device seems like a complete new device.

Distortion

Here, the attacker exploits the vulnerability of BLE protocol services like GATT, L2CAP (Logical Link Control and Adaptation Layer Protocol) or BLE data packets and tries to disrupt the services of the BLE devices.

- Fuzzing : Fuzzing involves writing invalid values to characteristics [24]. Characteristics are data fields which hold atomic values. As a consequence of fuzzing, the BLE server can start behaving abnormally, and in severe cases, it can even lead to the crashing of the GATT server. Prior to commencing the attack, a comprehensive understanding of the characteristics present in the victim's GATT server is required. This can be easily done by an active scan, but once the characteristic handle is obtained and is writable, then the attacker can write random values to it.
- Blue Smack : Both Bluetooth classic and BLE use L2CAP for data transmission services. In this attack, the attacker targets L2CAP protocol and disrupts its services. This is also known as the ping of death attack [25].

Surveillance

Due to the architectural design issues of the protocol and lack of proper security enforcement, attackers can gather information about a person's identity as well as personal data.

- Fingerprinting : Device fingerprinting is a technique of identifying a device uniquely using different device-specific features, such as MAC Addresses, Universal Unique Identifier (UUID), advertisement packets, GATT services, etc. [26].
- Blue Printing : Blue Printing is a technique to collect detailed information, such as device model, manufacturer, International Mobile Equipment Identity (IMEI), and software versions. It is not a severe attack, but it results in privacy leakage issues, as shown in [27].
- Blue-stumbling : It is the method of randomly searching for Bluetooth devices to find suitable targets to attack. It is mostly done in crowded places where a large number of Bluetooth devices are available. In this case, attackers mainly search for victims, marking the devices with more security flaws that could be potentially be exploited. This process, even though does not cause any harm to the victims directly, serves as the initial step to initiate an attack [36].
- Blue-Tracking is the method of tracing the location of a victim by following the signal of their Bluetooth Device. It is not meant to steal information from the victim. The attacker has no access to any content of the victim device [28].

IV. Challenges and Countermeasures

The Sweyn-Tooth vulnerabilities [31], one of the most recent sets of vulnerabilities, have the potential to affect devices using the BLE protocol. The vulnerabilities expose flaws in particular BLE SoC implementations, which enable an attacker within radio range to initiate deadlocks, crashes, buffer overflows, or completely bypass security.

One of the earliest works showing the vulnerabilities of medical devices is the seminal study by Halperinet al. [32], which introduced attacks on an Implantable Cardiac Defibrillator (ICD), compromising the confidentiality, integrity, and availability of the device. Similar attacks were also later shown in insulin pumps [33], Fitbit trackers [34], medical infusion pumps [35]. Several studies have also explored information disclosure vulnerabilities in Bluetooth-enabled wearable devices [36].

A proof-of-concept attack, executed by experts at Bitdefender [46], targeted a Samsung smartwatch that was paired with a Google Nexus smartphone. Exploiting sniffing tools, researchers were able to uncover the PIN used to protect the smartwatch and the smartphone connection. In this case, an attacker could easily perform a brute-force attack on the PIN, as the "key space" is composed of only 1 million possible key combinations. The vulnerability is in the Link Manager Protocol and can be remediated by the manufacturer by requiring a password for Bluetooth pairing, as well as implementing encryption for the data communication.

Concerning BLE fitness bands [40] and health devices [34], it has been shown that an attacker can very easily access a lot of personal data, read the various health sensor data [41] or even guess what the user is typing by analyzing the motion sensors data from wearable wrist devices [42].

Glucose monitors can be connected to companion smart apps on smartphones, which not only capture data, but also send alerts to patients. The technology can be exploited by individuals in close range, and MiTM and eavesdropping attacks can be executed [43]. During these attacks, data being communicated between the devices could be intercepted, decrypted, and captured.

A. *Mitigation strategies*

Given the open nature of wireless technologies, preventing all attacks and guaranteeing security is a very challenging task, however, there are several countermeasures that can be applied to provide a reasonable security level.

Several mitigation strategies designed specifically for BLE applications have been proposed over the years. Notably, in reference to [37], the authors present various sets of rules for users to help them perform actions safely, thereby minimizing the susceptibility to potential attacks. They describe how to use your BLE devices in your environment as well as underscore the significance of regularly updating the firmware of such devices. Of particular importance is the usage of a lengthy PIN during the authentication phase when establishing connections with other devices. Ensuring that this PIN is not only lengthy but also randomly generated enhances its resilience against brute-force attacks, akin to the practice employed in altering phone passwords, as also mentioned in [14]. The authors also suggest the adoption of link encryption for all data transmissions as a means to prevent eavesdropping, while the utilization of the maximum encryption key size is emphasized to fortify protection against brute-force attacks.

In recent times, there has been a notable emergence of BLE security testing frameworks aimed at evaluating the security of applications. One such framework, as described in [24], encompasses various software components designed to carry out attacks like MiTM, DoS by flooding, and fuzzing. The principal objective of this particular BLE security testing framework is to present an integrated approach for assessing the security of BLE networks through the execution of multiple attacks on the network and its associated devices.

Additionally, [38] introduces an innovative framework, known as MARC, which is specifically tailored to identifying MiTM attacks in HealthCare BLE systems. The primary purpose of this framework is to detect, analyze, and mitigate Bluetooth security vulnerabilities, with a specific focus on MiTM attacks targeting NiNo devices. To achieve this, a comprehensive solution has been proposed which utilizes four novel anomaly detection metrics for detecting MiTM signatures. These metrics involve the analysis of malicious scan requests, advertisement intervals, Received Signal Strength Indicator (RSSI) levels, and cloned node addresses.

The authors in [39] present an automated security assessment framework designed specifically for Wearable BLE-enabled Health Monitoring Devices. This framework encompasses four distinct stages, beginning with the initial phase of information gathering. During this stage, the focus is on identifying the assets, their interactions, and comprehending the overall system workflow. Subsequently, the threat modelling phase is executed, followed by a thorough vulnerability analysis, and ultimately, the exploitation phase.

The efficiency of this framework has been empirically evaluated by conducting tests on a variety of medical devices, such as the Athos Smart Apparel. This particular wearable system seamlessly integrates surface electromyography (sEMG) technology, Smart Fitness Trackers, and Electrocardiogram (ECG) trackers. The outcomes of these assessments have revealed interesting findings, underscoring the framework's value in enhancing the security posture of such health monitoring devices.

V. Conclusion

Maintaining a balance between security and design goals remains a challenging task and requires closer collaboration between manufacturers, security researchers, and clinicians. As the popularity of Bluetooth continues to grow and it is incorporated into more aspects of everyday life, it's very important that users understand the risks involved with using Bluetooth. Even more important is that they work to mitigate those risks by following the recommended security guidelines.

Both academia and industry researchers and practitioners are presently collaborating to address certain open research challenges aiming to enhance the performance of BLE, like the improvement and design of the physical layer, specifically the radio or PHY mode introduced in BLE v5.x. [44]. Additionally, the investigation of adaptive parameter settings [48] and the utilization of random back-off mechanisms to retry channel sensing for more efficient device discovery appears to be quite promising in identifying devices within crowded environments. Finally, research topics such as the role switching between central and peripheral devices based on events, the coexistence of BLE with other wireless technologies, as well as adaptive frequency hopping techniques to avoid interference, are expected to enrich our understanding, inform practical applications, and stimulate further research.

Acknowledgment

This research has been co-financed by the European Regional Development Fund of the European Union and Greek national funds through the Operational Program Competitiveness, Entrepreneurship and Innovation, under the call RESEARCH – CREATE - INNOVATE (project code:T2EDK-03093)

References

[1] R. Horton, "What We Can Learn From Bluetooth Medical Device Recalls," orthogonal.io/bluetooth [retrieved: August, 2023]

[2] P. A. Williams and A. J. Woodward, "Cybersecurity vulnerabilities in medical devices: a complex environment and multifaceted problem," Med Devices (Auckl), vol. 8, pp. 305—316, 20 Jul 2015. Doi: https://doi.org/10.2147/MDER.S50048

[3] "Medical devices market", www.fortunebusinessinsights.com [retrieved: August, 2023]

[4] "How bluetooth technology is enabling safe return strategies in a COVID-19 era", www.bluetooth.com [retrieved: August, 2023]

[5] K. Zetter, "It is insanely easy to hack hospital equipment". Available online: www.wired.com [retrieved: August, 2023]

[6] M. Kijewski, "Medical devices most vulnerable to hackers". Available online: www.medtechintelligence.com [retrieved: August, 2023]

[7] P. Paganini, Smartwatch Hacked, "How to access data exchanged with smartphone". Available online: www.securityaffairs.com [retrieved: August, 2023]

[8] T. Melamed, "An active man-in-the-middle attack on bluetooth smart devices". International Journal of Safety and Security Engineering, vol. 8, pp. 200-211, 2018. Doi: https://doi.org/10.2495/SAFE-V8-N2-200-211

[9] A. M. Lonzetta, P. Cope, J. Campbell, B. J. Mohd, and T. Hayajneh, "Security vulnerabilities in bluetooth technology as used in IoT," J. Sens Actuator Netw, 2018. Doi: https://doi.org/10.3390/jsan7030028

[10] "Bluetooth Low Energy A Complete Guide", www.novelbits.io [retrieved: August, 2023]

[11] A. Barua, M. A. Al Alamin, M. S. Hossain and E. Hossain, "Security and Privacy Threats for Bluetooth Low Energy in IoT and Wearable Devices: A Comprehensive Survey," in IEEE Open Journal of the Communications Society, vol. 3, pp. 251-281, 2022, doi: 10.1109/OJCOMS.2022.3149732

[12] W. Saltzstein, "Bluetooth wireless technology cybersecurity and diabetes technology devices," Journal of Diabetes Science and Technology, vol. 14, no. 6, pp. 1111-1115, 2020. Doi: 10.1177/1932296819864416

[13] M. Cäsar, T. Pawelke, J. Steffan, and G. Terhorst, "A survey on bluetooth low energy security and privacy," Computer Networks, vol. 205, p. 108712, 2022. Doi: https://doi.org/10.1016/j.comnet.2021.108712

[14] P. Cope, J. Campbell, and T. Hayajneh, "An investigation of bluetooth security vulnerabilities," IEEE 7th Annual Computing and Communication Workshop and Conference (CCWC), Las Vegas, NV, USA, pp. 1-7, 2017. Doi: 10.1109/CCWC.2017.7868416

[15] F.R. Maruf and A. Nasr, "Eavesdropping in bluetooth networks," International Journal of Current Engineering and Technology.www.researchgate.net [retrieved: August, 2023]

[16] S. Jasek, "GATTacking bluetooth smart devices," Tech. rep., SecuRing, p. 15, www.paper.bobylive.com [retrieved: August, 2023]

[17] Gattacker, "A Node.js package for BLE (Bluetooth Low Energy) Man-in-the-Middle & more". www.github.com/gattacker [retrieved: August, 2023]

[18] G. Kwon, J. Kim, J. Noh, and S. Cho, "Bluetooth low energy security vulnerability and improvement method," IEEE International Conference on Consumer Electronics-Asia (ICCE-Asia), Seoul, Korea (South), pp. 1-4, 2016. Doi: 10.1109/ICCE-Asia.2016.7804832

[19] Rosa, "Bypassing passkey authentication in Bluetooth low energy", 2013, www.eprint.iacr.org [retrieved: August, 2023]

[20] C. Gomez, J. Oller, and J. Paradells, "Overview and Evaluation of Bluetooth Low Energy: An Emerging Low-Power Wireless Technology Sensors," Sensors 12, no. 9, pp. 11734-11753, 2012 Doi: https://doi.org/10.3390/s120911734

[21] T. Martin, M. Hsiao, D. Ha, and J. Krishnaswami, "Denial-of-service attacks on battery-powered mobile computers," Second IEEE Annual Conference on Pervasive Computing and Communications, pp. 309-318, 2004. Doi: 10.1109/PERCOM.2004.1276868

[22] J. Uher, R. G. Mennecke and B. S. Farroha, "Denial of Sleep attacks in Bluetooth Low Energy wireless sensor networks," MILCOM IEEE Military Communications Conference, Baltimore, MD, USA, pp. 1231-1236, 2016, Doi: 10.1109/MILCOM.2016.7795499

[23] D. Cauquil, "You'd better secure your BLE devices, or we'll kick your butts!," www.virtuallabs.fr [retrieved: August, 2023]

[24] A. Ray, V. Raj, M. Oriol, A. Monot and S. Obermeier, "Bluetooth Low Energy Devices Security Testing Framework," IEEE 11th International Conference on Software Testing, Verification and Validation (ICST), Västerås, Sweden, pp. 384-393, 2018. doi: 10.1109/ICST.2018.00045

[25] R. Nasim, "Security threats analysis in bluetooth-enabled mobile devices". arXiv:1206.1482

[26] C. Zuo, H. Wen, Z. Lin, and Y. Zhang, "Automatic Fingerprinting of Vulnerable BLE IoT Devices with Static UUIDs from Mobile Apps," in Proceedings of the ACM SIGSAC Conference on Computer and Communications Security, pp. 1469–1483, 2019. Doi: https://doi.org/10.1145/3319535.3354240

[27] C. Herfurt, C. Martin and C. Mulliner, "Remote Device Identification based on Bluetooth Fingerprinting Techniques".www.researchgate.net [retrieved: August, 2023]

[28] P. Lloyd, "Blue Tracking". www.scribd.com/Blue-Tracking. [retrieved: August, 2023]

[29] T. Claverie and J. L. Esteves, "BlueMirror: Reflections on Bluetooth Pairing and Provisioning Protocols," 2021 IEEE Security and Privacy Workshops (SPW), San Francisco, CA, USA, 2021, pp. 339-351, Doi: 10.1109/SPW53761.2021.00054

[30] BLURtooth: "Exploiting cross-transport key derivation in Bluetooth Classic and Bluetooth Low Energy", arXiv:2009.11776

[31] Swentooth, Unleashing Mayhem over Bluetooth Low Energy, www.github.com/sweyntooth [retrieved: August, 2023]

[32] D. Halperin, T. S. Heydt-Benjamin, K. Fu, T. Kohno, and W. H. Maisel, "Security and privacy for implantable medical devices," in IEEE Pervasive Computing, vol. 7, no. 1, pp. 30-39, 2008. Doi : 10.1109/MPRV.2008.16

[33] J. Radcliffe, "Hacking medical devices for fun and insulin: Breaking the human SCADA system," in Black Hat Conference Presentation Slides. www.media.blackhat.com [retrieved: August, 2023]

[34] M. Rahman, B. Carbunar, and M. Banik, "Fit and vulnerable: Attacks and defenses for a health monitoring device," in Proceedings of the 6th Workshop on Hot Topics in Privacy Enhancing Technologies. arXiv 2013, arXiv:1304.5672

[35] Y. Park, Y. Son, H. Shin, D. Kim, and Y. Kim, "This ain't your dose: Sensor spoofing attack on medical infusion pump," in Proceedings of the 10th USENIX Workshop on Offensive Technologies.www.usenix.org/ [retrieved: August, 2023]

[36] S. S. Hassan, S. D. Bibon, M. S. Hossain, and M. Atiquzzaman, "Security threats in bluetooth technology," Comput. Secur. pp. 308–322, 2018. Doi: 10.1016/j.cose.2017.03.008

[37] S. Shrestha, E. Irby, R. Thapa, and S. Das, "A Systematic Literature Review of Bluetooth Security Threats and Mitigation Measures," in Computer and Information Science, vol. 1403, pp. 108–127, 2022. Doi: https://doi.org/10.1007/978-3-030-93956-4_7

[38] M. Yaseen et al. "A Novel Framework for Detecting MiTM Attacks in eHealthcare BLE Systems," Journal of Medical Systems vol. 43, p. 324, 2019. Doi: https://doi.org/10.1007/s10916-019-1440-0

[39] G. A. Zendehdel, R. Kaur, I. Chopra, N. Stakhanova, and E. Scheme, "Automated Security Assessment Framework for Wearable BLE-enabled Health Monitoring Devices," ACM Trans. Internet Technol, vol. 22, no. 14, pp. 1-31, 2021. Doi: https://doi.org/10.1145/3448649

[40] W. Zhou and S. Piramuthu, "Security/privacy of wearable fitness tracking IoT devices," Proc. 9th Iberian Conf. Inf. Syst. Technol. (CISTI), pp. 1-5, 2014. Doi: 10.1109/CISTI.2014.6877073

[41] O. Arias, J. Wurm, K. Hoang and Y. Jin, "Privacy and security in Internet of Things and wearable devices," IEEE Trans. Multi-Scale Comput. Syst., vol. 1, no. 2, pp. 99-109, 2015. Doi: 10.1109/TMSCS.2015.2498605

[42] H. Wang, T. T.-T. Lai and R. R. Choudhury, "MoLe: Motion leaks through smartwatch sensors," Proc. 21st Annu. Int. Conf. Mobile Comput. Netw., pp. 155-166, 2015. Doi: https://doi.org/10.1145/2789168.2790121

[43] M. Kijewski, "The Medical Devices Most Vulnerable to Hackers". www.medtechintelligence.com [retrieved: August, 2023]

[44] J. Seo, K. Cho, W. Cho, G. Park, and K. Han, "A discovery scheme based on carrier sensing in self-organizing Bluetooth Low Energy networks," Journal of Network and Computer Applications, vol. 65, pp. 72-83, 2016. Doi: https://doi.org/10.1016/j.jnca.2015.09.015

[45] J. Yang, C. Poellabauer, P. Mitra, and C. Neubecker, "Emerging applications and challenges of BLE," vol. 97, 2020. Doi: https://doi.org/10.1016/j.adhoc.2019.102015

[46] "PoC hack on data sent between phones and smartwatches",www.arstechnica.com [retrieved: August, 2023]

[47] "BlueBump Attack",bluebump-attack [retrieved: August, 2023]

[48] E. Park, M. S. Lee, H. S. Kim, and S. Bahk, "AdaptaBLE: Adaptive control of data rate, transmission power, and connection interval in bluetooth low energy," Computer Networks, vol. 181, 2020. Doi: https://doi.org/10.1016/j.comnet.2020.107520

Higher Education Institutions as Targets for Cyber-attacks: Measuring Employees and Students Cybersecurity Behaviours in the Estonian Academy of Security Sciences

Kate-Riin Kont
Internal Security Department, Estonian Academy of Security Sciences
Tallinn, Estonia
e-mail: kate-riin.kont@sisekaitse.ee

Abstract — **The purpose of this study is to identify the most common characteristics that make users vulnerable, either individually or in groups, and to determine whether there is a relationship between user behaviour and victimisation of a cyber-attack. This research should help characterise people who are more likely to become victims of various phishing and social attacks. For this purpose, students, employees and lecturers of the Estonian Academy of Security Sciences were investigated. A five-scale questionnaire was used as the methodology of the study, which considers the following behaviours: risky behaviour, conservative behaviour, risk exposure behaviour and risk perception behaviour. The results obtained show that users with risky behaviour are most exposed to social engineering attacks in social networks. Furthermore, the analysed groups of faculty and staff fall victim to these attacks less often than students. Finally, we concluded that people who spend more time in front of a computer and engage in riskier cyber behaviours are more vulnerable to attacks.**

Keywords – cyber security, user behaviour, risk, vulnerabilities, higher education institutions, staff, students.

I. INTRODUCTION

Across Europe, the number and sophistication of cyber-attacks and cybercrime is increasing. While nearly every major industry faces significant cyber security challenges, higher education is particularly vulnerable for several important reasons.

In particular, it has to do with the unique academic culture, known for its openness and transparency. Criminals can get into the researchers' network and see what is happening, what is being tested, and how those tests are going. Several master's and doctoral theses have taken place in closed defences, with no public access to them, although the university membership or a certain part of it has access. Such data is not only a target for espionage but also has economic value.

Another reason has to do with history – specifically, that higher education institutions have been online for a very long time. Universities have always been the main targets of cyber- attacks because universities have had access to the Internet for a relatively long time. They have always offered free public access, as research centres in their field, not only to their members but also to anyone who wishes, e.g. through their libraries. As a result, they have long been visible targets, and cybercriminals are likely to know their weaknesses very well. A few examples of cyber-attacks on universities show that such an attack can be not only detrimental to relations between countries but even life-threatening.

The University of Helsinki was hit by an exceptionally extensive cyber-attack on 22.03.2022. During the day, up to 2,500 comments were posted on the university's social media accounts from what appeared to be new fake profiles with few posts and followers. The content of the messages was clearly anti-Russian. Among other things, they demanded the withdrawal of the right to study from Russian students. There were 10–15 identical messages, so it could be assumed that it was an automated robot attack. The Russian state was probably behind the attack, and the messages were used to give the university the impression that there are anti-Russian sentiments in Finland or the University of Helsinki. Such attacks could be successfully used, for example, in the Russian media against Finland. Such a large and organised cyber-attack was exceptional at the University of Helsinki [1].

The most serious attacks are those on health care, for example, hospitals. In the Czech Republic, a cyber-attack took place in the middle of March 2020 on a hospital performing corona tests in the city of Brno. The malware locked the hospital's data and demanded a ransom to unlock it [2]. Another example had very serious consequences. Düsseldorf University Hospital failed to admit a woman brought by ambulance on 19.09.2020 after a cyber-attack froze the hospital's information system. The woman later died in the ambulance as it was diverted to another hospital 30km away. As claimed by Reuters, it was the first confirmed case anywhere in the world, in which a person has died as the direct consequence of a cyberattack [3]. However, it was not certain if the university hospital was the actual target of the attack or if it was collateral damage in an attack on the university. The ransom demands were aimed at Heinrich Heine University, not the hospital directly. The police contacted the attackers and informed them that the target of the attack was the hospital, not the university, and that the patient's life was in danger. After that, the attack was stopped and the authorities were given the encryption key, but it was too late [4].

In summary, higher education institutions are targets for cyber-attacks because their data is valuable and easily accessible. In addition to the fact that the personal data of students and staff held by universities presents an opportunity for ransom attacks, the latest research findings could become a target for international espionage. Therefore, it is critical that academic institutions provide resources for cyber security and protect themselves against potential attacks.

The current study examines the behaviour of students, lecturers (researchers) and employees of the Estonian Academy of Security Sciences regarding hybrid threats and possibilities to prevent risks related to cyber security. This study is part of a larger research conducted within the framework of the cooperation program on hybrid threats (HYBRIDC) between Estonian Academy of Security Sciences, Lithuanian Mykolas Romeris University, Academy of Public Security and Riga Stradins University. This questionnaire has been prepared in cooperation with the digital development department of the Estonian Academy of Security Sciences. The results of the study can be used to develop strategies and trainings to reduce errors related to the human factor in the cyber security of higher education institutions. " Th rest of the paper is structured as follows. In Section 2, we give a brief overview of how cyber security awareness among the members of higher education institutions has been studied so far, what have been the conclusions of these studies, and what recommendations have been made in the future. In Section 3 we shortly introduce the research design, methodology used, present the research questions and the course of the study. General results are pesented in Section 4. Finally, we conclude our work in Section 5.

II. LITERATURE REVIEW

Security in a higher education institution is completely different than in the private sector because it is an open institution. There are many access points and a lot of personal information about employees and students. Information security training, awareness raising, and cyber behaviour monitoring are not always top priorities for educational institutions. The contribution of lecturers, researchers and employees who engage in research and teaching work or provide administrative support to these activities are often considered to be the central figures of a higher education institution. Information technology (IT) employees deal with security to the extent that they have the human and time resources for it.

Several studies have shown that there is a human dimension to the causes of cyber-attacks in higher education institutions [5]-[9]. Analysing the data from these studies, it was discovered that the patron's ignorance and carelessness in password management is common, which contributes to higher education institutions becoming targets for cyber-attacks. The studies by Öğütçü et al. [5] and Benavides-Astudillo et al. [9] aimed to identify common characteristics that make users vulnerable to social manipulation, either individually or in groups. For this purpose, they conducted a survey among the employees and students of the higher education institution. Four scales that consider the following behaviours were studied: Risky Behaviour Scale (RBS), Conservative Behaviour Scale (CBS), Exposure to Offence Scale (EOS) and Risk Perception Scale (RPS). Öğütçü et al. [5] results showed that respondents' behaviour becomes more cautious the more they perceive threats. Respondents' use of risky technologies increases their exposure to crime, which in turn increases caution. It also appeared that the score of the group that participated in security training was higher than the score of the group that did not attend such training. This finding clearly shows that such training increases people's awareness. The data analysis showed that the respondents do not report the cybercrime they have experienced to the authorities because they do not know who to turn to. One of the most important findings of this study is that the higher the level of education, the greater their awareness of information security. A notable finding was that students (between the ages of 18 and 30) appear to be the group most at risk [5]. The results of a study conducted by Benavides-Astudillo et al. [9] with the same methodology showed that users with risky behaviour are most exposed to social manipulation attacks in social networks. It also concluded that the analysed faculty and staff groups fall victim to such attacks much less often than students and that people who spend more time online are more likely to fall victim to a social engineering attack [9].

III. RESEARCH METHODOLOGY

To find out the most common reasons that make everyday Internet users, such as students and employees of Estonian higher education institutions, undoubtedly vulnerable, either individually or in groups, the four-scale measure developed by Öğütçü et al. [5] was used. The RBS measures the risk behaviour of Internet users, e.g. whether various security measures are used to protect themselves as well as the people they live or work with. The purpose of the CBS is to measure the Internet user's actions and actions in protecting his personal information. The purpose of the EOS is to measure the exposure of users to any cyber security threat, highlighting the user's behaviour in relation to the risks, threats and effects resulting from the events. The RPS measures the level of risk or threat that befalls the Internet user and is related to the field of trust that the user has in the face of possible cyber-attacks [5], [9].

The scales and questions were developed based on existing literature and IT expert opinions of the Estonian Academy of Security Sciences. It is quite important to determine the level of awareness because awareness and behaviour are very closely related. According to this model, an individual's behaviour is determined by the perception of a threat and actions to resolve that threat. Awareness is a powerful weapon against social engineering attacks, so this study allows universities of applied sciences to use these findings to focus their cyber security training priorities. The survey consists of five parts: 1) questions that collect respondents' demographic data, 2) questions about user profiles related to IT and computer security, 3) questions dealing with risky issues related to IT behaviour, 4) questions about respondents' behaviour regarding information security and threats, and 5) questions that address users' exposure to cybercrime.

Answers could be given according to a 5-point Likert scale. The proposed scales were formulated depending on the questions asked. Total respondent scores were calculated by assigning 5 points for "Always", 4 points for "Often", 3 points for "Sometimes", 2 points for "Rarely", and 1 point for "Never" for the RBS and CBS questions. A higher score indicates that the respondent is very risk tolerant. For EOS, it is said that as the scores increase, the respondent is exposed to crime (negative experience) at a higher level. For RPS, "Very dangerous" is 5 points, "Dangerous" is 4 points, "Slightly dangerous" is 3 points, "Not dangerous" is 2 points and "I don't know" is 1 point. As the scores increase, it is understandable that the respondent considers related technologies more dangerous [5].

Based on the two main studies of RBS, CBS, EOS and RPS [5], [9], the following research questions were raised:

Is there a difference between the scales concerning their average score?

Is there a difference between the surveyed groups (lecturers, administrative staff, and students) concerning their average score?

Does the duration of time spent on the Internet affect the average score of the scales?

Does the cyber security training attendance affect the average score of the scales?

Invitations to participate were sent to the email addresses of 1,000 undergraduate students and 69 master students, 439 faculty members and 271 staff. The survey was conducted using LimeSurvey and was administered by sending a link to the online survey. Data collection lasted for two months, during which repeated reminders were sent. There were 363 total responses including non-completed. The data were screened and any results missing one or more responses were deleted, resulting in a sample size of n=277.

IV. GENERAL RESULTS

Tables 1 and 2, and Figures 1 and 2 show the results obtained based on the user's general information. Table 1 gives an overview of the demographic data of the users, and here information about the completed/uncompleted cyber training, the time spent on the Internet during the day, as well as the type of Internet access used can be found. Table 2 shows the survey averages for all four defined categories – Risky Behaviour Scale (RBS), Conservative Behaviour Scale – (CBS), Exposure to Offence Scale (EOS) and the Risk Perception Scale (RPS). A score of 1 is considered the lowest value and 5 is the maximum value for each survey question.

TABLE I. RESULTS OF THE USER PROFILE SECTION

Characteristic	Category	Number of respondents	Percentage
Gender	Male	120	43%
	Female	157	57%
Age range	19–25	68	30%
	26–30	27	9%
	31–40	58	19%
	41–50	81	27%
	51–60	32	11%
	61–70	9	3%
	70+	2	1%
Position	Vocational student	33	12%
	Undergraduate student	98	33%
	Graduate student	14	5%
	Lecturers	42	15%
	Administrative staff	71	26%
	Other	19	7%
Cyber security training completed	Yes	241	60%
	No	66	40%
Time spent on the Internet	1–5 hours/day	145	52%
	6–10 hours/day	123	44%
	11 or more hours/day	9	3%
Type of Internet access	Using Mobile Internet	133	48%
	Using public Wi-Fi network (Cafes, shopping centres)	1	1%
	Using private Wi-Fi network (Home)	15	5%
	Using remote connection of my organisation	128	46%

TABLE II. NUMBER OF QUESTIONS AND AVERAGES OBTAINED BY SCALE

Scale	Number of questions	Average score
RBS	20	2.610469
CBS	10	4.051264
EOS	7	1.38886
RPS	17	3.49777

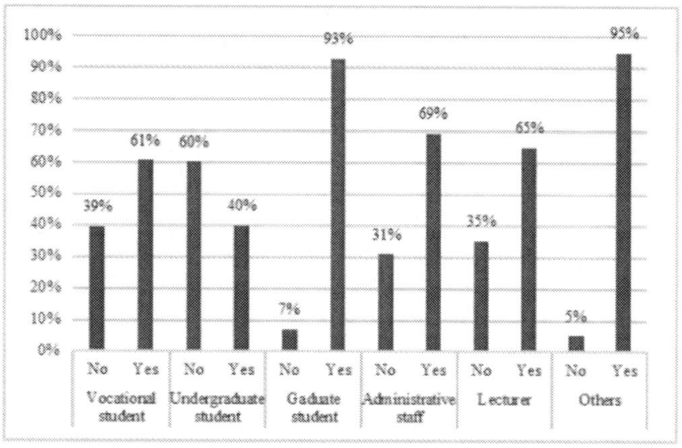

Figure 1. Results of the completed cyber security training

Figure 1 shows that the majority of students who have participated in cyber security training are master's students, and among the employees of the higher education institution, those who have identified themselves as "others", that is, research workers and external lecturers. Notably, 61% of vocational students and only 40% of applied higher education students have completed cyber security training. More than half of the teaching staff and employees have also completed the training. Nonetheless, this level is definitely not high enough.

Figure 2 shows the most eager Internet users in every studied group separately. While undergraduate students and lecturers are the most diligent Internet users in both 1–5 hours/day and 6–10 hours/day groups, the administrative staff is apparently overwhelmed with work in the 11 or more hours/day group.

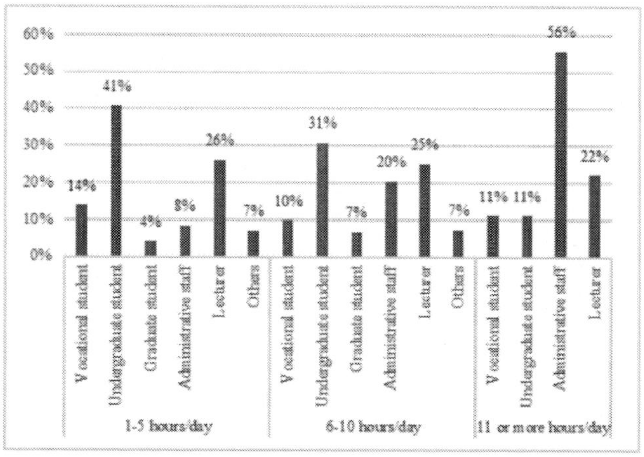

Figure 2. Time range of Internet use according to the position.

V. CONCLUSIONS

It is necessary to emphasise that people's behavior can contribute to making it easier to become victims of cyber-attacks, and it is by raising their awareness that it is possible to mitigate the consequences of cyber-attacks on universities. The model proposed here can be successfully applied to different higher education institutions – it helps quickly find out the cyber security training needs and develop the training policy which can be implemented at the right level of difficulty. Similarly, this model identifies the knowledge and skills of user groups, to deal with social engineering attacks.

REFERENCES

[1] K. Kirsi, "Helsingin yliopisto joutui laajan verkkohyökkäyksen kohteeksi: some-päivityksiin tullut jopa 2 500 venäläisvastaista kommenttia" [in English: "The University of Helsinki was the target of a large-scale online attack: up to 2,500 anti-Russian comments were posted on social media"], YLE News, 2022, March 22. https://yle.fi/a/3-12370984

[2] C. Cimpanu, "Czech hospital hit by cyberattack while in the midst of a COVID-19 outbreak," ZDNET, 2020, March 13. https://www.zdnet.com/article/czech-hospital-hit-by-cyber-attack-while-in-the-midst-of-a-covid-19-outbreak/

[3] D. Busvine and T. Kaeckenhoff, "Prosecutors open homicide case after hacker attack on German hospital," Reuters, 2020, September 18. https://www.reuters.com/article/us-germany-cyber-idUSKBN26926X

[4] M. Heikkilä, "Nainen kuoli ambulanssiin, kun kyberhyökkäys jumitti saksalaisen sairaalan tietojärjestelmän – syyttäjä avasi harvinaisen henkirikostutkimuksen," Woman dies in ambulance after cyber-attack freezes German hospital's information system - prosecutor opens rare homicide investigation"], YLE News, 2020, September 19. https://yle.fi/a/3-11553530

[5] G. Öğütçü, Ö. M. Testik and O. Chouseinoglou, "Analysis of personal information security behavior and awareness," Computer & Security, 2016, vol. 56, pp. 83–93. https://doi.org/10.1016/j.cose.2015.10.002

[6] L. Muniandy, B. Muniandy and Z. Samsudi, „Cyber Security Behaviour among Higher Education Students in Malaysia," 2017, Journal of Information Assurance & Cyber Security, 2017, pp. 1-13. DOI: 10.5171/2017.800299

[7] J. Yerby and K. Floyd, "Faculty and Staff Information Security Awareness and Behavior," 2018, Journal of The Colloquium for Information System Security Education (CISSE), vol. 6(1). https://cisse.info/journal/index.php/cisse/article/view/90

[8] Z. Othmana, N. Rahimb and M. Sadiq, "The Human Dimension as the Core Factor in Dealing with Cyberattacks in Higher Education," International Journal of Innovation, Creativity and Change. 2020, vol. 11(1). https://ijicc.net/images/vol11iss1/11101_Othman_2020_E_R.pdf

[9] E. Benavides-Astudillo, L. Silva-Ordoñez, R. Rocohano-Rámos, W. Fuertes, F. Fernández-Peña, S. Sanchez-Gordon and R. Bastidas-Chalan, "Analysis of Vulnerabilities Associated with Social Engineering Attacks Based on User Behavior," in Applied Technologies. ICAT 2021. Communications in Computer and Information Science, vol 1535, M. Botto-Tobar, S. Montes León, P. Torres-Carrión, M. Zambrano Vizuete, B. Durakovic (eds) Springer, Cham. https://doi.org/10.1007/978-3-031-03884-6_26